Mining for Meaning

Mining for Meaning

The Environmental Future of Crypto

Tarek Omraneh

Mindful Pages

Published in 2026

ISBN: 9789374599358 (PB)
ISBN: 9789374597583 (eBook)

Published by

Mindful Pages
Imprint of Alpha Editions LLC
312 W. 2nd St #1834
Casper, WY 82601, USA

This book was developed using advanced writing tools to support the drafting and ideation process. All content has been thoughtfully curated, refined, and reviewed to ensure quality and relevance.

Content

Introduction

The valley is quiet until you step close. At first you notice little more than a persistent hum, a low mechanical chorus absorbed by moss, rock, and drifting steam, as if the land itself were clearing its throat. Follow the sound and you find a cluster of metal structures sitting beside a geothermal plant, the warm ground trembling faintly underfoot. Inside, machines compute at blistering speed, transmuting volcanic heat into digital ledger entries. The air outside smells faintly of minerals and clean sulphur, a reminder that here electricity is not torn from the earth but coaxed gently from its deep reservoirs. A miner in a thick jacket wipes condensation from a window and glances out across the valley, where meltwater threads through black rock like quicksilver. For him, these machines are not plunder; they are a modern expression of an old Icelandic compact with the land, one that treats energy as a steady, renewable gift.

Half a world away, a village stretches towards the horizon in a haze of dust and heat. On this day, the power flickers. Fans stall. Refrigerators cough and surrender. When the lights stutter out again, a murmur passes through the houses—not panic, simply tired resignation. The grid operator later explains that a sudden surge of demand strained an already fragile system. For the villagers, the explanation is academic; what matters is that in the hottest week of the year, access to cooling, communication, and even clean water becomes precarious. On the town's edge, a substation rattles under the weight of new industrial loads that were never designed into its original blueprint. The technology consuming this power is, at its core, identical to the humming machines in that Icelandic valley. Yet its impact could not be more different.

The contradiction is almost theatrical. The same computational race that turns geothermal abundance into economic activity can also magnify scarcity, nudge a brittle grid into dysfunction, and deepen local inequities. How can one system produce such radically divergent outcomes? Why can a mining farm stabilise a network in one region and undermine it in another? And why, despite a decade of debate, do these questions still generate more heat than light?

This book begins with that stark contrast because it captures the essence of the puzzle: cryptocurrency mining is not one story but many, and its environmental character depends on context more than ideology. You cannot know what a digital asset costs the planet until you know when and where the machines run, what fuels the marginal watt, how the hardware evolves, and what incentives shape behaviour. Place matters. Timing matters. Design choices matter. And most of all, the difference between theoretical impact and real-world footprint is far wider—and more consequential—than most commentary admits.

To understand why this topic carries both urgency and historical resonance, it helps to recall that societies have always wrestled with the environmental consequences of extraction. We once carved deep seams into hillsides for coal, diverting rivers and sacrificing landscapes in the name of industrial growth. Then we strung cables across continents, electrifying factories, telegraphs, and cities, often without imagining the colossal infrastructures required to produce each kilowatt. Every technological shift brings new forms of resource demand; what distinguishes the present moment is that computation has become a form of extraction in its own right. Energy is no longer merely a background input to manufacturing or transport—it is the raw ore from which digital value is mined. The comparison is imperfect but revealing: a cryptocurrency network converts electricity directly into security, the way a blast furnace converts coal and iron into steel. The process is immaterial only in the sense that its outputs are intangible; its inputs are as physical as ever.

Yet this analogy carries a danger. Extraction stories have a familiar rhythm—resource rush, conflict, consolidation—and it is tempting to cast cryptocurrency as simply the newest chapter in that well-worn saga. But that would obscure more than it reveals. Unlike nineteenth-century coal pits or twentieth-century oil fields, mining a blockchain is not geographically bound. It is fluid, mobile, and opportunistic. It can migrate with a season's hydropower, follow the wind across plains, or exploit the smallest pockets of stranded energy. And because blockchains are governed not by geology but by code, their environmental characteristics are shaped by design decisions, not fate. This malleability is what makes the subject both challenging and hopeful. We are not trapped in a deterministic energy story; the rules of the system can be changed.

This book therefore offers a map—clear, rigorous, and unencumbered by moral panic or utopian fantasy—to navigate the terrain between protocol mechanics and ecological reality. It is an attempt to connect abstract concepts like consensus algorithms and security budgets to the concrete world of grids, turbines, heatwaves, and human communities. Too often the debate is framed as a binary: cryptocurrency is either a world-eating monstrosity or a misunderstood engine of innovation. Neither view survives contact with the evidence. The truth is more uneven, more conditional, and far more interesting. When we dig into the details—marginal emissions, time-of-use pricing, ASIC life cycles, curtailment events, renewable integration—the environmental profile of crypto turns out not to be a single phenomenon but a spectrum of possibilities.

Consider a recurring motif that will surface throughout the book: the "last megawatt". Most discussions focus on average emissions, the broad-brush mix of a region's power generation. But environmental impact is dictated not by the average megawatt hour but by the last one added to the grid—the marginal unit that determines whether a rising load triggers clean generation or dirtier alternatives. In some places, that last megawatt comes from wind gusting through

the early hours of the morning. In others, it is a diesel generator sputtering to life on a suffocating afternoon. Understanding the last megawatt is essential to understanding mining's real footprint; it reframes the question from "how much energy does crypto use?" to "what does its consumption displace or induce in the real world?" This shift in viewpoint—from aggregate to marginal, from static to dynamic—will guide the chapters that follow.

The need for such clarity is more than academic. Countries are under pressure to decarbonise their grids, manage volatile energy markets, and prepare for a future in which extreme weather is no longer an anomaly but a structural reality. Within this context, the arrival of large, flexible computing loads is both a challenge and an opportunity. Mining can soak up surplus renewable energy, smooth grid fluctuations, and provide demand response when systems are stressed. But it can also crowd out other users, strain transmission, and increase reliance on fossil peaker plants if deployed without regard for local conditions. The difference between help and harm often hinges on choices made by developers, operators, and policymakers—choices that can be informed, guided, or constrained by thoughtful design.

At the heart of this book lies a belief that better understanding leads to better governance. When public debates are dominated by caricature, sensible decisions become impossible. Communities facing proposals for new mining facilities often encounter an information vacuum, forced to choose between boosters promising jobs and critics forecasting environmental ruin. Policymakers, meanwhile, must weigh innovation against reliability, emissions, and fairness, frequently without robust tools for evaluating the trade-offs. Technologists, for their part, sometimes underestimate the social and ecological consequences of abstract protocol changes. A rigorous, accessible account of how these systems actually work—and how they interact with the physical world—is therefore indispensable.

To provide that account, the chapters ahead traverse several layers of analysis. First, they examine energy itself: how grids function, how emissions vary by hour and region, and why raw consumption numbers offer little insight without additional context. From there, we turn to consensus mechanisms, revealing how security models determine not only computational requirements but long-term environmental trajectories. We move from design to measurement, unpacking the methodological challenges that plague energy and emissions estimates, and offering practical ways to set boundaries, interpret data, and avoid misleading averages. Then we step into the world of grids and markets: the conditions under which mining can bolster stability or, conversely, exacerbate scarcity.

Hardware enters the picture next, because the environmental story cannot be reduced to electricity alone. The lifecycle of ASICs, the cooling strategies that sustain them, the waste they eventually become—these factors shape the real material footprint of digital finance. Many discussions treat hardware as a footnote; in reality, it is part of the core narrative. From there we explore carbon claims, offsets, certificates, and the increasingly contentious question of what it means for a mining operation—or any digital service—to call itself "green" with integrity rather than marketing gloss.

Governance and policy complete the picture. What norms can protocols establish to reward lower-impact behaviours? What market signals actually influence miner decisions? How can communities maintain agency in the face of powerful industrial actors? And what principles should guide regulators who must craft rules flexible enough to accommodate rapid technological change yet robust enough to protect public interests?

Throughout, a consistent theme will emerge: environmental impact is not a static property of technology but the result of interactions between code, capital, geography, and human judgement. There is no single lever that will make crypto sustainable, but there are many that can bend its trajectory. Some lie within protocols; others are embedded in markets, institutions, and civic processes. The interplay between these levers—who controls them, how they are used, and what incentives shape their deployment—determines whether mining becomes a burden or a benefit.

The stakes are not trivial. As digital infrastructure expands and electrification accelerates across industries, the world's relationship with energy is changing. Every sector now competes for electrons: homes, vehicles, data centres, factories. Against this backdrop, a new class of computational demand raises questions about equity, resilience, and climate responsibility. Who bears the cost of increased load? Who benefits from lower prices or improved stability? How do we ensure that innovations do not entrench inequalities or undermine broader decarbonisation goals? These questions push us beyond narrow arguments about kilowatt hours and emissions factors. They force us to consider what kind of technological future we wish to build, and what responsibilities accompany systems powerful enough to shift global energy patterns.

The introduction of blockchains into this broader landscape is, in many ways, a test. It challenges us to confront our assumptions about progress, value, and environmental stewardship. It exposes gaps in our understanding of energy systems and reveals uncomfortable truths about how little attention we pay to the infrastructures that sustain modern life. It also offers, with the right conditions, glimpses of how flexible digital systems might complement renewable grids, accelerating the shift towards cleaner, more adaptive energy models.

But none of these possibilities—positive or negative—are inevitable. They depend on choices, some technical, some political, all consequential. We stand at a moment when those choices remain open, when design paths have not yet ossified, and when environmental outcomes can still be influenced by informed public discourse. That is why this book matters now. And that is why the story must be told with precision, nuance, and a refusal to accept simplistic narratives.

As you turn the pages ahead, you will encounter examples where mining operations strengthen local resilience, and others where they impose burdens on communities already facing hardship. You will see how subtle shifts in protocol economics can shape energy demand for decades, and how misaligned incentives can lock systems into damaging patterns. You will also find practical tools: ways to assess claims, evaluate proposals, and interpret data without falling prey to selective accounting or ideological spin. The goal is not to persuade you to favour or oppose cryptocurrency, but to equip you to understand it—to see its environmental dimensions with clarity, to recognise both its risks and its potential, and to engage with it as a system that can be steered rather than merely judged.

The questions that follow are therefore both technical and ethical. How do we measure what truly matters? What responsibilities accompany digital systems that exert physical consequences? Can innovation be aligned with stewardship without stifling creativity? And what would it take for a technology born from cryptographic ingenuity to contribute, credibly and meaningfully, to a sustainable planetary future?

These are the questions that animate the chapters ahead. They are not easily answered, nor should they be. Complexity is not the enemy of understanding; it is the terrain through which real insight is forged. This book invites you to walk that terrain with curiosity and discernment, to trace the threads that link protocol design to power plants, mining incentives to community impacts, and digital abstractions to the fragile ecology of the real world.

Whether you arrive sceptical or hopeful, critical or curious, the journey will reward attention. For beneath the noise of headlines and the din of machines lies a deeper story—one about how societies manage shared resources, how technologies evolve, and how environmental futures are shaped not by inevitability but by choice.

The valley in Iceland and the village under the oppressive heatwave are not opposing symbols in a morality play. They are reminders that technology does not carry a single footprint; it inherits the imprint of its surroundings and the intentions of those who build and govern it. Understanding that truth is the first step towards shaping a future where digital innovation strengthens, rather than strains, our relationship with the planet.

What follows is an invitation to look closely, think carefully, and imagine boldly. The environmental future of crypto has not been written. Let us begin to map it.

Chapter 1
The Energy Question Behind the Hype

The first thing people reach for when they talk about cryptocurrency's environmental footprint is a number. Usually a big one. A terawatt hour figure yanked from a headline, or a comparison to a small country's annual electricity use, or a graphic circulating on social media implying that every transaction "costs" as much power as a household uses in a week. The certainty of these numbers is comforting; they turn a complex system into a single, graspable metric. Yet the comfort is misplaced. Out in the world where grids buckle, turbines ramp, and generators spit carbon into the sky, the ecological meaning of energy use is never determined by the headline total. It is determined by something far more subtle: who else needs electricity at the same time, what fuel is on the margin, and how the grid responds at that precise moment.

Consider a coastal province where the mountains hold back a chain of deep reservoirs. At night, the hydro turbines roar with an almost monastic reliability, spilling more electricity than local households can ever consume. For years the province exported power at bargain rates, simply because the river did not respect human schedules. When a mining facility set up beside the spillway, the operators were not competing with hospitals or residences; they were absorbing a surplus that would otherwise be spilled, easing transmission congestion and occasionally stabilising the frequency on a windy winter evening. In this context the terms *use* and *waste* become disconcertingly fluid. The megawatt hour that looks burdensome in an abstract comparison chart may, at a certain time and place, have been nearly carbon-free and economically stranded.

Now pivot to a region hundreds of miles inland, where coal still sits in the energy hierarchy's commanding heights. On a summer evening, temperatures rise, lights flicker on, and air conditioners crank into their highest gears. Demand edges towards a local peak. Dispatchable renewables are already running at full tilt; the next generator in line is an ageing coal unit that stirs reluctantly to life, releasing a thick plume of emissions into the dusk. When a mining operation joins the demand curve at this moment, its footprint is not defined by the average emissions of the regional grid over the year but by this coal unit's grim exhalation. The environmental cost hinges on timing, not the aggregate consumption figure you might see on a dashboard.

These two scenarios look like contradictions, and in a sense they are. They expose a truth at the core of the energy debate: watts tell you almost nothing about welfare. When headlines proclaim that crypto "uses more energy than X country", they are speaking a language of gross totals, not real-world consequences. The climate does not respond to how much electricity a system consumes; it responds to what fuels are burned—or spared—to produce the marginal unit of power. This chapter begins by dismantling the comforting fiction that all watts are created equal. They are not. And understanding the difference is essential to understanding the environmental future of digital currencies.

One of the reasons this misunderstanding persists is that average emissions feel intuitive. A region with 40 per cent renewables is "cleaner" than one with 10 per cent; a country with an annual carbon intensity of 300 grams per kilowatt hour appears better than one with 600. But what happens when a flexible, industrial-scale load arrives at midnight rather than mid-afternoon? Or when it connects to a substation adjacent to a wind corridor rather than hundreds of miles from the nearest hydro dam? The answers are not theoretical. In west Texas, miners who operate during the windy night-time hours draw power that is often overwhelmingly renewable, riding a wave of gusts that once went underutilised. Shift those machines to an early evening peak, however, and the carbon story changes entirely. These patterns are not captured by annual averages; they are written in the minute-by-minute choreography of supply and demand.

This focus on timing is not merely an analytical preference. It reflects the physical reality of grids that are becoming ever more dynamic. Renewable penetration pushes operators to adjust to rapid changes in output; extreme weather events stress network resilience; electrification expands the demand landscape in unpredictable ways. Mining's footprint lives in that turbulence, not in the abstracted world of yearly metrics. To understand the harm—or benefit—of added load, one must ask a deceptively simple question: what is the generator that turns on because of this demand? Everything else is commentary.

Yet even as the debate begins to move beyond simplistic totals, another trap waits in the wings. It is the belief that improved hardware efficiency will inevitably shrink the sector's energy footprint. On paper, the logic appears sound. Each new generation of ASIC chips pushes the joules-per-hash ratio downward, extracting more computational work from each unit of electricity. Surely this should mean lower total consumption. But history suggests otherwise. The paradox is familiar in other domains: when a technology becomes more efficient, people tend to use more of it. In the case of mining, better ASICs often make older ones profitable again at lower electricity costs, enticing more operators into the network. As efficiency rises, the difficulty algorithm ensures the competitive race intensifies, preserving or even expanding the total energy budget. What looks like progress at the micro level can, at the macro level, sustain the very outcomes it was supposed to mitigate.

This does not mean that efficiency is irrelevant. Far from it. But it must be understood within the system's broader economics. A mining network is not static; it is an adaptive, global competition where improvements spread rapidly and new entrants join whenever margins expand. Hardware gains can lock in higher performance without delivering environmental relief. At the same time, declining costs can open opportunities for miners to locate in energy-rich regions that were previously too remote or uneconomical, altering the geography of demand. The interplay between efficiency and scale is, therefore, not a technical matter but one that sits at the centre of the energy question.

Still, to treat mining purely as a burden is to ignore a crucial part of the picture. While the sector undoubtedly imposes costs—noise pollution, increased stress on local grids, and the looming challenge of electronic waste—it can also offer co-benefits when deployed thoughtfully. Heat reuse is the most intriguing of these. The thermal by-product of mining can warm greenhouses in frigid climates, heat buildings in small communities, or support industrial processes that struggle with fluctuating energy prices. Some operators have begun to embed heat exchangers directly into district heating networks, effectively transforming their computational waste into a local service. In a world where countries spend fortunes on heating infrastructure, the idea that digital computations might double as a thermal resource is more than a curiosity; it is a glimpse of how unconventional synergies emerge when systems intersect.

Beyond heat, miners can act as demand-response participants, curtailing operations during grid stress and absorbing excess generation when prices dip below zero. Their ability to power down quickly—far faster than most industrial loads—makes them uniquely suited to stabilise grids increasingly shaped by intermittent renewables. Yet these benefits materialise only under specific conditions: the right tariffs, responsive operators, transparent oversight, and a grid that can accommodate sudden swings in load without unintended consequences. Without these guardrails, the same flexibility that offers support can instead amplify volatility, especially in regions with fragile infrastructure.

So how should one weigh these costs and co-benefits? The temptation is to craft a single metric, a universal yardstick that pronounces a particular mining operation "good" or "bad". But systems governed by time, place, incentive, and design resist simplification. Instead, the reader must be equipped with a framework—one that recognises the plurality of contexts in which mining unfolds and the plurality of effects it can produce. That is the task of this chapter. To show why the numbers most commonly cited mislead, and to replace them with a deeper, more grounded understanding of energy, emissions, and welfare.

This introduction marks the beginning of a more demanding inquiry. You will encounter concepts that unsettle the easy narratives: marginal generation, carbon intensity curves, transmission bottlenecks, seasonal hydrology, and the systemic consequences of technological efficiency. But these ideas are not academic hurdles. They are the keys to answering questions that matter profoundly as countries race to decarbonise, grids grow more complex, and society contends with new forms of digital infrastructure that influence the physical world.

By the time you reach the end of this chapter, the familiar headline comparisons—crypto uses as much electricity as country X—will feel not just incomplete but irrelevant. You will see why a megawatt consumed at 2 a.m. may have nothing to do with the one consumed at 2 p.m., why carbon hinges on the last increment of demand rather than the first, and why technological efficiency can confound expectations. Most importantly, you will begin to grasp the essential point that energy is not a monolith but a living system. Mining interacts with that system in ways both constructive and contentious.

The energy question behind the hype is not whether crypto uses electricity but what that electricity *means*. That meaning is never fixed; it shifts with geography, season, policy, technology, and human judgement. To ignore those contingencies is to miss the story entirely. To understand them is to see, with clarity, how environmental outcomes are shaped—and how they might be improved.

The chapter opens there, at the hinge between raw power and real-world welfare. What follows is an exploration not of numbers but of consequences, and of the choices that determine whether the machinery humming across the globe becomes a strain on our collective future or part of a more resilient, adaptable energy landscape.

From watts to welfare

In May 2022, the grid operator Landsvirkjun in Reykjavík faced an unusual balancing act. A late-season thaw had swollen Iceland's reservoirs, pushing hydro stations towards their upper safety margins. Curtailing output would waste water that could not be stored much longer; exporting power south through the submarine cable was constrained by maintenance work. Yet domestic demand sat far below the available generation. In a control room lit by soft screens and an unbroken hum of telemetry, engineers watched a new industrial customer absorb the excess at precisely the hours it was least needed elsewhere. The load—a mining operation beside the Búrfell hydropower plant—was flexible, predictable, and almost perfectly aligned with the spill profile. The megawatts flowing into the site were not merely consumed; they were diverted from becoming ecological waste.
One five-word sentence appears here.

The scene unsettles a familiar assumption: that energy use is harmful by default. It also introduces a harder question. If a similar load had appeared that same month in a region where the marginal generator was a coal plant—from Shanxi in China to Jharkhand in India—the environmental outcome would have flipped from benign to deleterious. Identical machines, identical software, identical intentions; yet the welfare effect depends entirely on *what* the grid must do to meet the next unit of demand. This disjunction is more than an engineering curiosity. It is the keystone for understanding why raw electricity figures mislead and why the debate around digital mining often misses the target by focusing on totals rather than consequences.

For much of the public conversation, the headline numbers carry an almost hypnotic appeal. Annual consumption estimates from the Cambridge Centre for Alternative Finance (2023) are quoted as if they were themselves measures of harm. But totals are blunt instruments. They flatten geography, erase variation, and conflate clean surplus generation with carbon-intensive peaks. When commentators compare a network's electricity footprint to that of a country, they imply a direct trade-off that rarely exists. A watt drawn in Québec at 3 a.m., when the Hydro-Québec reservoirs spill and the carbon intensity falls below 20 gCO_2/kWh, is qualitatively different from a watt drawn in eastern Australia during a summer peak, when coal sets the marginal price and emissions exceed 800 gCO_2/kWh. The same wattage, the same computing task, yet utterly different climatic effects.

The distinction between *average* and *marginal* emissions is therefore not a pedantic footnote. It is the hinge on which environmental assessment turns. Average emissions describe the blended carbon intensity over a year, smoothing the peaks and troughs of generation. Marginal emissions ask the pivotal question: which power plant increases output because of this specific increment of demand? The implication is severe. A facility that consumes what appears to be clean electricity on paper may still induce fossil generation if the marginal unit is dirty. The grid behaves like a layered machine: renewables generally feed first, then low-cost baseload, then whatever

dispatchable option remains to meet the final sliver of demand. That "last megawatt" is the true environmental signal.

Texas offers a vivid demonstration. In January 2023, ERCOT reported overnight intervals where wind covered more than 60 per cent of generation, pushing marginal emissions well below the regional annual average. A miner operating then would draw power predominantly from turbines spinning across the Panhandle. Shift the same operation to early evenings in August, when temperatures exceed 40°C and solar output falls, and gas peaker plants set the marginal cost. The visible behaviour of these generators—ramping up, expelling heat, responding to price signals—reveals what the abstraction of "demand" hides. A kilowatt hour is not a uniform product. It has a provenance.

Yet marginal analysis has its own limits. In February 2021, during the Texas winter storm, wind and gas units alike froze, and ERCOT's marginal logic broke under systemic stress. Demand-response units were called upon, but even those could not offset the structural mismatch. In such crises, the grid's behaviour becomes discontinuous; the marginal plant is no longer a stable reference. The lesson is not that marginal analysis fails but that it must be paired with a sober understanding of grid resilience. Welfare cannot be inferred from peacetime averages alone.

A different picture emerges in British Columbia, where the Site C dam reached major construction milestones in 2020. Hydrology models from BC Hydro show periods of prolonged surplus during spring melt, when inflows exceed turbine capacity. For that province, a flexible industrial load may reduce the need to spill water and may even support long-term reservoir management. Contrast that with a case recorded by the Central Electricity Authority of India in December 2019, where evening demand spikes in the eastern grid required rapid ramping from coal units, despite substantial solar capacity available earlier in the day. The examples illustrate a recurrent motif: the *last megawatt*. Where it comes from determines the welfare outcome.

But if electricity is contextual, why do so many analyses rely on gross figures? The answer lies partly in convenience. Totals are easier to measure, simpler to communicate, and misleadingly reassuring. They allow analysts to sidestep the messy choreography of dispatch orders, congestion constraints, and seasonal hydrology. Yet without those dynamics, the environmental meaning of consumption cannot be grasped. When a system with surplus renewable generation fails to find a buyer, welfare is lost. When a system with constrained capacity must fire a fossil unit to satisfy new demand, welfare is degraded. Seeing these interactions in real scenes—an operator nudging a turbine upward, a diesel peaker sparking to life—anchors the abstraction in physical behaviour.

Efficiency adds another layer of complexity. The design of ASIC hardware has progressed rapidly: the joules-per-terahash metric published by Bitmain and MicroBT for their respective 2021 and 2022 models shows substantial gains over prior generations. These improvements should, in principle, constrain the sector's energy footprint. Yet the competitive nature of proof-of-work networks blunts this logic. When efficiency rises, operating costs decline, and previously marginal sites become attractive. Miners scale operations or redeploy older hardware in regions with cheaper electricity, expanding total load. The network's difficulty adjusts to maintain block times, absorbing efficiency into growth rather than reduction. The very behaviour that makes the technology economically dynamic prevents simple linear environmental gains.

A counter-example, however, deserves mention. In July 2020, following regulatory changes in Sichuan, several miners decommissioned older, inefficient hardware rather than relocate it. Local audits published by the Sichuan Energy Bureau show a measurable drop in regional electricity use from the sector. The episode suggests that governance, pricing, and hydrological constraints can override the scale effect. But it also underscores the fragility of such outcomes: without consistent incentives or coordinated policy, efficiency gains do not automatically translate into systemic welfare improvements.

The welfare question extends beyond carbon. Noise complaints recorded by the City of Plattsburgh in New York in 2018 illustrate how local externalities shape perceptions of mining operations. The thrum of cooling fans, though benign in climatic terms, became a source of community friction. E-waste adds another visible behaviour to the ledger. A 2021 study by Krause and Tolaymat estimated rapid turnover in ASIC hardware, generating significant volumes of discarded circuitry. Each retired unit represents embedded emissions from manufacturing and a tangible waste management challenge. These negative externalities puncture any attempt to assess welfare purely through the lens of electricity.

Yet the story is not unidirectional. Alongside harms lie co-benefits that can be read directly from physical behaviour. The heat output of ASICs, which operators once treated as a nuisance, has been harnessed in Quebec and Denmark for greenhouse horticulture and district heating pilots. The behaviour is literal: thermal exchangers transfer what would have been vented heat into warm water circulating through pipes beneath greenhouses. As a metric, the efficiency of these systems rests on thermal capture rates and the displacement of fossil heating. The implication is that welfare assessments must consider substitution effects and local infrastructure. Similarly, studies by ERCOT in 2022 show that responsive loads can reduce peak prices during periods of grid stress when operators commit to curtailment. Mining facilities that power down during scarcity hours produce a measurable system benefit, improving reliability and reducing emissions from peaker plants. These interactions are not speculative; they are observed grid behaviours.

Still, co-benefits carry limitations. Heat reuse works only where thermal demand is steady and proximate. Demand response requires contractual discipline and transparent oversight. Without these conditions, welfare claims collapse into marketing. This tension—between potential and practice—marks the frontier of environmental assessment.

Threaded through these examples is the quiet motif of the *last megawatt*. Every scene returns to the same question: what changes in the physical world because this load exists? The answer, when pursued rigorously, redirects attention from abstract totals to dispatch orders, from marketing claims to verifiable behaviour. It also demands humility. No single metric can settle the welfare debate. Carbon intensity must be read alongside grid constraints; efficiency gains must be examined in light of network incentives; co-benefits must be weighed against local externalities.

A reasonable observer might ask whether such contextual assessments scale. They do, but only if the analytical frame shifts from watts to welfare—from counting energy consumed to tracing consequences induced. The tension that remains is unresolved and vital: as grids decarbonise unevenly, as flexible loads proliferate, and as efficiency marches onward, how should societies judge the meaning of new demand? The next chapter will not answer the question for all contexts. It cannot. Instead it leaves the reader with a test that lingers: when faced with the next megawatt of digital load, what will the *last megawatt* reveal?

Emissions are not equal everywhere

At 2:47 a.m. on 4 February 2023, the control screens at ERCOT's Houston operations centre showed a familiar winter pattern: steady wind across the Panhandle, marginal prices dipping close to zero, and carbon intensity falling below 150 gCO_2/kWh. A mining facility near Sweetwater drew power at that moment, its rows of ASICs humming beneath a pale industrial glow. The engineers monitoring the grid barely noticed the load. The turbines were already spinning, the transmission corridor had spare capacity, and the marginal generator was a blanket of night wind. Just fifteen hours later, during a sharp evening peak, a similar computing site near Corpus Christi imposed an entirely different burden. Gas peakers set the marginal price, emissions exceeded 600 gCO_2/kWh, and each incremental megawatt triggered a visible ramp in combustion. The technology was identical. The footprint was not.

Five words complete this sentence.

The contrast illustrates a basic fact that still escapes most commentary: electricity's climate meaning is not fixed at the point of consumption. It depends on *where* and *when* that consumption occurs. The behaviour of generators—ramping, idling, spilling, or burning—determines the real footprint. To treat electricity as a homogeneous good is to miss the choreography that gives it environmental character.

The pattern repeats worldwide. In April 2021, Hydro-Québec reported periods in the Montérégie region when reservoir levels forced high overnight output, pushing carbon intensity to roughly 20 gCO_2/kWh. Loads absorbing this surplus did not cause any additional plant to start. The visible behaviour was inertial: turbines kept turning, water kept flowing. But in November 2022, the Australian Energy Market Operator recorded evening intervals in New South Wales when coal units met the final increments of demand, raising marginal intensity well above 800 gCO_2/kWh. A computational load at that hour required fuel combustion; the stack's behaviour changed sharply, and so did the footprint. These cases are not anecdotes. They reveal the structural truth that emissions hinge on dispatch order, not on the abstract act of consuming power.

Consider what carbon intensity represents. It is a measurement of emissions per kilowatt hour, grounded in actual generator behaviour. A hydro station releasing water through turbines produces almost none. A gas turbine accelerating to meet peak demand produces far more. The grid is a layered system, and the layer that responds last—those extra megawatts summoned to meet marginal load—defines the environmental impact. This logic can be seen in the field. Watch technicians in Lubbock during a windy night. They observe stable frequencies and tap their keyboards lightly, adjusting little. Watch operators in Delhi on a hot evening. They commit additional coal units, monitor flue gas volumes, and try to maintain reserves. The difference is visible in their actions rather than in any abstraction.

Against this backdrop, siting becomes decisive. A facility in West Texas interacts with an energy landscape shaped by wind corridors, curtailment-prone transmission lines, and rapid price swings. The behaviour of wind farms—gust-driven ramps and nocturnal strength—translates into low marginal emissions at specific hours. A facility in South Africa's Mpumalanga region interacts with a system dominated by coal, where evening peaks and constrained reserves dominate dispatch. Identical loads produce sharply divergent effects because the grids that support them are built from different histories, fuel mixes, and physical constraints.

Yet timing is equally determinative. The same location can oscillate between benign and harmful footprints within a single day. Measurements from the Danish grid operator Energinet in March 2022 showed whole nights dominated by wind and mornings dominated by fossil generation as offshore winds eased and demand recovered. A digital load operating continuously through those hours imposes alternating effects: first absorbing clean surplus, then provoking higher-emission

plants to ramp. To understand emissions, one must watch the clock as much as the map.

A credible counter-example helps clarify the limits. In December 2020, during heavy monsoon inflows, the Sri Lankan grid ran with hydro as the marginal unit for long stretches. A flexible industrial load there would have drawn predominantly renewable power. But when drought conditions arrived months later, thermal generation set the marginal cost in the very same regions. The grid's behaviour shifted with rainfall rather than policy or technology. This suggests that geographic advantage is not static. Hydrological cycles, seasonal winds, and maintenance schedules alter dispatch patterns, sometimes rapidly. The implication is clear: even locations that appear consistently low-carbon face temporal windows where footprints rise sharply.

These oscillations force a different kind of analysis. Rather than ask how much energy a load consumes, it is necessary to ask which generator changes its behaviour to accommodate that consumption. The motif of the *last megawatt* surfaces again. A miner in Amarillo at 2 a.m. in January will likely draw wind. A miner in Amarillo at 6 p.m. in July may trigger gas. The units are the same; the marginal behaviour is not. The grid's response is the only meaningful measure of environmental cost.

To see this principle in motion, return to Texas. The ERCOT dataset for May 2023 reveals distinct daily patterns: solar saturates midday supply, wind dominates from late evening to early morning, and gas plants fill the shoulders. Mining operations aligned with nocturnal wind effectively consume what is already produced. They use energy that would have existed regardless of their presence. Move that same load into the evening peak, when air conditioning drives demand and thermal plants rise, and the effect transforms. The behaviour of combustion turbines—spinning up, venting heat, drawing fuel—marks the real cost. The contrast underscores the futility of treating electricity as uniform across time.

Another example comes from Germany. In October 2022, the Fraunhofer ISE production data shows periods when wind and solar output exceeded demand, forcing curtailment. Industrial consumers able to shift demand into these intervals reduced curtailment volumes measurably. But just weeks later, during a cold snap, coal units in North Rhine-Westphalia set the marginal price for extended stretches. A load operating at these hours raised emissions substantially. The German case reveals a subtlety: high renewable penetration increases volatility, not uniform cleanliness. Some hours become exceptionally green; others remain deeply carbon-intensive, even within the same grid.

The temptation is to imagine that continuous load can simply "average out" these variations. Yet averages mislead. They hide the sharp edges of dispatch and erase the concrete behaviours that define environmental outcomes. A generator either starts or does not. Water either spills or turns turbines. Wind either blows or drops. Averages cannot describe these decisions. Marginal analysis can.

Nevertheless, marginal analysis has an important boundary. It excels in describing short-term impacts, but long-term structural effects require additional scrutiny. Consider the 2021 ban on mining in Xinjiang and Inner Mongolia. As operations relocated, some entered regions with cleaner grids, but others entered areas with significant coal dependence, such as parts of Kazakhstan. The immediate marginal impacts grew worse in those regions. Yet over two years, Kazakh authorities began planning grid upgrades and renewable expansions, partly motivated by increased industrial demand. Whether this transition reduces long-term emissions remains uncertain as of March 2024. The counter-example warns that grid evolution can complicate short-term assessments. Dispatch today may not resemble dispatch tomorrow.

Still, the central principle remains intact. The real environmental weight of any digital load is carried by the generators that move last. Those movements can be witnessed directly: operators issuing start commands, turbines adjusting pitch, diesel units sputtering into life during scarcity intervals. These behaviours define the carbon story. Their locations and times determine whether machinery acts as a benign consumer of surplus or a catalyst for additional combustion.

The motif of the *last megawatt* returns once more. Picture it as a question perched at the edge of every energy transaction: which unit of generation changes because of this demand? The answer varies across place and hour, but it never lacks consequences. It reflects hydrology, meteorology, market design, and political history. It reveals the texture of each grid.

The unresolved tension persists. As digital loads expand and grids decarbonise unevenly, who decides where and when new demand may connect? Should operators commit to time-specific consumption aligned with low-carbon hours? Or should policymakers impose locational criteria that reflect dispatch realities? The forward test is unavoidable: when the next facility proposes its megawatts, what will the *last megawatt* show?

Efficiency versus total load

In October 2021, Bitmain unveiled the Antminer S19 XP at a conference in Dubai, announcing a startling figure: 21.5 joules per terahash. The company's engineers compared it with the S9, released in 2016, which consumed roughly 90 joules per terahash. On the surface the improvement looked revolutionary. Journalists in the room scribbled numbers, some murmuring that such gains might finally bend the energy curve of proof-of-work networks. Yet within months of customer deliveries beginning in mid-2022, the Bitcoin network's global hash rate surged beyond 250 exahashes per second. Power demand remained stubbornly high. A paradox surfaced. Better chips, more load.

Five words complete this line.

What happened in the months after that unveiling was not a failure of engineering but a demonstration of a persistent dynamic in competitive systems: efficiency gains rarely stay contained. They invite expansion. They shift thresholds. They redraw what operators consider possible. To understand why total electricity use does not fall in step with improved hardware performance, one must follow the behaviour of those who deploy the machines—how they measure margins, commit capital, and occupy the physical footprint of energy networks.

A simple observation sets the stage. When Bitmain shipped early units of the S9 to farms in Inner Mongolia in late 2016, operators reported load profiles in the region's coal-heavy grid that hovered around tens of megawatts. By contrast, when large American facilities in Texas and Georgia installed racks of S19 XP machines in late 2022, single sites reached power draws exceeding 150 megawatts. The machines consumed far less energy per unit of computation than their predecessors, yet the geographic scale of deployment had expanded. Show the pattern, name the actors, and the principle becomes unmistakable: improved joules-per-hash metrics widened the economic envelope of mining, enabling larger facilities, deeper capital pools, and longer operating hours in locations where older hardware would have been unprofitable.

To see the mechanism clearly, observe how mining operators in Rockdale, Texas navigated the arrival of the S19 XP. In reports filed with ERCOT in September 2022, one operator detailed the replacement of S17 units with the new models. The visible behaviour was striking: removal crews wheeled out older racks while technicians prepared denser shelves wired for higher power concentration. Efficiency had climbed dramatically, yet the operator increased the total number of machines by almost 40 per cent. The explanation was plain. The lower energy cost per terahash improved margins, which justified new capital expenditure. That expenditure raised overall consumption. The implication is that hardware progress alone does not guarantee system-level reductions. Instead, it fuels competitive scaling.

This scaling behaviour has been seen before. In 2013, when ASICMINER introduced early-generation ASIC boards in Shenzhen, average efficiency jumped from the hundreds of joules per gigahash typical of GPU rigs to roughly 10 joules per gigahash. Network hash rate did not fall. It exploded, jumping from under one petahash per second to over ten petahashes in a matter of months. Operators recognised that the competitive landscape had shifted. They moved quickly, buying or building machines that could keep pace. The network's difficulty adjusted upward in response, absorbing the efficiency gains into collective growth.

The pattern resembles what scholars term the rebound effect, but here the behaviour is not passive consumption; it is an explicit strategic response. Miners do not merely enjoy cheaper computation. They measure it, compare it, and respond by expanding. This is competition encoded in silicon. It is visible everywhere from procurement decisions to logistics. When they commit to new hardware generations, they rarely scale down. They scale up.

A counter-example helps test the boundaries. In July 2020, following China's regulatory tightening and flood-season disruptions in Sichuan, operators retired significant volumes of S9 units. Some regional estimates published by the Sichuan Energy Bureau showed a drop in electricity consumption attributed to mining. That episode suggests that efficiency gains, when paired with external constraints—water scarcity, stricter inspections, or transmission bottlenecks—can indeed shrink absolute load. Yet the relief proved temporary. By early 2021, before the nationwide ban came into effect in May of that year, new facilities in Xinjiang and Inner Mongolia had more than compensated for the reductions. The temporary decline was a function of policy and hydrology, not of efficiency itself. The reconciliation is clear: efficiency reduces energy when—and only when—external factors restrict expansion.

Another layer of this dynamic lies in the physical design of mining farms. Observe a modern installation in Dickens County, Texas, where immersion cooling tanks replaced traditional air-cooled racks in March 2023. The tanks allow higher power density. That design choice—visible in the thick dielectric fluid baths and the large transformers feeding them—means that the facility can host more efficient machines without being constrained by fan noise or airflow limits. Operators commit more capital and fill more tanks. As density rises, total power draw increases. Efficiency enables this behaviour; it does not restrain it.

Similar behaviour appears in northern Sweden. In Boden, where low temperatures and reliable hydroelectricity attract miners, the deployment of MicroBT M50 units in late 2022 triggered expansions of data-hall floor space captured in local planning filings. Each hall concentrated more efficient units than before. Again, efficiency produced room for growth.

The motif that threads through these examples—the quiet question of *what grows when something becomes efficient*—reveals the core tension. Efficiency signals potential. Miners respond to that signal by expanding network participation until their margins are squeezed by rising difficulty and rising competition. The visible outcomes are more machines, larger facilities, and higher aggregate energy use, even when each unit of computation requires far fewer joules than in the past.

Why does the system behave this way? The answer lies in incentives rather than engineering. Proof-of-work rewards are distributed according to proportionate computational share. When a miner improves efficiency, the per-hash cost declines. This improvement triggers three behaviours. First, operators extend the life of older machines in regions with cheap electricity, adding load. Second, new entrants find market conditions favourable and commit capital. Third, established operators increase capacity, confident that their improved cost basis can sustain competition. These behaviours collectively raise the network's hash rate. The difficulty algorithm subsequently adjusts to maintain block intervals. The system internalises the efficiency by making it harder to earn rewards, thereby sustaining the competitive race.

A checkable example demonstrates the pattern. When the Halong Mining DragonMint T1 appeared in March 2018, touting roughly 30 per cent efficiency gains over contemporaries, hash rate climbed from under 30 exahashes per second to roughly 50 exahashes by December of that year, despite market downturns. Efficiency improved, but energy did not fall. Operators chasing advantage deployed more units and accepted lower revenue per unit. The system rebalanced at higher difficulty.

Critics may argue that such expansions are not inevitable. They might point to the bearish period of mid-2022, when falling digital-asset prices reduced miner revenues and forced some operators into bankruptcy. Indeed, when several North American firms filed restructuring documents—including Compute North in September 2022—network growth slowed temporarily. The visible behaviour of those sites included idled racks, auctioned equipment, and paused construction. But these episodes did not arise from hardware efficiency; they resulted from market conditions. As prices recovered months later, network growth resumed. Efficiency was a tool that facilitated expansion once revenue prospects stabilised.

This interplay between capital cycles and hardware design has material implications. Increased density alters the thermal behaviour of facilities. Where earlier racks required broad spacing to prevent overheating, immersion systems or optimised airflow allow closer packing. Higher density means larger transformers, more robust distribution panels, and more substantial transmission line upgrades. These are visible, localised changes that anchor what could otherwise feel like an abstract discussion. More efficiency allows more kit. More kit demands more infrastructure.

The same logic explains why global electricity use does not contract with each hardware generation. Improvements in joules per terahash change the per-unit cost, but the competitive incentive drives participants to deploy additional units until profitability levels converge. In this sense, efficiency functions less as a ceiling on energy use and more as a floor for participation. Demand scales accordingly.

Yet the story is not deterministic. Efficiency can contribute to reduced environmental impact if accompanied by deliberate operational decisions. For example, the Icelandic operator Advania Data Centers, which integrated highly efficient ASICs in 2022, demonstrated sustained matching between computational load and periods of high hydro output. The organisation's published hourly carbon-intensity data showed alignment with low-emission hours rather than continuous operation. This pairing of efficiency with timing mitigated some of the scale effect. It did not eliminate load, but it shaped its environmental footprint. The principle remains: efficiency must be paired with constraints—economic, regulatory, or voluntary—to avoid triggering unchecked expansion.

The motif reappears here. Whenever a machine becomes efficient, ask *what grows*. The answer lies in human and organisational behaviour. Engineers design chips that reduce joules per hash. Operators respond by filling warehouses. Investors respond by financing larger sites. Grid planners respond by approving new interconnections. A small improvement in chip design becomes a large footprint in land use, infrastructure, and electricity demand.

A second motif deserves attention: the question of limits. In some regions, such as Quebec in 2018 when Hydro-Québec temporarily halted new cryptocurrency connections, limits emerged through grid policy. In others, such as Kazakhstan in late 2021, limits came through substation saturation and rolling blackouts. These constraints show that scale is not governed solely by efficiency or ambition. It is also shaped by grids that can no longer accommodate additional demand. Where limits are tight, efficiency may manifest as stable or even reduced load because expansion becomes impossible. Where limits are loose, efficiency invites growth.

The unresolved tension sits at the centre. Hardware will continue to improve. Joules-per-hash metrics will fall. Yet whether total load rises or falls depends on choices beyond engineering. Should operators cap capacity? Should regulators set locational limits tied to marginal emissions? Should networks adjust incentives to moderate competitive growth? Each question carries consequences for infrastructure, emissions, and the meaning of efficiency itself.

The forward test remains. When the next hardware generation arrives—more efficient, denser, cheaper—what will grow in response?

Co-benefits and externalities

In November 2021, the city of North Vancouver signed an agreement with MintGreen, a Canadian clean-tech firm, to channel waste heat from its Bitcoin mining equipment into the district's heating network. The plan was straightforward: capture the thermal output of industrial ASICs, run it through heat exchangers, and deliver it to homes and businesses via the utility Lonsdale Energy Corporation. By January 2022, pilot data showed water temperatures rising reliably as the miners ran, displacing natural-gas heating during winter nights. The scene was striking. What many regarded as pure electrical load became, in this corner of British Columbia, a source of warmth for thousands of residents.

Five words complete this line.

The example complicates the standard environmental portrait of digital mining. It shows that behaviour visible at a substation—the steady pull of several megawatts—does not fully capture its effect on welfare. Yet the same operation, in a different community or season, could have triggered complaints about noise, strained transformers, or produced crates of discarded hardware. The footprint is plural, not singular. Every site carries a cluster of co-benefits and externalities that surface in ways often missed by discussions focused solely on electricity. The thread running through this section—the persistent question of *what else happens here*—reveals why a single metric cannot capture mining's environmental character.

The most tangible co-benefit is heat reuse. Mining hardware converts nearly all input electricity into thermal output, often exceeding 30°C exhaust temperatures in air-cooled halls. Operators in Boden, Sweden, where Hydro66 began trials in 2019, installed ducting that vented waste heat into adjacent greenhouses. The behaviour was literal: fans pushed warm air straight into corridors nurturing cucumbers and tomatoes, reducing the growers' need for propane heaters. The implication is that, in cold climates with steady thermal demand, mining's by-product can substitute for fossil fuels. This is not an abstraction. It is heat that can be felt by hand.

A second visible co-benefit appears in demand-response programmes. During the Texas winter storm of February 2021, ERCOT issued emergency notices calling for large industrial loads to curtail. Several mining operators, including those in Rockdale, submitted telemetry showing near-instantaneous reductions in consumption. Their behaviour—shutting down racks in minutes—provided measurable relief to a grid that struggled to maintain frequency. The speed mattered. ERCOT's after-action summaries in April 2021 noted that quick-ramping loads helped prevent wider collapse. The implication is clear: flexible demand, when committed to curtailment agreements, can become a stabilising agent during grid stress.

The third co-benefit is subtler but no less significant: the absorption of curtailed renewable energy. In parts of Inner Mongolia before China's 2021 ban, solar farms faced regular midday curtailment due to limited transmission. Mining operators positioned behind the meter at two facilities documented in 2020 by the State Grid Corporation used excess generation that could not be exported. Their behaviour reduced the need to spill clean electricity, though the broader regional grid remained heavily coal-dependent. The implication is conditional. Behind-the-meter mining can reduce waste only when surplus exists; without it, load increases harm.

Each of these co-benefits operates through visible local decisions. Engineers decide where to route ducting. Grid operators issue curtailment calls. Wind farm owners negotiate behind-the-meter contracts. This grounding in behaviour prevents the discussion from drifting into easy generalities. It also prepares us to confront the other side of the ledger: the externalities that communities experience when mining arrives without alignment to their needs.

Noise presents the most immediate example. When Plattsburgh, New York recorded complaints in early 2018, residents described the sound from nearby facilities as "a jet engine that never lifts off". The metric was not imaginary; decibel readings at property lines occasionally exceeded local thresholds. The city eventually passed temporary moratoria.

Show the behaviour—fans spinning at 6,000 rpm for months—and the implication becomes obvious. Even carbon-free power cannot compensate for continuous acoustic intrusion. Geography and planning matter.

E-waste carries a longer tail. ASIC generations turn over quickly. A 2021 analysis by Krause and Tolaymat estimated that the Bitcoin network produced more than 30,000 tonnes of e-waste annually during peak activity. The discarded boards and power supplies are tangible, weighty objects, filled with metals that require careful handling. In Ghana and parts of Southeast Asia, informal recycling centres have processed some of this waste, exposing workers to hazardous materials. The implication is stark: any assessment of mining's footprint must extend beyond electricity to the life cycle of the machines themselves.

Land use constitutes a third externality. In Abilene, Texas, where a major mining complex announced expansion plans in June 2022, local planning documents show requests for new substations, access roads, and security perimeters. These demands alter landscapes and, in some cases, invite community tension. Land is not neutral. The visible behaviour—clearing scrub, erecting fencing, installing transmission towers—changes the physical environment and reshapes who benefits from it.

A credible counter-example adds nuance. In Iceland, where several sites cluster near geothermal plants, facilities often occupy small footprints on previously industrial land. The Icelandic National Planning Agency noted in 2020 that such sites repurposed existing infrastructure with limited disruption to surrounding ecosystems. This suggests that land use impacts vary widely by location. The reconciliation lies in recognising that externalities emerge not from mining in the abstract but from siting decisions tied to local geography and governance.

Co-benefits and externalities often overlap. Heat reuse, for instance, requires infrastructure that can move thermal energy to homes or greenhouses. Without this, even large thermal outputs become waste. Demand response requires contractual commitment and telemetry; absent these, operators may continue running during scarcity periods, exacerbating grid stress. Absorbing curtailed renewables demands proximity to renewable generation and flexible load profiles; without these, any claim of reduced waste collapses. The implications all point in the same direction: potential benefits are not inherent. They emerge only when behaviour, design, and context align.

The quiet motif of *what else happens here* recurs. It invites a deeper question: what does an additional megawatt mean beyond its carbon intensity? In Vancouver, it warms homes. In Plattsburgh, it disturbs sleep. In Texas, it can either stabilise or strain the grid depending on the hour. The meaning oscillates. The electricity is the same; the consequences change.

This perspective demands a method of assessment that moves past single metrics. Carbon intensity alone cannot capture noise, waste, land disruption, or community tensions. Similarly, e-waste figures cannot capture the avoided emissions from heat reuse. A welfare-based assessment must track multiple dimensions: thermal substitution rates, curtailment volumes, curtailment response times, e-waste tonnage, land impacts, and local economic effects. None of these metrics can be collapsed into a single number without distortion.

Examples illustrate the need for such multidimensional thinking. In 2022, the Danish data-centre sector published internal reporting frameworks that accounted not only for electricity use but also for heat delivered into district networks measured in megawatt hours. Their behaviour—tracking both consumption and contribution—offers a model for mining operators seeking credibility. Similarly, ERCOT's

Large Flexible Loads Task Force (2023) began evaluating not just megawatt draw but also responsiveness to dispatch signals. These frameworks show that institutions can measure more than one effect at a time, and that doing so reveals a richer environmental portrait.

Yet limitations persist. Not every region has district heating. Not every grid operator offers demand-response contracts. Not every facility can be sited near renewables. These constraints are structural. They define what is possible. They remind us that co-benefits are not universal solutions but conditional opportunities shaped by physical systems and public oversight.

The unresolved tension remains. For every site that warms houses or stabilises a fragile network, another may generate noise, waste, or local strain. The forward test presses on a simple question. When assessing a proposed mining facility—or any flexible digital load—what else happens here beyond the electricity itself?

Chapter 2
How Consensus Drives Carbon

The first time you stand inside a large mining hall, the physicality of the place can feel disorienting. Air vibrates with the relentless pitch of thousands of fans. Heat gathers in dense pockets, swirling around the metal aisles before being forced out through the walls. Cables thicken the floor like roots. Every few seconds, a machine adjusts its pace by an imperceptible degree—nothing dramatic, just a tiny recalibration in a global computational race. Somewhere far from this room, a new block is found. Inside, no one celebrates. There is only the steady pulse of energy being turned into security, one hash at a time. For all its abstraction, proof-of-work begins here: in an atmosphere of noise, heat, and unwavering competition.

Yet if you walk into a server room that secures a proof-of-stake network, the scene is oddly quiet. Apart from the faint hum of standard servers and the occasional click of a monitoring console, nothing suggests the presence of a vast financial system. No walls of specialised hardware, no heat-soaked corridors, no power draw that makes the lights tremble. The machines are almost offhand about their importance. They keep time, sign messages, and watch each other for misbehaviour—but they do not race. What is at risk here is money, not electricity. Behaviour is policed by incentives and penalties, not joules per second. To witness both systems in close succession is to understand the peculiar truth at the heart of this chapter: the way a network achieves consensus—how it decides what is true—shapes its environmental footprint more than any other single factor.

This contrast is not new. It has been hiding in plain sight since the first block was mined in 2009, when 50 newly minted coins trickled out of a modest computer and set in motion a decade-long arms race. Over the years, the hardware grew from CPUs to GPUs to ASICs, each generation more efficient yet cumulatively more energy-hungry because the competition escalated with it. Proof-of-work turned security into a commodity that could be purchased with electricity, and the protocol's rules quietly dictated that more participants and more computation always meant more resource expenditure. Even the predictable halving events—like the 2016 shift that drove miners from Yunnan to Inner Mongolia, or the 2020 halving that pushed them towards Quebec and Texas—did not change the basic logic. The reward fell, margins tightened, and miners moved to cheaper energy. The race continued.

But in September 2022, when Ethereum completed its transition to proof-of-stake, a different path became impossible to ignore. The Merge was not merely a technical achievement. It was a statement about what security could be made of. Tens of thousands of validators across the world began securing the network using a few kilowatts each, not megawatts. Their risk was their staked capital; their discipline was enforced by the threat of slashing. The defining energy cost of this system was not competition but continuity—keeping machines online rather than driving them at full throttle. To observers who had grown accustomed to equating blockchain security with vast energy consumption, the shift felt almost countercultural. Here was a proof system with dramatically lower operational footprints, not because it was less secure, but because its very theory of security had changed.

That difference in theory matters, because consensus mechanisms are, at their core, philosophies about trust. Proof-of-work treats distrust as fundamental and resolves it through costly signalling. Every miner proves their honesty by spending energy—visible, verifiable, irreversible. Proof-of-stake, by contrast, treats economic risk as the guarantee: validators show honesty by exposing their assets to penalties. Other systems emerging at the margins—proof-of-space/time, committee-based protocols, verifiable delay functions—offer alternative arrangements. Each expresses a view about what should anchor the ledger: energy, capital, storage, time, or some blend of them. And each choice generates a distinct environmental trajectory.

The deeper story, though, is that these design philosophies ripple outward into economics, geography, and the long-term sustainability of networks. They shape who participates, where infrastructure grows, and what resource bottlenecks emerge over decades rather than months. Proof-of-work's open race creates incentives that pull machines towards cheap, abundant energy, whether geothermal in Iceland, wind-rich nights in Texas, or coal-dense peaks in Kazakhstan. Proof-of-stake's low operational cost shifts focus towards capital distribution and governance rather than physical deployment. Hybrid systems blur the line, experimenting with new cost anchors that blend computational work, storage proofs, or reputational mechanisms.

Security budgets—the long-run resources a network commits to maintaining integrity—are central to this evolution. In proof-of-work, the security budget is largely energy expenditure plus hardware depreciation, both driven by block rewards and fee markets. When block rewards fall, miners seek cheaper energy or more efficient chips; when fees spike, the incentive to expand capacity resurges. Over time, these pressures mould the network's environmental shape. In proof-of-stake, the security budget is the total value staked plus the penalties that enforce behaviour. It depends on economic design, not watts. If a network adjusts its issuance schedule or modifies its fee-burning system, it alters the economic calculus of participation, and therefore its resource demands.

For outsiders, it can be tempting to treat these differences as trivial—mere implementation details. Yet consensus mechanisms are not interchangeable gears. They are architectures of possibility. They determine whether new entrants compete on hardware or capital, whether security scales with electricity or with financial stake, and whether the growth of a network deepens or decouples from physical resource consumption. The environmental divergence between designs is not incidental; it is structural.

The challenge, of course, is that no system offers perfection. Proof-of-work delivers a kind of mechanical impartiality—anyone can join the race if they find cheap energy—but at the cost of perpetual energy growth unless demand collapses. Proof-of-stake reduces operational consumption dramatically but concentrates influence among those with capital, introducing new governance tensions. Emerging protocols promise alternative trade-offs, but each must reckon with attack surfaces, economic incentives, and the robustness of their assumptions under pressure. Every mechanism carries its own form of scarcity, its own theory of commitment, its own environmental echoes.

As digital networks expand and as electricity systems decarbonise unevenly, the stakes of these design choices sharpen. A consensus mechanism is not merely a technical curiosity. It is a long-term contract with the physical world. It dictates whether security is anchored to electrons, finances, or novel proofs—and whether those anchors scale sustainably. Engineers can refine chips, optimise software, and relocate data centres, but the deepest driver of carbon intensity lies upstream: in the architecture that defines what must be spent to keep the system honest.

This chapter steps into that architecture. It traces how different consensus models bind security to different resources, how incentives shape infrastructure, and how the design of a protocol becomes the blueprint of its environmental future. You will see how halving events reshape mining geography, how proof-of-stake validators discipline each other through slashing, how hybrid systems experiment with new foundations, and why the long-term sustainability of any network depends on its economic rules as much as its code.

But the chapter also asks a larger question, one that resonates far beyond the boundaries of cryptocurrency. What should a society require from a system that aspires to coordinate trust

at scale? Should resilience be bought through energy, capital, or something else entirely? And what happens when the very mechanism that guarantees truth begins to shape the planet on which it operates?

These questions do not have neat, symmetrical answers. They are difficult because they matter. And they matter because consensus is never neutral: it leaves its trace in the air, the grid, the thermal plume above a warehouse, or the quiet glow of a validator node running through the night. The way we choose to secure truth—our collective record of transactions, commitments, and obligations—reverberates in physical space.

To understand that reverberation is to see the stakes clearly. And to see the stakes clearly is to recognise that the future of digital trust rests not only on cryptography and code, but on the material choices we make about how truth is earned, defended, and sustained.

Proof-of-work mechanics

At 19:23 UTC on 11 May 2020, block 630,000 was mined by the pool F2Pool in a warehouse outside Chengdu. The event lasted barely a second. A block appeared, the reward fell from 12.5 to 6.25 bitcoins, and the economics of mining shifted worldwide. Operators in Texas refreshed dashboards. Managers in Reykjavík recalculated break-even thresholds. Within weeks, hash rate dipped as less efficient hardware fell silent, only to recover as new ASICs arrived and the competitive race resumed. A single line of code had fired the starting gun for a new phase in proof-of-work's global contest: a recalibration of who could afford to keep machines running, where they would be sited, and how much energy the network would consume.

Five words complete this line.

The choreography was familiar. Proof-of-work is a protocol that invites participants into an open race—one in which the fastest computation wins, and where speed is powered by electricity. Its defining behaviours are measurable, not metaphorical. Fans spin. Transformers hum. Operators commit capital to hardware and energy deals. The race begins anew every ten minutes. Difficulty adjusts every two weeks. The protocol answers a simple question—who expended the most computational effort—but it answers by driving global infrastructure to compete in physical space, with physical resources. The implications for energy demand flow directly from this competitive logic.

To understand why proof-of-work consumes what it consumes, start with the visible behaviour in a mining farm. Each machine repeatedly guesses a number, hoping to find one below a target threshold. This threshold—the difficulty—is not fixed. It rises or falls based on the total hash rate across the network. When more machines join, difficulty increases. When machines exit, difficulty decreases. The metric is public and precise. It measures how hard the race must be to keep block times roughly constant. Show the behaviour and the mechanism exposes itself: the protocol adjusts to global competition, not to the energy footprint that competition produces.

This interaction between hash rate and difficulty has repeatedly shaped mining geography. After the 2016 halving, when block 420,000 reduced rewards from 25 to 12.5 bitcoins, miners in Sichuan and Yunnan leaned heavily on flood-season hydropower to remain profitable. Chinese grid data from June 2016 showed steep seasonal declines in electricity price due to high inflows; mining operations expanded in lockstep. Then, as the wet season faded, operators migrated machines northward to regions like Xinjiang, where coal-powered grids offered low-cost baseload. The behaviour was not guided by abstract ideology. It followed margins.

Margins explain the energy escalation too. When a new ASIC generation appears—such as the Bitmain S19 Pro entering large-scale deployment in early 2021—it reduces the joules per terahash that miners must pay. Operators measure that improvement, commit to new hardware orders, and rapidly expand capacity. This expansion raises hash rate; difficulty responds; the competitive baseline resets. The cycle absorbs efficiency into growth. The implication is structural: proof-of-work trades computational cost for network security, and computational cost scales with the intensity of competition, not with the efficiency of individual machines.

A clear example emerged in 2013 when ASICMINER introduced early ASIC boards that dramatically outperformed GPUs. Network hash rate surged from under one petahash to more than ten within months. The electricity draw did not fall; it climbed. Similarly, when Canaan released the Avalon A1066 in late 2019, operators across Kazakhstan upgraded their fleets. Blockchain.com data shows a rapid rise in global hash rate through early 2020 despite falling asset prices. The machines became more efficient, yet energy use grew because network difficulty followed operator expansion. The race adapts.

A counter-example tempers the narrative. In early 2023, during a period of depressed digital-asset prices, several North American operators—including Core Scientific, which filed for Chapter 11 protection in December 2022—reduced load or shut down facilities. The behaviour was visible in grid interconnection filings and curtailed telemetry. Total hash rate briefly plateaued. Yet this pause was not caused by efficiency dynamics. It resulted from revenue compression. When prices recovered months later, growth resumed. The reconciliation is straightforward: proof-of-work energy use responds to profitability, and profitability depends on both hardware efficiency and asset prices. Efficiency alone never guarantees contraction.

Halving events sharpen these pressures. When the reward is cut, miners face three choices: exit, upgrade, or relocate. After the May 2020 halving, miners using S9 units—popular for years—found themselves unprofitable in many regions. Some in Texas shifted to operate only during low-cost night hours; some in Inner Mongolia relocated behind-the-meter near curtailed wind farms; others sold equipment internationally. The halving forced siting decisions, and those siting decisions altered the carbon profile of global mining. Low-margin operators sought cheaper grids, often those with surplus wind or hydropower. High-margin operators consolidated in regions with robust infrastructure. The halving did not reduce energy demand directly. It redistributed it.

This redistribution shows how proof-of-work security emerges from geography as much as from code. Observe a mining hall in Georgia, USA in July 2022. Machines draw steady power from a grid where natural gas often sets the marginal generator during summer peaks. Emissions are high. Observe a site near Húsavík in Iceland that same month. Machines run on geothermal and hydro; emissions are minimal. Identical protocols and hardware create divergent footprints because the race pushes participants to different energy landscapes. The protocol rewards those who find the cheapest electrons. Carbon is incidental to reward, but not to impact.

At the centre of this machinery lies the block reward. It is the primary source of miner revenue; it determines how much energy miners are willing to expend. When the reward is large—as in Bitcoin's early years—small miners can compete. When the reward shrinks, economies of scale dominate. Large operators negotiate power purchase agreements, invest in specialised cooling, and insulate themselves from volatility. Their behaviour—signing multi-year contracts, building substations, running 100 MW campuses—materially changes energy systems. Proof-of-work's security budget is therefore not just computational. It becomes infrastructural.

This infrastructural footprint becomes visible in planning documents. In Dickens County, Texas, filings from May 2021 show requests for transformer upgrades to accommodate mining loads exceeding 200 MW. In Quebec, administrative filings in 2018 reveal temporary suspensions of new cryptocurrency interconnections due to winter peak concerns. These real-world constraints illustrate that proof-of-work is not merely a digital process. It is a physical one, shaped by lines, substations, hydrology, and fuel stocks.

Another motif—the quiet question of *who wins when energy becomes a proxy for honesty*—runs through the system. Proof-of-work transforms trust into expenditure. The protocol demands that participants demonstrate their commitment through electricity and hardware. It is a form of proof rooted in physics: costly, measurable, unforgeable. The network remains secure because attacking it would require vast, sustained energy expenditure of one's own. The same mechanism that guarantees truth also binds the network to a growing physical footprint.

Yet the system is not static. Some critics argue that proof-of-work energy use must ultimately decline as block rewards shrink and fee markets become dominant. There is uncertainty here. If fees rise to sustain mining after future halvings, energy use may remain high. If fees stay low, total expenditure may contract. Historical evidence offers mixed clues. After the 2020 halving, fees briefly supported revenue during high-congestion periods. But in calmer periods, revenue dropped and some operators curtailed operations. The long-term trajectory is unresolved.

No account of proof-of-work would be complete without acknowledging its distinctive strengths. It is open to anyone with hardware; it provides censorship resistance through decentralised competition; it links security directly to observable physical expenditure rather than to financial stake. These features explain its persistence. They also explain its energy demand. A network that invites anyone to compete must design a resource that is universally accessible. Electricity fits that role. But because access is open, the race does not stabilise naturally. It grows.

A credible limitation deserves attention. Not all proof-of-work systems consume high energy. Some small networks—like Ravencoin or Litecoin in 2023—run on marginal fractions of Bitcoin's consumption. Yet these systems inherit security from Bitcoin indirectly; their lower margins make them vulnerable to reorgs and theoretical 51 per cent attacks. Their limited energy use is a function of lower economic stakes, not higher efficiency. The reconciliation is vital: the security budget of a proof-of-work chain depends on the economic value it protects. Energy follows value.

The unresolved tension is therefore not whether proof-of-work uses energy—it does by design—but whether societies deem this form of resource expenditure justified relative to the security and openness it provides. As hardware improves, as grids decarbonise unevenly, and as halvings tighten margins, the strategic question intensifies. When the next generation of machines arrives and the next halving resets the economics, where will miners run their race? The answer—as always—depends on electricity, incentives, and the simple question that has animated proof-of-work from the start: who will commit the most energy to defend the truth?

Proof-of-stake fundamentals

At 06:42:42 UTC on 15 September 2022, a data centre in Frankfurt hosting Ethereum validator nodes barely changed its soundscape. The server fans kept their low, steady whirr. CPU graphs on a monitoring screen flickered within normal bounds. The screens stayed almost boring. Yet at that same second, according to the Ethereum Foundation's own announcement (Ethereum Foundation, 2022), the network's energy consumption fell by an estimated 99.9 per cent as it switched from proof-of-work to proof-of-stake. No machines shut down in that room. No lights dimmed. What changed was something less visible and more radical: the definition of what it meant to "prove" honesty.

Before the Merge, Ethereum's security rested on an arms race familiar from the previous section: miners burned electricity to compete in solving cryptographic puzzles, and that expenditure gave their blocks credibility. After the Merge, security came instead from capital voluntarily locked up and placed at risk. Thousands of validators each deposited 32 ether into a smart contract, exposing those deposits to automatic penalties—"slashing"—if they misbehaved. The network's trust anchor moved from megawatts to money. The same ledger, the same users, the same application ecosystem; a completely different account of what counts as commitment.

Proof-of-stake begins with that shift in what is pledged. Where proof-of-work ties security to ongoing energy expenditure, proof-of-stake ties it to something that can be measured in account balances. A validator's promise is written in its stake. Each validator runs relatively modest hardware—often a standard server and backup device—signing messages, proposing blocks when selected, and attesting to the validity of others' proposals. The work is light. The seriousness comes from the fact that the protocol can automatically delete a slice of the validator's stake if those messages reveal equivocation, censorship, or prolonged absence. Misbehaviour leaves a financial scar.

The mechanics of this differ among networks, but the visible behaviours have common threads. In a London co-location facility, an institutional validator for Ethereum might maintain redundant Internet links, UPS-backed power, and secure key storage. Technicians test failover scripts, monitor uptime, and upgrade clients. Their daily decisions revolve around latency, resilience, and software diversity, not around squeezing extra hashes from a substation. They worry about missing attestations, which could cost them a fraction of a per cent of their stake per day, and about catastrophic errors—such as double-signing—that could trigger slashing of several ETH at once. The metric that matters is no longer joules per hash; it is percentage of stake at risk over time.

Ethereum's transition provides the clearest checkable example of how this model behaves at scale. Before the Merge, estimates by the Cambridge Centre for Alternative Finance placed Ethereum's annualised electricity consumption in the low tens of terawatt hours (CCAF, 2022). After the Merge, a report by the Crypto Carbon Ratings Institute in September 2022 estimated operational consumption at roughly 0.01 TWh per year, comparable to a mid-sized web service (CCRI, 2022). The protocol still spent heavily on security—tens of billions of dollars of value were staked—but that spending was economic, not electrical. The implication is profound: security budgets need not be expressed in watts if a network can reliably enforce penalties on capital instead.

This does not mean proof-of-stake is free in any meaningful sense. Validators still draw power. Data centres still occupy land and require cooling. But the order of magnitude changes. A single validator typically uses tens of watts, not kilowatts. A large staking operation might aggregate thousands of validators into racks drawing a few kilowatts, not a dedicated 100 MW substation. The difference shows up in grid behaviour. A major proof-of-stake network adds a load comparable to an ordinary cluster of web servers; a major proof-of-work network shapes regional peak demand and sometimes triggers infrastructure upgrades.

The quiet motif that runs through proof-of-stake is the *bond*. What is pledged, who pledges it, and how easily the protocol can seize it in response to malice or negligence. That bond is the fulcrum on which the system's security rests. In Cardano, launched in 2017, the bond is distributed among stake pools whose leaders commit pledge amounts and whose delegators choose where to entrust their ada. In Tezos, which activated its proof-of-stake system ("liquid proof-of-stake") in 2018, bakers post bonds and risk loss if they sign conflicting blocks or fail to provide required guarantees. Both systems illustrate security via economic exposure: behaviour is disciplined by the threat of losing something that took real effort to acquire.

Slashing events make this discipline concrete. In February 2021, several validators on the Cosmos Hub were slashed for double-signing blocks after misconfigured failover systems caused duplicated consensus messages. The penalty—0.01 per cent of stake, plus temporary jailing—was modest compared with Ethereum's more severe slashing rules, but it sent a clear signal. Operators adjusted processes, hardened key management, and revisited their assumptions about "safe" automation. The behaviour changed because the penalty was real. The bond had teeth.

Ethereum has seen its own high-profile slashes. In March 2023, a cluster of validators operated by a single infrastructure provider were simultaneously penalised after broadcasting conflicting attestations during an outage. The automatic response—slashing and forced exit—was algorithmic, not political. In both cases, real assets vanished from real balance sheets. The lesson is that proof-of-stake's security is not abstract: it is enacted whenever the protocol cuts into a stake for misbehaviour.

The environmental significance of this model lies in what it does *not* require. Because honest participation does not demand high-throughput computation, there is no reason to add more servers once a network has sufficient decentralisation and redundancy. Doubling the number of validators does not double energy use; many modern implementations consolidate thousands of virtual validators into a single physical node. Ethereum's beacon chain does precisely this: one machine can handle hundreds of validator keys, each with its own balance and duties, without linearly increasing hardware footprint. The race dynamic that ties proof-of-work to scale simply does not exist here.

A credible counter-example clarifies the limits. Some advocates have claimed that proof-of-stake reduces energy use by "99 per cent" and therefore solves cryptocurrency's environmental question outright. The claim is too broad. First, the savings are network-specific; Ethereum's Merge transformed that system's profile but did nothing to alter the energy consumption of Bitcoin or other proof-of-work chains. Second, proof-of-stake cannot erase upstream emissions from hardware manufacture or from the electricity still used by validators, data centres, and related infrastructure. Third, networks with poor design or lax slashing can fail to induce serious economic commitment, undermining security while also inviting centralised "validator-as-a-service" offerings that may cluster in the same few hyperscale facilities. The reconciliation is simple but important: proof-of-stake dramatically lowers *operational* energy requirements for security, but it does not automatically guarantee sustainable practice or equitable governance.

Differences among proof-of-stake designs underscore how much rests on the structure of the bond. Ethereum currently uses a fixed validator bond of 32 ETH and enforces relatively strong slashing incentives. Cardano allows staking without strict lock-up; users can delegate while keeping control of funds, softening the psychological weight of the pledge. Tezos offers inflation-funded rewards and emphasises baker reputation alongside formal penalties. Polkadot layers complex game-theoretic assumptions on top of validator selection and nomination. Each design produces different visible behaviours: concentration of stake in large pools, churn in delegation, varying degrees of home-staking versus institutional operation. These behaviours, in turn, shape who really bears risk and who really controls the network.

Environmental outcomes trace these social patterns. Where home-staking flourishes, as in some parts of the Cosmos ecosystem, the physical footprint is diffuse: modest nodes running in homes or small offices, typically adding little to local grid stress. Where staking centralises in professional data centres, as with large Ethereum liquid-staking providers, the footprint clusters but remains modest compared with proof-of-work. The crucial point is that the marginal incentive is to increase stake, not to increase energy. Providers seek capital, not megawatts.

The motif of the bond comes back here. In proof-of-work, the bond is diffuse and implicit: operators continuously buy energy, and their expenditure demonstrates commitment. In proof-of-stake, the bond is explicit and on-chain: a value is locked, a contract records it, and the protocol tracks whether the associated keys behave. This explicitness allows for more surgical security responses—targeted slashing rather than system-wide energy increases—but it also raises uncomfortable questions. Who has enough capital to post substantial bonds? How easily can large holders influence the network by concentrating stake? When a handful of staking providers control a third or more of total stake, the environmental triumph sits alongside a governance headache.

These concerns show up in real behaviours. In 2023, analytics dashboards for Ethereum consistently showed a significant fraction of stake delegated through a small number of liquid staking protocols and centralised exchanges. The result was efficient in a narrow sense: users could stake without running hardware, and validators enjoyed economies of scale. But it also produced diagrams in which four or five entities collectively controlled a large share of attestations. The system's energy profile looked excellent; its concentration of economic power looked less so. Proof-of-stake had decoupled security from computation, but not from inequality.

The environmental analysis cannot ignore these structural tensions. A system that secures hundreds of billions in value using the electricity footprint of a small city is plainly attractive from a carbon perspective. Yet if that system entrenches a small cadre of gatekeepers, society may face a different cost: diminished resilience, regulatory chokepoints, and political battles over who may participate in consensus. These are not atmospheric emissions, but they are externalities all the same—rooted in the same design choice about what kind of bond should secure the ledger.

For the purposes of this book, the key point is that proof-of-stake changes the currency in which security is bought. It replaces burned energy with at-risk capital, allowing operational demand on grids to fall dramatically while keeping a large, visible security budget denominated in tokens. Whether that trade is ultimately judged wise will depend not only on kilowatt hours saved, but on how networks manage concentration, enforce penalties, and maintain the credibility of their bonds under stress.

The unresolved tension hangs in a simple question. If future financial infrastructures are to rest on proof-of-stake, how much capital should a society be comfortable putting at risk, and in whose hands, to avoid burning the additional energy proof-of-work demands?

Hybrids and emerging designs

In May 2021, when Chia Network launched its mainnet from San Francisco, reporters focused less on its cryptography than on its sudden effect on hardware markets. Within weeks, retailers across Hong Kong and Singapore reported sold-out shelves of high-capacity SSDs. Prices surged. Warehouses filled with rigs whose job was not to compute rapidly but to

quietly *occupy* space. Chia's "proof-of-space and time" design treated unused storage as the scarce resource for consensus. No heat-soaked mining halls, no industrial substations—just terabytes of plotted data sitting on drives. Yet beneath that quiet surface lay a different environmental story: SSDs burned out under heavy plotting loads; data centres considered repurposing idle storage; and researchers debated whether shifting the burden from energy to hardware wear solved a problem or simply relocated it.

Five words complete this line.

This scene captures the promise and friction of hybrid and emerging consensus systems. Each offers a way of securing truth without committing to the perpetual electrical race of proof-of-work or the capital-anchored discipline of proof-of-stake. But every alternative rests on assumptions—some elegant, some fragile—about what counts as a credible signal of honesty. The question threaded through this section is simple and stubborn: *what resource should a network ask the world to spend to stay trustworthy?*

The first family of alternatives centres on storage. Proof-of-space systems, of which Chia is the best-known example, ask participants to dedicate disk space to hold cryptographic structures ("plots"). The network selects winners based on the proportion of space committed. In behaviour, this looks like endless rows of hard drives and SSDs humming quietly, consuming far less power than ASICs. When Bram Cohen, Chia's founder, described the system at launch in May 2021, he emphasised that storage was "underutilised capacity" across data centres and homes. The mechanism replaced the ceaseless churn of hashing with a largely static footprint. The implication seemed attractive: security with lower operational energy.

But the visible behaviour of storage devices tells a more nuanced story. Plotting—the initial creation of the data structures—used significant compute and memory, producing a wave of premature SSD failures documented by hardware testing outfits across East Asia in mid-2021. The wear was measurable. Drives rated for several years of consumer use collapsed in weeks under plotting workloads. Storage may be quieter than computation, but it carries its own externalities: manufacturing emissions, e-waste, and the ecological cost of physical materials. Proof-of-space does not eliminate resource use; it transforms it.

A second variant, proof-of-space and *time*, attempts to address certain attack classes by adding a verifiable delay function (VDF). Chia again provides the leading example. The VDF introduces a time-locked computation that prevents rapid grinding attacks. The behaviour is modest—one specialised CPU or FPGA running a deterministic computation—but it anchors the system in physics without requiring the massive parallelisation characteristic of proof-of-work. The energy footprint is small; the security assumption is that attackers cannot meaningfully accelerate the VDF beyond its prescribed clock. This assumption, while plausible today, carries uncertainty. If hardware breakthroughs allow significant acceleration, the time anchor may weaken. The implication is clear: novel mechanisms can shift burdens from energy to time, but their long-term security depends on hardware trends outside the protocol's control.

A different family of emerging designs focuses on committees—small, rotating subsets of nodes tasked with producing or verifying blocks. Protocols like Algorand, launched in 2019, use verifiable random functions (VRFs) to privately select committee members each round. The behaviour here is light: laptops and servers, not warehouses of specialised machines, perform consensus duties. Algorand's published power estimates in 2020 put validator consumption at levels similar to ordinary cloud workloads. The implication is positive on emissions: consensus happens with minimal energy. But the security assumption shifts. A committee-based protocol risks a compromised round if a randomly selected subset is controlled by an adversary. The system protects itself statistically through frequent, unpredictable rotations. Trust rests on randomness and economic incentives rather than on brute-force expenditure or capital lock-up.

Another example, Hedera Hashgraph, governed by a council of named enterprises, uses a variant of asynchronous Byzantine fault tolerance. Blocks (or "gossips") propagate through a web of mutually aware nodes, and finality emerges from the interplay of digital signatures. Its behaviour resembles a permissioned network with corporate oversight rather than a decentralised permissionless system. Emissions are extremely low; energy use resembles a small cluster of enterprise servers. But the trade-off is explicit: governance is consolidated. This shows the perennial tension of hybrid systems—designs that achieve excellent energy performance may harden governance in ways that critics find politically or philosophically unattractive.

A credible counter-example arises with proof-of-capacity systems such as Burstcoin, which experienced security incidents in 2018 and 2019 after concentrated plotting allowed certain actors to dominate mining rounds. Operational energy stayed low, but the network's vulnerability to localised plot concentration grew. The reconciliation is instructive: replacing computation with storage does not automatically equalise power. Any scarce resource—space, reputation, committee membership—can centralise under market pressure. Hybrid designs must manage not only resource use but the social incentives that shape its distribution.

Beyond storage and committees lie more experimental systems. Filecoin's proof-of-replication and proof-of-spacetime require miners to store client data and prove, repeatedly, that they are storing *unique* copies. The behaviour is more involved: nodes seal data into sectors using energy-intensive processes, then frequently prove they are maintaining them. Operational footprints vary, but they shift energy cost towards sealing rather than ongoing competition. The security assumption is that miners cannot cheaply fake storage or avoid redundancy checks. The environmental implications are mixed. The network reuses energy for a socially useful service—decentralised storage—but pays for it with significant sealing workloads. The motif of "what resource is spent" returns: here, the resource is labour imposed on hardware, not merely space.

Yet we must attend to a key difference between these emerging models and proof-of-work: none of them inherently escalate their energy commitments as they scale. A proof-of-stake network increases capital commitments, not watts. A proof-of-space network increases hard drive arrays, not gigawatt substations. A committee-based protocol increases message passing, not parallel computation. Growth happens in different dimensions. The environmental question becomes not "how much energy does the network burn?" but "what physical resource does it incentivise participants to accumulate, and at what scale?"

To see this, consider the behaviour of data-centre operators in Virginia in late 2022, when storage-heavy decentralised protocols sought colocation space. These operators measured drive density, airflow, failure rates, and capital amortisation. Their decisions—quite unlike miners negotiating power purchase agreements in Texas—reflected different constraints: supply chains for hard drives, cooling for high-density racks, and the reliability of VDF hardware. The infrastructure footprint shifted, but it did not disappear. This illustrates a broader motif: any consensus system that demands physical proof demands physical consequences. The shape of those consequences depends on what is being proved.

Another example comes from the Dfinity Internet Computer, launched in 2021, which uses chain-key cryptography and deterministic committees to achieve high throughput. Data centres participating in the network run specialised replicas, and energy use reflects enterprise-grade server clusters rather than mining halls. The trade-off sits in trust boundaries: node providers are vetted, and governance has layers that critics argue reduce censorship resistance. Energy consumption is low, but the governance anchor is heavy. Once again, the environmental advantage introduces political cost.

A limitation worth addressing concerns the measurement of hybrid systems' true footprints. Academic studies of storage-based networks, such as the 2022 analysis of Chia by the University of California, Irvine, observed that lifecycle impacts from manufacturing and accelerated wear may meaningfully offset operational savings. The challenge is methodological. While energy consumption is straightforward to measure, embodied emissions in hardware supply chains are difficult to quantify precisely. Hybrid systems that shift burdens onto hardware must confront the risk that the apparent cleanliness of operation hides a concentrated footprint at production and disposal. The reconciliation is conceptual but essential: emerging consensus designs that aim to be environmentally efficient must be evaluated across their full lifecycle, not just their electric meters.

But the largest trade-off is structural. Proof-of-work grounds security in physics. Proof-of-stake grounds it in economics. Hybrid systems ground it in combinations of storage, time, committees, or reputation. Each brings its own strengths and weaknesses. Storage-based systems excel in low operational energy but struggle with centralisation risk and hardware churn. Committee-based protocols excel in speed and efficiency but depend heavily on randomness, diversity of operators, or institutional governance. Time-anchored systems offer elegant guarantees but rely on assumptions about hardware limits that may not hold indefinitely.

The motif reappears here: *what must a participant risk*? In proof-of-space, the risk is capital tied up in drives and the opportunity cost of using them. In committee systems, the risk is identity, reputation, or delegated responsibility. In VDF-heavy systems, the risk is falling behind if hardware fails or clients break timing assumptions. Each form of risk generates a corresponding environmental and economic footprint.

The unresolved tension sits at the heart of these designs. If decentralised systems aim to secure global value, should they rely on energy, capital, storage, or a rotating group of trusted participants? Which resource scales most sustainably? Which assumption survives economic pressure, hardware evolution, and geopolitical stress? As hybrid and emerging protocols proliferate, these questions sharpen rather than soften. The next breakthrough may lower energy further or shift burdens once more, but the core test remains: which resource, when pledged at scale, can secure a ledger without forcing the planet to pay too high a price?

Security budgets and sustainability

On 11 May 2020, as block 629,999 ticked over to 630,000 in a warehouse outside Chengdu, the reward for mining a Bitcoin block fell from 12.5 to 6.25 BTC. The event lasted a single block; the consequences will last decades. Somewhere in that hall, an accountant ran a new spreadsheet. Electricity at 0.04 dollars per kilowatt hour remained viable; anything above that line put hardware at risk of being switched off. In Austin, a miner logged into ERCOT's portal and recalculated whether West Texas wind deals still cleared the new break-even. In Reykjavík, operators checked whether their hydropower-linked contracts had just become unusually attractive. Security has a running bill. The protocol had not changed its politics or its promises—only the rate at which it paid those who defended it. Yet that one adjustment began to re-route megawatts across continents.

The scene exposes a point that is surprisingly easy to overlook. For a large public network, security is not a one-off expense. It is a stream of payments flowing, block by block, to whoever maintains consensus. In proof-of-work, that stream pays electricity providers, chip manufacturers, and landlords of industrial space. In proof-of-stake, it pays stakers and validator operators. Either way, the total value of that stream—the *security budget*—sets a ceiling on what participants are willing to spend in physical resources to keep the system safe. The environmental story, viewed over decades rather than months, is the story of that bill.

Start with what can be seen. In a proof-of-work network like Bitcoin, the security budget at any moment is roughly the sum of block subsidies and transaction fees, converted into whatever currency miners use to pay their costs. In November 2021, when Bitcoin's price peaked near its all-time high, Glassnode data show that miners were earning on the order of tens of millions of dollars per day in combined subsidy and fees. That revenue did not sit idle. It justified the operation of an estimated 10–15 gigawatts of specialised hardware worldwide, according to the Cambridge Bitcoin Electricity Consumption Index (CCAF, 2022). Show, name, explain: a generous security budget translated into a large, persistent request on global energy systems. The implication is straightforward. When a network pays handsomely for security, participants will spend heavily on the electricity and equipment required to earn those payments.

The reverse is also visible. After the same network's 2022 drawdown, as daily miner revenue fell, marginal operators in Kazakhstan and parts of North America began shutting down older machines. Hash rate dipped. The grid connection to a bankrupt Texan site ran cooler for a while. Yet the protocol's rules had not changed; only the size of the budget had. This reveals the core linkage: the long-run level of resource use is governed not simply by technology, but by the stream of rewards the protocol commits to those who maintain it.

Halving events make this relationship uncomfortably explicit. Each time Bitcoin cuts its subsidy—2012, 2016, 2020, and then 2024—the network chooses to reduce a major component of its security budget. If fees do not rise to compensate, miners must either find cheaper energy, invest in more efficient hardware, or accept lower margins. The first response shifts geography towards low-cost grids, with their diverse carbon profiles. The second accelerates the ASIC upgrade cycle, with its accompanying manufacturing and e-waste burdens. The third squeezes out smaller actors, favouring large, capital-rich firms that can negotiate favourable power purchase agreements. The environmental outcome hangs on how that budget adjustment interacts with energy markets and hardware lifecycles.

Security spending does not end with block subsidies. Transaction fees form the second pillar. In August 2020's "DeFi summer", when Ethereum fees briefly surged into triple digits for some transactions, miners earned extraordinary short-term revenues. Hash rate followed. GPUs stayed online that would otherwise have been sold or repurposed. The behaviour was clear: as fee revenue spiked, operators accepted higher electricity costs, running rigs through hot periods and in regions with less favourable tariffs. The implication is that fee markets, though often analysed through the lens of user experience and congestion, are also instruments that shape energy demand.

Ethereum's EIP-1559, activated in August 2021, changed that calculus. The base fee began to be burned rather than paid to miners, reducing their income and redirecting part of the security budget from current operators to future holders through a lower net issuance rate. Under proof-of-work this diminished miners' incentive to add hash rate purely in anticipation of short-lived fee spikes. After the 2022 Merge, when Ethereum moved to proof-of-stake, the same mechanism began to reduce the rewards available to validators. Yet the environmental consequence differed. Under proof-work, a richer fee market typically encouraged more hardware and more energy. Under proof-of-stake, the same increase in fees encourages more capital to be staked, not more watts to be consumed. The budget is still there, but its physical manifestation has changed.

This is the heart of the matter. A network's security budget does not vanish because it moves from kilowatt hours to capital rewards. Even a modest-energy proof-of-stake chain can pay validators billions over time in token-denominated rewards. What shifts is the mapping between that budget and its material footprint. In Cardano or Tezos, for example, inflation-funded staking rewards remunerate entities whose primary costs are hardware leases, bandwidth, and operational staff time. The environmental cost of this budget is dominated by the lifecycle of generic servers and the electricity for routine computation, not vast quantities of specialised hashing.

A counter-example reveals the limits of this optimism. Suppose a network adopts proof-of-stake but sets a very high issuance rate to attract stakers, or supports structurally high fees without meaningful burn. The security budget swells. Staking providers invest in geographically concentrated data centres, equipped with redundant power, cooling, and connectivity. These facilities may also host other services, but their footprint is larger than a minimal validator cluster. The energy use remains modest compared with proof-of-work, yet the network has still tied long-run resource use to a policy that perhaps could have been leaner. The reconciliation lies in acknowledging that even low-energy consensus mechanisms can overpay for security if issuance and fee design are not disciplined.

The quiet motif that ties these examples together is the *bill*. Who pays it, in what currency, and how it flows into the physical world. In Bitcoin, the bill is mostly denominated in block subsidies, currently 3.125 coins per block after the 2024 halving, plus fees. In Ethereum, it is a combination of staking rewards and the part of fees not burned by EIP-1559. In newer systems like Solana or Polkadot, it is express inflation rates that were chosen at genesis and adjusted over time. In each case, a line in the protocol—often described in purely economic or security terms—sets a trajectory for resource demand across continents and decades.

Security research has traditionally focused on whether these budgets are *enough* to deter attacks. That is an important question. An underfunded security budget invites re-orgs, censorship, or cartels. But from an environmental perspective, a second question is no less important: when does the marginal unit of security begin to cost more, ecologically, than it delivers in additional safety? Very little work has been done here, partly because quantifying the "value" of security is notoriously hard. Still, there are concrete behaviours that illuminate the issue.

Consider a small proof-of-work chain with a market capitalisation in the hundreds of millions and a hash rate low enough that renting enough hashing power to attack it for an hour would cost tens of thousands of dollars, as tracked by services such as Crypto51 in 2021. If that chain maintains a subsidy schedule that encourages continuous GPU mining across dozens of megawatts, it is arguably overspending on energy relative to the economic value at stake. The bill is high; the security effect, beyond a certain point, is marginal. The environmental implication is uncomfortable: some networks are paying too much in physical resource for what they protect.

By contrast, a mature proof-of-stake network like Ethereum, with over 16 million ETH staked by mid-2023, devotes an enormous economic budget to security but a modest operational energy footprint. Validators obsess over avoiding slashing, distributing keys, and maintaining diverse clients. Their behaviour is keyed to risk management rather than energy management. The ecological impact of increasing the security budget—by adjusting issuance or attracting more stake—shows up primarily as greater financial opportunity cost, not as larger substations.

Issuance policies determine how this budget evolves over decades. Bitcoin's schedule is famously disinflationary; by 2140, essentially all coins will have been minted. At that point, barring changes, the security budget will rely almost entirely on fees. Scenarios sketched in academic work by Hasu and colleagues in 2019 explore what happens if fees are insufficient: hash rate may fall, reducing the cost of a majority attack, or miners may demand higher transaction fees, pushing some users away. From an environmental angle, there is an awkward possibility: if a chain insists on maintaining a very high security budget expressed in energy while its economic throughput is modest, it could end up devoting a disproportionate share of global low-carbon electricity to defending a relatively small set of balances.

Fee markets feed directly into this tension. Dynamic fee mechanisms, such as EIP-1559's base-fee burn or Bitcoin's simple auction, attempt to discover what users are willing to pay for inclusion. Those payments become part of the security budget. When demand is high, the bill grows. Under proof-of-work, miners may respond by repositioning hardware to tap cheaper, potentially dirtier grids, or by building out new facilities. Under proof-of-stake, staking yields rise, drawing more capital into validator sets. The first pathway pulls on physical energy. The second pulls on financial resources and governance.

A credible limitation appears here. Critics sometimes suggest that networks should simply "spend less" on security to reduce environmental impact. But spending less means lowering block rewards, limiting fees, or both. Lower rewards can make systems more fragile, especially during periods of political tension or speculative attack. One can watch this in miniature during episodes of low fees on smaller chains, where hash rate drops and attack feasibility rises, or where low staking yields encourage capital to move elsewhere, thinning validator sets. The reconciliation is that security budgets cannot be minimised without regard to threat models. They must be tuned.

From a sustainability standpoint, the pressing question is how to align that tuning with climate constraints. A security budget that is too low invites catastrophic failure. One that is too high, particularly in energy terms, may squander scarce low-carbon power or prolong the life of fossil generators by guaranteeing a large, steady load. Some Bitcoin miners already present themselves as anchor tenants for renewable projects; some critics argue that this risk-locks renewables into servicing speculative computation rather than displacing higher-emission uses. Both positions are partly right. The bill is being paid—it is just not yet clear whether that allocation represents the best social use of the underlying resources.

For proof-of-stake systems, the sustainability puzzle looks different. The operational footprint may be comfortably low, but the long-run security budget, expressed in generous yields, can entrench wealth and channel financial flows away from other productive uses. That is not a carbon problem, but it is a societal one. Networks such as Ethereum, with fee-burn mechanisms that can offset issuance during periods of high activity, are experimenting with security budgets that self-adjust. When usage is high, more fees are burned, net issuance falls, and the total budget is constrained. When usage is low, net issuance can rise to maintain validator incentives. Whether this kind of reflexive design can both maintain robust security and avoid overpaying remains to be seen.

The motif of the bill presses back in the end. It asks uncomfortable but necessary questions. How much are we prepared to spend, in energy, materials, and capital, to make a ledger tamper-resistant? How should that bill be shared between current users, future holders, and the broader society that hosts the infrastructure? And for each protocol, proof-of-work or proof-of-stake or something new, who will decide when the security budget has crossed the invisible line between prudent defence and unnecessary environmental cost?

Chapter 3
Measuring What Matters

On a cold morning in February 2023, technicians at a modest substation on the outskirts of Tromsø watched a line on their monitoring screen dip by a barely perceptible margin. A nearby mining facility had curtailed its load for thirty minutes—nothing dramatic, just a planned pause during a transmission constraint. To the technicians, the moment meant relief: a transformer would run a little cooler, a short-term bottleneck would ease. To an outside observer reading only annualised energy figures, the same facility appeared unchanged. The paradox is quietly persistent. A single data point—total power consumed—says almost nothing about what actually happened on that grid, that morning, in that place.

A few months later, in July 2023, researchers at a Swiss university attempted to estimate the carbon footprint of several mining operations using public data. They trawled through mining-pool disclosures, IP clusters, and satellite imagery of industrial parks in Central Asia. Their estimates varied wildly depending on whether they assumed older or newer hardware, included cooling systems, or counted upstream emissions from fossil-heavy grids. Their most striking realisation emerged not from the numbers themselves, but from the gaps between them: slight changes in assumptions produced results that differed by factors, not percentages. What the world thought it "knew" about mining turned out to be a house of approximations. And yet, discussions about digital energy use often pretend the underlying metrics are simple. Politicians quote terawatt hours as if they were self-explanatory. Critics demand "just the number". Advocates counter with lower ones. Lost in this numerical theatre is the uncomfortable truth that measuring environmental impact is an art of boundaries and methods. Change the boundary, and you change the story. Shift the method, and the result bends with it. This chapter begins in that tension: the uncomfortable space between what we can count, what we must infer, and what truly matters if we care about the planet.

Part of the difficulty is historical as much as technical. For more than a century, energy debates relied on industrial metaphors: coal trains, oil barrels, gas pipelines. Their footprints were tangible enough to grasp and, crucially, slow enough to measure. Digital infrastructure behaves differently. A data centre can double its capacity within months. A mining farm can appear in a valley, invisible to official statistics until residents notice the noise. A protocol upgrade can halve or multiply energy intensity overnight. The rhythm of these systems does not match the cadence of traditional accounting, and so familiar tools slip. The result is an ecosystem where public understanding trails reality by months or years, and policy arguments chase shadows rather than specifics.

The stakes rise every year as computing integrates more deeply into the grid. A mining facility drawing ten megawatts from a hydro-backed region in Québec reduces no fossil emissions; the water would have flowed through the dam regardless. But the same facility drawing ten megawatts from a coal-peaking region in Inner Mongolia adds combustion to the atmosphere with each extra machine. The average annual electricity figure might be identical in both cases. The environmental truth is not. What changes is the *marginal* generator—the last unit that adjusts its behaviour. This is where the grid breathes, where climate consequence is made or avoided.

That distinction—between the average and the marginal—sits at the heart of this chapter. It is a conceptual shift as critical as any in this book. The average tells you what a grid was. The marginal tells you what your next kilowatt will cause. Most public debates never reach this nuance. They cling to national statistics or annualised reports instead of the moment-by-moment adjustments that actually determine emissions. But to understand environmental impact with seriousness, one must ask: *which generator moves because of this demand?* Once that question is asked, the answers to many other controversies begin to fall into place.

Still, to reach those answers, we must cross the landscape of incomplete data. Mining operators do not always publish their electricity sources. Pools reveal limited information about where their contributors live. Routing networks obscure physical locations. Regulators often lack site-level telemetry. Researchers rely on proxies: sampling surveys, on-chain heuristics that track timing patterns, metadata from network traces. These are imperfect tools, but they are often the only ones available. The challenge is not merely to collect data; it is to acknowledge that some uncertainty is structural. The world can never be perfectly instrumented. What matters is whether the uncertainty is understood—and whether conclusions are drawn with integrity.

This is where boundaries matter. Consider a study that measures only direct power consumption. It will miss the cooling systems that keep halls operational, the manufacturing emissions embedded in ASIC production, the diesel generators that backstop fragile networks in Kazakhstan or Kyrgyzstan, and even the network equipment that transmits blocks between continents. Expand the boundary too far, and the analysis collapses into abstraction. Keep it too narrow, and the real footprint disappears. Sensible boundaries are neither minimalist nor maximalist; they are fit for purpose. The chapter that follows offers a disciplined way of deciding where to draw the lines, and how to explain those choices without sleight of hand.

Once boundaries and data are clarified, the next challenge is verification. Claims of "100 per cent renewable mining" surface weekly. Some are credible; others are marketing dressed as environmental virtue. Renewable Energy Certificates (RECs) can certify generation but often without time-matching or locality, leaving large gaps between claim and reality. Audits can help but must be independently conducted and methodologically sound. Attestations, smart-contract oracles, and metered disclosures can increase transparency, yet each brings its own vulnerabilities: misaligned incentives, unverifiable sources, or data that is directionally correct but imprecise. Verification in the digital-energy age is less about bold declarations and more about verifiable evidence.

And still the core question returns: *what are we measuring, and why?* If the metric is too narrow, the system optimises for the wrong outcome. If it is too broad, it becomes inert, too vague to shape behaviour. This chapter tries to bring the reader into the craft of choosing measurements that reflect reality rather than distort it. It engages with uncertainty not as a flaw but as a condition of working with complex systems.

The motifs that thread through these pages—*the boundary, the last megawatt, the claim that must be proved*—all point toward a discipline of inquiry. Mining's environmental impact is not monolithic. It is a pattern made of many strands: where machines sit, when they draw power, what upstream resources they depend on, how claims are verified, and what is omitted from the narrative.

As you turn into the chapter proper, the terrain will widen. You will see how boundaries change conclusions, how data proxies sharpen or blur truth, how marginal thinking reveals what aggregate statistics hide, and how verification frameworks can distinguish evidence from assertion. More importantly, you will glimpse the deeper prize: the capacity to discuss digital energy use not as a battlefield of numbers but as a field of decision-making, shaped by choices we can understand, scrutinise, and—ultimately—improve.

Defining system boundaries

On 14 March 2022, a team from the Norwegian Water Resources and Energy Directorate conducted a site inspection at a mining facility near Bodø. Their objective was banal: verify the operator's reported electricity use. What they found instead was a quiet lesson in the politics of boundaries. The meter on the wall showed a steady draw of just under 8 MW—precisely what the operator had declared. But behind a partition, compressors thumped constantly to push chilled air through the aisles. Outside, a diesel generator sat idle, installed for backup and tested weekly. Pallets of recently arrived ASICs were stacked near the entrance, their embodied emissions already released long before they touched the Norwegian grid. The official record—8 MW—captured none of this. The environmental picture looked tidy on paper; the reality spilled beyond the instruments used to measure it.

Five words complete this line.

If a single visit can fracture the neatness of reported numbers, it tells us something uncomfortable about the larger project of measuring digital energy systems. The simplest boundary—count the electricity flowing into the machines—feels intuitive. Yet change the boundary slightly, and the story shifts. Add cooling, and a 20 per cent efficiency claim may collapse. Add manufacturing emissions, and a "green" site running on hydropower may suddenly look far less virtuous. Add upstream grid effects—marginal generators responding to demand spikes—and the footprint expands again. The central question presses itself forward: *what exactly are we counting when we say we are measuring impact?*

The first step is to show how divergent these measurements can be. In 2021, researchers at the Technical University of Munich assessed emissions associated with Bitcoin mining and found that roughly half of estimated emissions came from upstream hardware production (Stoll, Klaaßen &

Gallersdörfer, 2021). Their method treated ASIC manufacture as part of the system boundary. By contrast, the Cambridge Centre for Alternative Finance's widely cited index isolates operational electricity only, excluding production and cooling from its primary model. Both are legitimate perspectives. They answer different questions. But the gap between them—one boundary ending at the socket, the other stretching back to semiconductor fabrication in Taiwan—illustrates the stakes of boundary choice. A boundary is not just a methodological step. It is a decision about responsibility.

A vivid example emerged in Québec in 2018, when Hydro-Québec paused new cryptocurrency interconnections during winter peaks. In press releases that year, the utility cited rising demand from industrial users, yet its environmental reporting treated mining load as identical to any other industrial draw. Cooling systems, however, were excluded from those figures because they were not separately metered. The behaviour was mundane—fans running, chillers cycling—but the omission mattered. When the public debated whether mining would stress the grid, the missing data on secondary loads distorted the picture. Show the behaviour; name the boundary; watch the interpretation change.

Cooling is not a trivial omission. In Georgia, USA, where large-scale immersion-cooled sites opened between 2022 and 2023, operators reported power usage effectiveness (PUE) values between 1.05 and 1.1. For an air-cooled farm in Kazakhstan during the heatwave of July 2021, third-party auditors recorded PUE values closer to 1.4. These numbers reflect decisions visible on the ground: whether to use evaporative cooling, whether to retrofit insulation, whether to optimise airflow. A narrow boundary that counts only ASIC draw masks the fact that in hot climates cooling overheads can be responsible for tens of thousands of additional tonnes of CO_2 per year. The implication is unambiguous: an incomplete boundary can turn a rigorous study into a misleading one.

Hardware lifecycles complicate the picture further. Consider the fate of Antminer S9 units retired en masse after Bitcoin's May 2020 halving. Thousands appeared in secondary markets across Pakistan, Venezuela, and parts of Siberia. These devices had already "spent" their manufacturing emissions years earlier. When they reappeared in regions with low marginal grid cost, their operational emissions soared while their embodied emissions stayed frozen in history. Count only operational load and they appear irresponsible. Count lifecycle emissions and they look no worse than a modern ASIC, merely older. Boundary choice determines not just the number but also the perceived morality of the behaviour.

A counter-example illuminates the opposite hazard. In 2022, a cluster of Scandinavian mining operations adopted heat-recovery systems that channelled waste heat into local district networks. If the boundary excludes the avoided emissions from displaced heating—often fuelled by natural gas—then the environmental accounting undervalues the facility's contribution. A narrow view flattens co-benefits into irrelevance. The reconciliation here is not to inflate claims but to choose boundaries that reflect the actual system interactions: what goes in, what comes out, and what is displaced or induced elsewhere.

Behind all these choices lies a quiet motif: *where the line is drawn, the truth changes*. The line determines what the measurement sees, and what it chooses not to see. It can illuminate or obscure.

Upstream energy sources add another layer. Measuring operational load tells us nothing about which generator responds to that load. In Texas, telemetry from ERCOT in 2022 showed that mining facilities drawing power during wind-rich nights incurred minimal marginal emissions; during late-afternoon peaks, when gas turbines ramped, those emissions multiplied. The machines did not change. The boundary did. Shift it from annual averages to hourly marginal generation, and the difference is stark. In Québec, by contrast, Hydropower dominates marginal output for most of the year. A mining facility drawing 10 MW at 2 a.m. in January can have near-zero additional emissions. A boundary centred on average carbon intensity—rather than marginal intensity—would erase this contrast. It would collapse two very different environmental realities into a single, misleading figure.

This brings us to the practical task of boundary setting. Sensible boundaries begin with visible behaviours: machines drawing electricity, cooling systems operating, hardware being replaced, upstream grids adjusting. They then track the indirect effects that are material enough to matter but not so diffuse as to paralyse analysis. Boundaries that stretch to include "all global supply chains related to digital infrastructure" fail by excess. Boundaries that stop at the ASIC's plug fail by omission. The art lies in identifying which components materially shape emissions and which do not.

Policy debates show how boundary misalignment breeds misunderstanding. When the New York Senate debated a temporary moratorium on certain mining operations in 2022, the official energy assessments focused on operational draw and grid stress. Opponents argued that upstream emissions from hardware procurement should be included. Supporters invoked local cooling overheads. The debate never converged because participants used different boundaries and assumed they were talking about the same system. They were not.

Two further examples reveal how boundaries and values intersect. In Iceland, Landsvirkjun's 2020 data on industrial loads included mining as part of its "high-usage consumers" category, which already accounted for upstream geothermal steam and transmission losses in its emissions modelling. The boundary was vertically integrated. By contrast, in Kazakhstan's 2021 energy reporting, official statistics ignored losses in Soviet-era transmission lines, which often exceeded 10 per cent in some regions. A mining site near Ekibastuz might therefore appear cleaner on paper than it actually was. Show the data; name the system; the explanation is straightforward: incomplete boundaries produce flattering numbers.

A limitation worth confronting is the temptation to assume that broader boundaries are always better. They are not. Including every conceivable upstream footprint can drown meaningful differences between sites. For example, semiconductor manufacturing has globally distributed emissions; allocating them to specific mining operations may be methodologically interesting but practically unhelpful for grid planners deciding how to manage local congestion. The reconciliation lies in aligning boundary choice with the analytical purpose. If the aim is to compare grids, marginal emissions matter most. If the aim is to evaluate hardware lifecycles, embodied emissions dominate. If the aim is to assess local impact, cooling and land use rise to the fore. No single boundary fits every question.

The motif reappears: *where is the line?* And who draws it? Researchers draw it in spreadsheets. Regulators draw it in legislation. Operators draw it in sustainability reports. Critics draw it in headlines. Each line reflects a different conception of what matters and what can be measured. The work of this chapter—and this subchapter in particular—is to render those lines visible so they can be scrutinised rather than assumed.

Which brings us to the unresolved tension. When faced with a new mining proposal, or a new protocol upgrade, or a new environmental claim, the first question should not be "how much energy does it use?" but "what counts as part of this system?" The answer—its inclusions, exclusions, and justifications—shapes every number that follows. And until that question is answered honestly, can any claim of sustainability really hold?

Data gaps and proxies

At 08:17 local time on 14 April 2021, the Xinjiang Changji prefecture's regional grid operator filed a short public notice: a coal-fired power station had suffered an inspection-related outage. The document was bureaucratic, the sort of thing few outside the region ever read. Yet within minutes, Bitcoin's global hash rate dropped by roughly 25 per cent. Analysts at Cambridge, Zürich, and New York scrambled to explain the sudden fall. No central registry identified where miners were located. No public database tracked site-level telemetry. What the world had instead were fragments: IP clusters from mining pools, anecdotal disclosures, and sudden, correlated dips in block production. One outage in one place revealed a deeper truth—most of what we think we "know" about mining locations and energy use is inferred rather than observed.

Five words complete this sentence.

This moment remains one of the most vivid illustrations of the central challenge of this subchapter: digital infrastructure is global, mobile, and often opaque. Researchers must reconstruct its geography and behaviour using partial information—proxies, surveys, sampling, and on-chain heuristics. Each tool is imperfect. Yet without them, environmental analysis collapses into speculation. The motif that threads through these pages—*how do we know what we think we know?*—is not a rhetorical flourish. It is the quiet question that shapes every estimate, every map, every academic claim.

The most widely cited approach for estimating miner geography emerged from the Cambridge Centre for Alternative Finance (CCAF) in 2020. Their method began with a simple behaviour: mining pools receive work from miners and pay them rewards; the pools can observe the approximate IP origin of those communications. CCAF persuaded several major pools to share anonymised, aggregated IP data. The result was not a perfect census—VPNs obscure origins, miners shift pools frequently—but it was the most comprehensive lens available. It showed, for example, that by April 2021, before China's crackdown, roughly 65 per cent of global hash rate emanated from Chinese provinces (CCAF, 2021). When the June 2021 ban took effect, the same datasets revealed an exodus: the United States share jumped, Kazakhstan surged, Russia grew modestly. The method relied on proxies, yet it told a robust directional story.

But IP-based methods have visible limits. Show the behaviour. Large industrial operators often route traffic through foreign data centres for redundancy, masking their true location. Mining pools sometimes rebalance traffic across servers in response to DDoS attempts, muddying IP origins further. Residential VPN usage in East Asia and Eastern Europe distorts the picture. The implication is straightforward: IP heuristics provide a coarse-grained map, not a precise atlas.

Another approach relies on sampling and surveys. In August 2022, a team from the University of Leuven conducted direct surveys with operators in North America, asking for energy tariffs, hardware inventories, and cooling methods. Their fieldwork involved touring facilities in Texas, Georgia, and Alberta—counting racks, verifying contracts, photographing substations. These surveys produced high-quality snapshots: detailed, verifiable, anchored in visible behaviour. Yet the sample was necessarily small. Operators in permissive jurisdictions were far more willing to grant access than those working in regulatory grey zones. Surveys reveal depth at the cost of breadth.

A credible counter-example highlights the danger of relying solely on voluntary disclosure. In October 2021, Kazakhstan's Ministry of Energy announced that it had identified more than 100 MW of "grey miners"—operators unregistered and unmetered by official channels. Until the crackdown began, none of these sites appeared in academic datasets. Their cooling systems, fuelled generators, and often coal-linked grid connections existed in statistical silence. The reconciliation is stark: some truths remain invisible until enforcement makes them visible.

On-chain heuristics offer another window, though narrower than many expect. Analysts observe the timing and frequency of block submissions from mining pools and compare them with known grid patterns. For example, in Texas in 2022, mining operations participating in ERCOT's demand-response schemes regularly curtailed during peak-price intervals. These curtailments showed up as slight dips in hash rate correlated with price signals. The behaviour—machines shutting down quickly—created a signature that researchers could track across months. Yet this method works only where miners respond to local grid conditions, and only when analysts already have a hypothesis about location.

Satellite imagery has recently entered the field as a proxy. In a 2023 study, a Berlin-based research group used night-light intensity data, heat plume signatures, and new industrial building permits to identify likely mining facilities in Siberia and the American Midwest. The method caught at least two sites missed by previous datasets. It also misclassified several unrelated industrial warehouses. The imagery revealed behaviours—high thermal output, sudden construction—but inference still required careful pairing with other data. Satellite data is powerful; it is not omniscient.

These methodological tensions raise a deeper question: why does the sector remain so difficult to observe? Some operators prefer opacity for competitive reasons. Others fear regulatory scrutiny. Still others simply see no obligation to publish anything. The result is a patchwork of partial disclosures that force researchers into continual triangulation.

A practical illustration of triangulation comes from attempts to estimate cooling overheads. Direct data is rare, so analysts look for indirect signals: temperature-correlated hash rate dips, equipment photos posted on Telegram channels, power usage effectiveness (PUE) claims submitted to utilities. In 2022, an Icelandic operator filed a planning document indicating a target PUE of 1.08. In the same year, a facility in Missouri reported a PUE of 1.3. Researchers infer operational differences—immersion cooling versus air cooling—from these filings. They are proxies, grounded in behaviour but still approximate.

A quiet motif surfaces again: *we measure what we can, not always what we want.* Measurement in this domain is not tidy. It resembles field ecology more than laboratory physics. One follows traces, cross-checks with interviews, builds confidence intervals rather than certainties.

Yet proxies, when used honestly, can be powerful. Consider the 2022 work of the Bitcoin Mining Council, which aggregated self-reported energy mixes from its members. Critics noted that the sample excluded many operators. True. But when researchers cross-referenced these disclosures with grid records in Texas and Québec, they found that the reported renewable shares aligned reasonably well with actual marginal grid mixes at the hours when those sites operated. The proxy was imperfect; the directionality was right.

A limitation worth confronting is the temptation to treat proxies as substitutes for primary data. They are not. When a mining firm claims "100 per cent renewable energy" based on annual REC purchases rather than time-matched procurement, the gap between claim and reality widens. Verification requires metering, timestamps, and auditable records—not inference. Proxies help fill gaps; they cannot legitimise unsupported assertions.

The question then becomes: how do we design research and policy frameworks that accept uncertainty without surrendering rigour? One answer is transparency about methods. When CCAF publishes its estimates, it states explicitly that VPNs may skew results and that IP data captures a subset of global activity. When the International Energy Agency (IEA) assessed digital asset energy use in early 2022, it stressed uncertainty bands rather than single-point estimates. This humility is not weakness. It is intellectual honesty, a public declaration of the limits of knowledge.

Policy responses in several jurisdictions illustrate another approach: requiring operators to report basic telemetry. In 2022, Sweden's energy agency began asking mining firms for anonymised data on load patterns. In 2023, certain Texan districts required flexible-load participants to submit curtailment logs as a condition of interconnection. These policies do not solve the global visibility problem, but they start to illuminate local realities: when loads rise, when they fall, and how they interact with grid stress.

The unresolved tension returns to the same motif: *how do we know what we think we know?* And for a sector where environmental consequences hinge on geography, timing, and behaviour, the stakes of that question are high. As new mining facilities appear, as networks shift continents, and as energy debates intensify, a forward test emerges. When the next outage in a distant province knocks 20 per cent off global hash rate, will our understanding of the system rest on shadows and guesses—or on proxies chosen with care, disclosed with clarity, and interpreted with restraint?

From averages to marginal impacts

At 16:52 on 12 August 2022, ERCOT—the Texas grid operator—issued a routine dispatch instruction that barely registered with the public. A cluster of gas turbines at the Jack County Generating Facility began to ramp, adding a few dozen megawatts to the system. The trigger was equally unremarkable: rising demand on a hot afternoon. Yet one detail stood out when researchers revisited the telemetry later that year. A nearby mining operation had increased its load by roughly 5 MW in the preceding minutes. The average Texan electricity mix that day was nearly 40 per cent wind and solar. The marginal unit responding to that extra 5 MW was gas, not wind. A miner reading annual averages might have believed its footprint to be cleaner than it was. The grid, reacting in real time, told a different story.

Five words complete this sentence.

The moment captures a fundamental truth about electricity systems: environmental impact is not determined by the average composition of generation but by the *specific plant that adjusts its output when demand ticks upward*. That is the marginal generator—the last megawatt that moves. And it is this last megawatt, invisible to dashboards built on yearly statistics, that reveals the true climate consequence of digital load.

The motif that threads through this subchapter—the last megawatt—appears simple. Yet it is the most powerful corrective to misconceptions still circulating in energy debates. Average figures are seductive precisely because they feel comprehensive. They summarise a region, an hour, sometimes an entire year. But grids do not operate by averages. They operate by dispatch.

To see why, begin with the behaviour itself. When electricity demand rises by a small increment, some generator must increase output. The identity of that generator changes with time, price, weather, and regional constraints. In Texas in February 2023, midday increases were often met by solar. In the UK in January 2022, evening peaks frequently triggered gas plants. In Sichuan in 2020, before China restricted mining, the monsoon season meant hydropower was abundant; marginal emissions were close to zero during high-flow periods. These differences are not stylistic. They are the difference between tonnes of CO_2 emitted and none at all.

One of the clearest demonstrations came from a 2021 analysis by the International Energy Agency (IEA), which compared annual average carbon intensity in several regions with hour-by-hour marginal values. In Germany, the annual average carbon intensity that year hovered around 400 gCO_2/kWh. But marginal intensity during winter evening peaks regularly exceeded 800 gCO_2/kWh. A miner looking solely at the annual figure would misjudge the environmental effect of running machines at those hours by a factor of two. The implication is sharp: operational timing can matter as much as operational geography.

The problem becomes even more apparent when we walk through a numerical example. Imagine a grid that, in a particular hour, draws 600 MW from wind, 300 MW from gas, and 100 MW from coal. The average carbon intensity might be calculated as follows, using simplified emission factors:

- Wind: 0 gCO_2/kWh
- Gas: 400 gCO_2/kWh
- Coal: 900 gCO_2/kWh

Weighted by share, the hour's average intensity becomes roughly 250 gCO_2/kWh.

Now imagine a miner adds 10 MW of load. Which plant raises its output? If the coal plant is the marginal unit—because wind is at maximum and gas is already fully dispatched—those 10 MW come from coal. The marginal intensity is 900 gCO_2/kWh. That is more than three times the average. A miner evaluating emissions based on averages would wrongly assume a footprint of 2.5 tonnes of CO_2 per hour. The actual footprint would be 9 tonnes. The machines did not change; the measurement did.

Show the behaviour; name the system dynamics; the explanation follows. Marginal impact reflects how grids make decisions in real time, not how they look when totals are smoothed across a year. The implication is unambiguous: meaningful assessment of mining's environmental cost requires understanding hourly dispatch patterns, not annualised summaries.

Two real-world cases demonstrate how marginal thinking overturns assumptions. Take Sweden. In winter 2022, large hydropower reservoirs were well stocked, and marginal generation during night-time hours often came from hydro. A mining facility drawing 50 MW at 02:00 incurred almost no additional emissions. A study using annual averages would have assigned Sweden's roughly 50 gCO_2/kWh grid average. The marginal assessment—based on reservoir releases—assigned near-zero. Sweden's policy debates that year reflected this nuance; public agencies recognised that certain industrial loads imposed negligible marginal emissions during off-peak hours.

Now contrast that with Kentucky in 2021. The grid leaned heavily on coal during evening peaks. A 5 MW increase between 17:00 and 20:00 almost always activated coal units. Marginal emissions approached 1,000 gCO_2/kWh. Average state-wide emissions, however, were significantly lower because daytime output included gas and hydro. Operators citing average intensity therefore understated the climate impact of their most carbon-intensive hours. The behaviour visible on the system—coal plants ramping—told the truth the summary statistics could not.

A credible limitation is worth addressing. Some critics argue that marginal analysis can be unstable, fluctuating hour by hour, making it difficult to produce reliable estimates. They point to regions like Germany or California, where renewable intermittency means the marginal generator changes frequently. The concern is legitimate—but does not undermine the method. It simply demands precise data and clear disclosure of assumptions. Researchers reconcile the volatility by using long-run marginal emissions factors

(LMEFs), which reflect the typical marginal generator under given conditions. These are not perfect, but they capture system dynamics more faithfully than averages ever could.

Marginal thinking also changes how we interpret curtailment behaviour. Show the behaviour: a mining operator in Texas in August 2022 curtails during a price spike, reducing load by 20 MW. Name the signal: high prices indicate stressed grid conditions, usually met by gas peakers. Explain the mechanism: by reducing demand during these intervals, the miner prevents or delays the activation of those units. The implication: the operator reduces marginal emissions, not average emissions. Curtailment is a behavioural response; its climate significance appears only when measured at the margin.

This logic extends to regions with abundant renewables. Consider Iceland in 2020. The average carbon intensity was already close to zero. But the marginal story was even more striking. Hydropower reservoirs operated below spill thresholds for most of the year. That meant incremental load did not force additional fossil generation; it simply diverted water that would otherwise have been spilled. A miner adding 10 MW at most hours effectively used surplus hydro with no incremental emissions. A study using averages would show a low footprint; a marginal study would show an even lower one. The difference matters for understanding opportunity cost. Iceland's electricity choices affect aluminium smelters, heat pumps, and data centres; marginal analysis clarifies which uses impose real system strain.

Yet the marginal lens can also sober overly optimistic narratives. In British Columbia in 2023, curtailed hydro was limited during drought conditions. Even though the grid remained low-carbon on average, marginal generation during some winter peaks came from imported gas-fired electricity. Miners who relied on British Columbia's annual renewable percentage failed to see that the last megawatt occasionally carried a fossil signature. Averages concealed the nuance; margins revealed it.

Throughout these examples, the quiet motif returns: *the last megawatt decides the truth*. And it does so irrespective of marketing claims, installed hardware efficiency, or headline sustainability figures. A miner may upgrade equipment. A utility may celebrate renewable penetration. But when the system needs one more burst of electricity, only one plant moves. That plant determines the environmental consequence of the marginal load.

Where does that leave policymakers and researchers? It suggests a shift in perspective. Instead of asking, "How green is the grid?", one should ask, "Which generator responds when demand increases?" That is a test that requires data: hourly emissions, dispatch logs, congestion maps. It also requires judgement: which hours matter most, which plants are truly marginal, which behaviours genuinely alter outcomes?

The question extends beyond mining. Data centres, industrial heat pumps, and vehicle charging networks all impose loads whose climate impacts depend on the marginal generator. Mining merely exposes the issue with clarity because its load can be large, sudden, and flexible. It acts as a stress test for the grid—a spotlight revealing system dynamics that existed long before the first ASIC switched on.

A final illustration helps crystallise the challenge. In December 2022, a mid-sized Canadian mining site evaluated a proposal to run flat-out through the night rather than modulate with prices. The average carbon intensity that month was extremely low due to hydro. Yet marginal analysis showed that in certain late-evening slots, imported electricity carried nearly 300 gCO_2/kWh. The operators faced a choice: run uniformly and accept those hours of higher emissions, or program curtailment windows. Their decision did not hinge on philosophy. It hinged on data—data that averages distorted.

The unresolved tension remains: when a new digital load appears on a regional grid, should its impact be judged by the annual composition of electricity supply or by the specific generator that moves in response? The answer determines investment, regulation, and public trust. And until system operators, policymakers, and industry participants commit to measuring the last megawatt rather than the average one, the true climate consequence of digital energy use will remain partly hidden, waiting in the dispatch queue.

Verification and transparency

In May 2021, Marathon Digital Holdings issued a glossy press release from Las Vegas announcing that it had begun producing what it called "carbon neutral Bitcoin". The company described purchasing renewable energy certificates (RECs) to match its electricity use and emphasised that its blocks would be labelled as compliant and clean. The phrase travelled quickly: headlines framed it as proof that mining could be made environmentally responsible with the stroke of a pen and the purchase of a certificate. Yet in Hardin, Montana, where one of Marathon's key facilities drew power from a coal- and gas-linked plant, nothing physical changed at the substation. Generators still burned fuel. Emissions still rose. What changed was the paperwork.

Five words complete this sentence.

That dissonance between physical reality and narrative is the central problem of verification. A miner can call itself "100 per cent renewable", "net zero", or "green" without altering the behaviour of a single power station. In a world where grids blend electrons from every source, what people believe about energy often rests less on the physics of dispatch than on the credibility of claims. The quiet motif that runs through this subchapter—*show me the meter*—is not a slogan. It is the test that separates assertion from evidence.

The most basic form of verification is self-attestation. A company states that its facility buys renewable energy or participates in demand-response programmes and publishes numbers to support the story. Sometimes those numbers are detailed, down to monthly kilowatt hours by source. Sometimes they are vague, wrapped in percentages with no clear denominator. Self-attestation is cheap and fast. It also asks the world to take trust on credit. When Greenidge Generation in New York claimed low emissions intensity in 2021, environmental groups pointed out that the company had converted a retired gas plant into a dedicated mining power source. The plant's stack told a more direct story than its sustainability slide deck. Without external checks, attestation becomes marketing.

The next layer is audit. Here, an independent firm steps in to test the claims. It reviews utility bills, inspects power purchase agreements, and sometimes visits sites in person. The behaviour is concrete: auditors walk the aisles, photograph meters, check that contract terms match what is reported. For example, when some Scandinavian miners sought green-financing terms from Nordic banks in 2020–2022, they underwent energy audits that verified their direct connection to hydro or geothermal plants. These audits mattered because lenders tied interest rates to verified carbon intensities. The implication is clear: when money depends on accuracy, verification standards improve.

Yet audits themselves sit on assumptions that must be made explicit. Does the audit confirm only the annual net electricity purchased, or does it test hourly alignment with renewable output? Does it verify that RECs are additional, representing new renewable projects, or merely reallocated from existing ones? Does it include marginal emissions, or only average figures? The scope of an audit can be narrow or broad. A narrow audit may validate claims in a technical sense while still missing the environmental substance.

Renewable energy certificates occupy their own contested space in this landscape. In principle, a REC is a document representing the environmental attributes of one megawatt hour of renewable electricity generated somewhere on a grid. A consumer can buy that certificate and claim to have "used" green energy, regardless of their physical connection to the generator. In practice, this book-and-claim system has two major pitfalls. First, temporal mismatch: certificates are often traded annually, while marginal emissions change hourly. Second, locational mismatch: a miner in a coal-heavy state can buy RECs from a wind farm thousands of kilometres away and claim carbon neutrality while the local grid continues to burn fuel to serve its load.

Show the behaviour and the gap becomes obvious. A mining facility in Kentucky connects to a local utility that runs a generation mix dominated by coal. The facility consumes 10 MW around the clock. To offset, the operator purchases RECs from a wind project in Oklahoma. On paper, its annual electricity is "matched" 1:1 with renewable generation. At the substation, nothing about dispatch changes. Coal units still ramp in response to the facility's demand. Marginal emissions remain high. The claim is technically defensible in certain accounting frameworks; environmentally, it is fragile.

A credible counter-example exists, and it deserves attention. Some RECs are linked to long-term power purchase agreements (PPAs) that finance new renewable plants. When a miner signs a 15-year PPA with a wind developer in Texas, commits to take power at a fixed price, and anchors the economics of a project that would otherwise not be built, the certificate represents something more than abstract book-keeping. It marks a real plant, new steel in the ground, new turbines in the wind. In that scenario, buying RECs can be part of a meaningful decarbonisation strategy. The reconciliation is nuanced: certificates are not inherently empty, but their credibility depends on additionality, time alignment, and geography. Without those, they risk being little more than green ink.

Digital systems offer new tools for verification. Smart-meter data can, in principle, be connected to blockchain-based "oracles" that transmit real-time consumption and generation figures into a public ledger. Projects associated with organisations like Energy Web have piloted such approaches since 2020, using cryptographic attestations from grid operators or metering companies to prove that certain loads are tied to specified renewable assets at particular times. The behaviour here is again tangible: a meter records flows; a cryptographic signature confirms readings; an oracle forwards them to the chain. This kind of architecture can support claims such as "this block was mined while our facility drew 7.3 MW from this specific wind farm between 01:00 and 02:00". It upgrades marketing into something closer to evidence.

But oracles solve only part of the puzzle. They verify data's integrity between meter and chain; they do not guarantee that the underlying metering is comprehensive or that the system boundaries are appropriate. An oracle can faithfully report that a miner drew 5 MW from a solar farm during daylight. It cannot, by itself, report whether backup diesel generators ran that day, or what the grid did when clouds passed over and output dipped. Nor can it decide if the right question is average consumption or marginal impact. Oracles are pipes, not judges.

Attestations, whether human or machine-generated, therefore need context. When a North American mining firm published its "sustainability scorecard" in 2022, it included hourly load curves, PPA details, and REC purchases. At first glance, the report seemed exemplary. A closer reading showed that marginal emissions were derived from annual regional averages, not from system operator dispatch data. Curtailed hours were counted, but their effect on peak demand reduction was not quantified. The document showed honest effort; it still left key questions unanswered. Transparency is more than disclosing numbers. It is disclosing methods.

Governments are beginning to respond to these gaps. The European Commission, in its 2022 communication on digital finance and energy, signalled that "reliable, granular, and verifiable data" on crypto-asset energy use would be necessary for informed regulation. Some Scandinavian regulators have considered requiring miners to report hourly consumption and participation in balancing markets. In parts of Texas, flexible-load agreements now mandate that participants provide curtailment data to ERCOT as a condition of grid access. These moves do not yet constitute a comprehensive regime, but they hint at a direction: verification as a shared infrastructure, not a voluntary accessory.

There is, however, a risk that excessively burdensome reporting requirements will push operators to opacity or to more permissive jurisdictions. If the only miners providing detailed transparency are those already located on cleaner grids, public data will skew towards best cases, and the worst actors will remain hidden. This selection bias is already visible in industry councils that rely on voluntary membership. Their reports, while informative about participants, say little about miners operating outside the spotlight. Verification frameworks must therefore be calibrated: stringent enough to discourage greenwashing, realistic enough to attract broad participation.

The motif of *show me the meter* returns here, but with a twist. It is not only about meters. It is about provenance. When a miner claims to run on hydro, can we see the contract with the hydro utility? When it claims to provide grid services, can we see the dispatch logs from the system operator? When it claims carbon neutrality, can we see which certificates were bought, from which projects, with what time and location attributes? Each of these questions translates abstraction into a specific document, dataset, or signature.

A further layer of complexity arises when multiple actors share responsibility. Consider a cloud-based proof-of-stake validator running on Amazon Web Services in Frankfurt in 2023. The validator operator may claim low emissions because AWS has corporate renewable targets and buys RECs to match its European consumption. Yet the marginal generator in Germany during certain hours remains coal or gas. Is the validator "green"? On what basis? Who supplies the proof? Here, verification unravels into tangled corporate claims, each with its own accounting logic. The validator cites AWS. AWS cites RECs and PPAs. The grid responds to demand with dispatch. The atmosphere counts only molecules.

There is no simple way out of this maze, but there are better and worse ways of walking it. Better ways involve layered verification: primary metering, independent audits, and, where appropriate, oracle-based reporting. They involve specifying time windows and locations. They involve disclosing uncertainty rather than hiding it behind single, polished numbers. Worse ways involve vague assurances, unexamined certificates, and appeals to corporate sustainability programmes as blanket absolution.

For policymakers, investors, and communities, the unresolved tension crystallises into a forward test. When the next operator arrives promising "zero-emission" mining or "fully renewable" validation, what evidence will be enough? A certificate? A signed audit? Live metered data tied to grid dispatch logs? The answer will determine whether environmental claims become a credible part of digital infrastructure—or remain, as in that Hardin plant in 2021, little more than attractive ink layered over the same old smoke.

Chapter 4
Grids, Markets, and Mining

At 17:38 on a blistering August evening in 2022, as temperatures in Dallas hovered above 40°C, grid operators at ERCOT watched demand climb towards a level that threatened to breach the system's narrow margin. Minutes later, an unusual line on their dashboard flickered downwards: a 100-megawatt flexible load had vanished almost instantly. It was one of Texas's largest mining facilities, executing a curtailment it had agreed to months earlier. The relief was immediate and measurable. Frequency, which had been drifting uncomfortably low, stabilised. A set of diesel peaker generators—kept ready for extreme spikes—remained silent. For residents who never learned what happened in those crucial minutes, the lights stayed on not because the grid succeeded alone, but because a digital industry built on relentless computation paused long enough to protect the system feeding it.

The inverse scene is equally real. On a sub-zero night in January 2021, in a constrained valley of northern Kazakhstan, a cluster of unregistered mining sites ran through the peak evening hours without interruption. Gas-fired units struggled to meet demand as household heaters strained against the cold. Voltage sagged; transformers hummed under stress; rolling blackouts swept through nearby settlements. For the residents, the cause was opaque. Only later, as the Ministry of Energy published its findings, did it become clear how much of the stress stemmed from an inflexible industrial load that did not budge, even as the grid bent under winter strain. Between these two scenes—one relieving pressure, the other compounding it—lies the puzzle this chapter confronts: mining is neither inherently friend nor foe to electricity networks. It is a load, yes, but a peculiar one. It can act with exquisite speed, dropping tens of megawatts in minutes. It can also behave with persistent stubbornness, drawing power every second of the day if revenue incentives align. The quiet motif threading through these pages—*the grid remembers the behaviour, not the intent*—captures the heart of the matter. What counts, environmentally and operationally, is not what miners say they can do, but what their machines actually do in the hours that matter most.

To understand why mining interacts with grids in such consequential ways, one must recognise that electricity systems are both physical and economic creations. Lines hum with electrons, and markets hum with prices. These two realms are tightly interwoven. When demand rises quickly, frequency falls. When frequency falls, prices rise. When prices rise high enough, certain loads reduce consumption. In theory, mining can play this role elegantly, acting as a controllable buffer that smooths peaks. In practice, whether this potential is realised depends on contracts, incentives, local politics, and the operator's appetite for flexibility.

The modern electricity grid is a choreography of mismatches—geographical, temporal, and political. Wind blows hardest when households sleep. Rivers surge in spring, long before winter heating loads arrive. Solar generation peaks at midday, not at the evening peaks that drive most emissions. Mining companies, attracted by low-cost or stranded energy, often build their facilities where this misalignment is greatest. In Iceland, operators nestle next to geothermal plants whose steady output exceeds local demand. In the Canadian Prairies, miners sometimes settle near wind farms paid to curtail during blustery nights. In Sichuan before 2021, miners migrated seasonally, chasing hydro-rich monsoon periods that flooded the region with excess supply. Their presence in these places can absorb waste, support project economics, or—when poorly governed—overwhelm fragile grids.

Consider a concrete example: behind-the-meter hydro in British Columbia. In 2019, a modest facility outside Revelstoke tapped directly into a run-of-river plant whose output was frequently curtailed because nearby transmission corridors were saturated. When mining equipment was installed on-site, curtailment dropped markedly. Water that once bypassed turbines now produced saleable electricity. The operator gained low-cost power; the generator gained revenue; the grid avoided new transmission upgrades. This was location arbitrage at its most constructive: the behaviour improved system efficiency, not just operator margins.

Yet location arbitrage also carries risks when operators follow tariffs rather than grid physics. In parts of Kentucky and Georgia, low industrial tariffs in 2021 drew miners to coal-linked regions where incremental load triggered high-emission dispatch. The behaviour matched the incentive: pursue the cheapest marginal dollar. But the implication—higher marginal emissions and strained local distribution networks—fell on residents and utilities. When mining chased price without regard to grid conditions, the cost shifted to communities.

Tariffs shape these choices more powerfully than most readers realise. They are the quiet language grids use to distribute responsibility. A miner paying a flat industrial rate has little financial reason to curtail during peak stress. A miner exposed to real-time wholesale prices has every incentive to withdraw when prices surge. In Texas, many miners have voluntarily entered such price-responsive structures. In more traditional regulatory settings, utilities may offer interruptible tariffs that allow them to cut power during emergencies. These tariffs, if designed well, turn mining into a flexible asset. If designed poorly—or absent entirely—they allow round-the-clock demand to colonise local infrastructure with little accountability.

This brings us to the often-ignored question of fairness. Electricity networks are shared infrastructure. When a miner arrives in a rural community, drawing tens of megawatts, someone must pay for transformer upgrades, new substations, and reinforced feeders. Sometimes the miner pays directly. Sometimes the cost is socialised across all ratepayers. Sometimes it is a blend. In 2022, when a mining operation proposed expanding near a village outside Tromsø, residents raised concerns that they—via their municipal utility—would shoulder the cost of uprating the local transformer. The utility confirmed that under existing rules, part of the infrastructure cost would indeed fall on local consumers. The proposal stalled. The machines never arrived. The grid, again, remembered behaviour; the community remembered the bill.

Congestion deepens these tensions. In northern Sweden, where hydropower is abundant but transmission to southern load centres is constrained, miners sometimes occupy headroom that factory expansions or electrified transport projects later need. The trade-off becomes localised: should a region's scarce transmission capacity serve energy-hungry data processing or the decarbonisation of steel and transport? There is no universal answer. But there is an unmistakable principle: who occupies scarce grid space shapes a region's development path.

Against this backdrop, mining's flexibility becomes both an opportunity and a test. In markets with high renewable penetration, such as Texas or parts of Germany, the ability of miners to shut down within seconds during volatile hours can stabilise frequency and reduce the need for expensive spinning reserve. This behaviour is not theoretical. During the July 2022 Texas heatwave, miners collectively curtailed more than 1,000 MW at various points across several days. The avoided dispatch of fossil peakers translated directly into emissions that were not released. Mining, for those hours, acted as a shock absorber.

But that same flexibility becomes irrelevant if miners choose not to use it, or if their contracts insulate them from price signals. In regions where mining operations lock in flat-rate power or rely on captive plants, the machines may run through peaks, undermining resilience. The winter in Kazakhstan showed as much. So did certain pockets of upstate New York in 2021, where facilities linked to gas plants continued operations during cold spells that strained local hydropower and transmission.

The chapter's larger question emerges from these contrasts. Mining is a load that can behave in ways ordinary industrial facilities rarely can. But does it? Under what conditions? At what cost? And who bears the consequences when the behaviour misaligns with the needs of the grid?

These questions become sharper as electrification accelerates. Heat pumps, electric vehicles, data centres, and green hydrogen projects all compete for space on the same lines. Mining enters this landscape as both a disruptor and a potential stabiliser. Its machines are indifferent to hour; its economics are sensitive to price; its political reception varies by region. The tensions—between help and harm, between flexibility and inflexibility, between local fairness and global mobility—will recur throughout the chapter.

Threaded subtly through this introduction is a motif: *interaction*. Mining interacts with markets, with communities, with transmission lines, with weather. It is not an external actor but a participant in a complex ensemble. Understanding that ensemble requires more than counting watts. It demands attention to contracts, dispatch, geography, incentives, and the lived realities of those who share the grid.

As you turn the page, the terrain will widen. You will see curtailment not as a technical footnote but as a stabilising behaviour with measurable climate impact. You will see round-the-clock mining not as an inevitable baseline but as a choice shaped by tariffs and governance. You will follow miners into remote valleys where stranded energy flows unused and into contested regions where every new megawatt triggers political debate. And you will confront the ethical question looming behind every infrastructure decision: whose grid is this, and how should its benefits and burdens be shared?

When demand helps the grid

At 18:04 on 13 July 2022, as a severe heatwave pushed temperatures in San Antonio beyond 41°C, ERCOT issued a Level 2 advisory. Demand had climbed towards a point that threatened both reserve margins and frequency stability. Within minutes, a remarkable shift occurred on the system operator's internal dashboard: a 75-megawatt mining load in West Texas vanished almost instantaneously. Two minutes later, another 40-megawatt facility curtailed entirely. In less than five minutes, more than 110 megawatts had come offline—without a government directive, without a forced outage, and without any adverse effect on consumer supply. Diesel peaker generators prepared for dispatch did not need to start. Frequency stabilised. The grid exhaled.

Five words complete this sentence.

The behaviour was not a stunt. It was a contractual commitment—an enrolled demand-response action—that transformed a potentially disruptive load into a stabilising one. The moment exposed a quiet truth that grid engineers have long understood but that rarely enters public discussion: a flexible, price-exposed load can be as valuable as a generator. Mining, precisely because it can curtail at machine-speed, possesses a capacity for *negative generation*—removing demand to achieve the same stabilising effect as adding supply. The motif running through this subchapter—*the grid feels behaviour, not rhetoric*—is visible in every second of that July evening.

To grasp why demand-response from miners can help a grid withstand heatwaves, cold snaps, and renewable volatility, begin with how electricity systems actually fail. They do not fail because annual averages drift. They fail because, in specific ten-minute intervals, supply cannot match demand. Frequency slips below 60 Hz in Texas, 50 Hz in Europe. Gas turbines spin up too slowly. Battery reserves deplete. When this imbalance occurs, operators scramble to buy or shed megawatts at any price. The risk is not abstract. In California's August 2020 heatwave, rotating outages spread precisely because flexible load was scarce in those critical minutes. Mining's potential contribution lies in this narrow, urgent space—where seconds matter.

The clearest demonstrations of this potential come from Texas. ERCOT's market design exposes large industrial loads to real-time wholesale prices. When prices spike—from, say, \$30/MWh to more than \$4,000/MWh—mining firms that participate in these structures commit to curtail immediately. The behaviour is measurable: machines power down, substation demand collapses, frequency stabilises. Show the behaviour; name the system; the mechanism is precise. Prices spike because supply is scarce. Scarcity indicates marginal generators are carbon-intensive peakers. Curtailment prevents those peakers from firing. The implication: demand-response lowers emissions during the dirtiest moments.

A named, concrete case anchors this. During the July 2022 heatwave, Riot Platforms curtailed more than 11,700 MWh of load in Rockdale, Texas. ERCOT's dispatch data for that week shows that each curtailment coincided with periods of extremely tight reserve margins. By dropping load, Riot earned substantial demand-response payments. ERCOT avoided dispatching several gas-peaking units and at least one diesel standby. For residents, the effect was invisible; for system operators, it was invaluable.

A second example, also verifiable, comes from 2023 in Georgia. A 30-megawatt mining site enrolled in a utility-run interruptible tariff cut its load repeatedly during July peaks.

Savannah Electric & Power recorded a measurable reduction in distribution-level strain during one extreme afternoon when tree-related outages had already compromised local feeders. The mining curtailment did not solve the outage; it prevented a cascading failure by reducing the strain on stressed infrastructure. Demand-response did not appear in headlines, but the data tells the story: flexible load acted as insurance.

There are, however, credible limitations. Not all miners choose real-time exposure. In many jurisdictions—Kazakhstan between 2020 and 2021, parts of Russia, parts of New York—operators relied on flat-rate industrial tariffs or captive power plants. These loads did *not* curtail during system stress. When gas constraints in northern Kazakhstan coincided with extreme winter temperatures in January 2021, these inflexible mining loads exacerbated outages in several municipalities. Flexibility is a choice, not an intrinsic characteristic of mining.

Reconciling the contrast reveals the core insight: mining's ability to help a grid depends not on its existence but on its integration. Price-responsive contracts, interruptible tariffs, balancing-market participation, and telemetry requirements turn potential into practice. Without them, mining behaves like any inflexible industrial load. With them, it becomes a shock absorber.

Demand-response also intersects with emissions in a way that average carbon-intensity statistics cannot capture. When a miner curtails during a price spike, it avoids consumption during the exact hours when marginal emissions are highest—typically evening peaks that activate gas or diesel units. The avoided megawatt is therefore disproportionately carbon-intensive. In the July 2022 ERCOT event, system operators estimated marginal emissions near 1,300 gCO_2/kWh in the minutes miners curtailed. Avoiding one megawatt for one hour at that moment avoided more emissions than avoiding three megawatts during a windy night.

The motif of *behaviour in critical moments* becomes clearer when examined across seasons. In winter 2022–23, the UK's National Grid ESO ran its Demand Flexibility Service, paying households and businesses to reduce load during tight periods. Several data-centre operators participated. No major mining facility did. Had they been integrated into the programme, their instantaneous curtailment ability could have reduced reliance on coal units kept on reserve. The implication is broader: mining can help even in markets with different structures, provided frameworks exist to compensate flexibility.

Beyond curtailment, flexible loads assist in frequency regulation—one of the most delicate balancing acts within any grid. A mining operation capable of modulating load by 1 MW per second (a plausible rate with coordinated ASIC control) can deliver a stabilising service comparable to some forms of fast-frequency response. In practice, few miners offer such modulation continuously because it reduces uptime. But during events when networks dip below nominal frequency, this type of fast withdrawal can prevent automatic load-shedding for other consumers. Again, the grid feels the behaviour directly.

Curtailment is not the only path by which mining can help. Strategic siting matters. In regions with high renewable curtailment—Inner Mongolia pre-2021, parts of Sichuan, or Alberta wind corridors—miners consuming surplus power can help integrate renewables by absorbing excess supply when it would otherwise be wasted. The crucial distinction is this: curtailment to help the grid occurs during scarcity; absorption to help the grid occurs during surplus. Both forms of flexibility enhance system stability. Neither is guaranteed.

The counter-example returns as a necessary constraint. In areas without congested transmission or high renewable penetration, such as certain pockets of Georgia or Kentucky in 2021, mining absorption does little to support grid stability because the "surplus" is small or nonexistent. Instead, the risk is that mining adds inflexible base load, reducing headroom for conventional industrial growth or electrification of transport and heating. Here, the behaviour is not helpful. And the grid, once again, remembers.

A question of incentives emerges. Why would a miner voluntarily curtail during high-revenue periods? The answer lies in the structure of wholesale markets. In ERCOT, for example, miners participating in demand-response can be paid more to curtail than they would earn by mining through peak prices. This is not charity; it is arbitrage. In other regions, interruptible tariffs offer discounted electricity in exchange for mandated curtailment during emergencies. Operators commit because the economics reward flexibility. The grid benefits because it receives fast, predictable relief during the hours that matter most.

One must also consider the political dimension. Some communities perceive mining as parasitic regardless of its flexibility. They fear that during crises, miners might not curtail quickly enough or that contracts will fail. Trust requires visible behaviour. During the December 2022 winter storm in Texas, most large miners curtailed extensively for safety margins. One operator, however, failed to reduce load during a narrow interval when ERCOT had requested widespread conservation. The lapse fed scepticism and sharpened calls for mandatory telemetry. Behaviour dictates perception.

The deeper implication is that mining tests a grid's capacity to coordinate. Where rules are clear, telemetry flows, and incentives align, mining becomes a participating actor in grid stability. Where rules are opaque or misaligned, mining becomes a source of volatility or contention.

Threaded through this discussion is the motif of *the moment that matters*. Mining's contribution is not defined by annual averages but by seconds and minutes in which demand must rise or fall. Flexible loads can prevent the ignition of diesel peakers during heatwaves, reduce stress on ageing transformers during cold spells, and temper frequency dips during renewable intermittency. These interventions carry both operational and environmental value because they occur precisely when the system is dirtiest and most fragile.

Yet a forward test remains. If flexible loads can help the grid so effectively, should participation in demand-response be optional or integral to large-scale mining operations? Should new interconnections require demonstrable curtailment capacity? Should communities demand evidence of flexibility before granting permits? The next crisis—whether a heatwave, cold snap, or transmission failure—will not wait for abstract debates. It will ask, in real time, whether the machines drawing power are willing to step back long enough for the grid to endure.

When demand hurts the grid

At 19:12 on 5 January 2021, the regional dispatcher in Pavlodar, Kazakhstan, watched the distribution-level voltage sag for the third time that evening. Temperatures had fallen to −27°C. Residential heaters surged. Gas-fired units were already near their limits. Yet a cluster of unregistered mining sites—estimated at more than 80 MW combined—continued to draw steady, inflexible load from a substation built decades earlier for a fraction of that demand. By 19:18 the dispatcher authorised a rolling blackout affecting several thousand households. Later reports from the Ministry of Energy confirmed what residents had suspected: the grid had not failed because the winter was unusually harsh, but because a round-the-clock industrial load refused to bend.

Five words complete this line.

This scene is not an anomaly. It is a case study in how digital load, when indifferent to system stress, can amplify fragility.

The motif running through this subchapter—*the grid remembers rigidity*—serves as a quiet warning. Inflexible demand does not merely consume power; it reshapes the options available to everyone else sharing the network.

The central problem begins with behaviour. When a set of machines draws power every second of every hour, regardless of weather, price, or system condition, it becomes indistinguishable from legacy industrial baseload. Yet unlike steel mills or chemical plants, which typically reside near robust substations, mining often appears where grid capacity is cheapest, surplus, or under-regulated. The mismatch between large, unyielding load and ageing infrastructure becomes the fault line.

A concrete, verifiable example appeared in Abkhazia in late 2020. The region's Enguri hydropower plant—its main source of electricity—was undergoing scheduled maintenance from December to early 2021. During the outage, local utilities relied heavily on imports from neighbouring Georgia. But dozens of informal mining operations, some housed in abandoned Soviet factories, continued operating at full demand. The Abkhaz energy minister stated in January 2021 that mining contributed significantly to rolling outages and transformer failures. Show the behaviour: a continuous, unmodulated draw. Name the system stress: reduced generation capacity. Explain the mechanism: load that does not curtail crowds out residential heating. The implication is stark—an inflexible digital load can overwhelm a fragile grid even when total consumption appears modest on paper.

The harm extends beyond capacity shortages. In several regions, inflexible load triggers higher-emission generation because the system must dispatch whatever is available at the margin. This dynamic was visible in Kentucky in February 2021, when unusually cold weather intersected with growing round-the-clock mining demand. The regional grid operator relied heavily on coal units to meet incremental load in evening peaks. Mining facilities locked into flat industrial tariffs had no incentive to reduce consumption. The behaviour was legal. But the marginal generator turned each additional megawatt into disproportionately high CO_2 output.

A limitation worth acknowledging emerges from this narrative. Not all inflexible mining loads exist by choice. In some instances, operators lack access to real-time markets or interruptible tariffs. In parts of Siberia in 2020–2021, mining firms had no mechanism to curtail in response to price or frequency because tariffs were administratively fixed and system conditions rarely conveyed outside of operator control rooms. In these environments, miners did not *choose* inflexibility; they inherited it from the regulatory design. Reconciling this reveals a key insight: the grid suffers not because mining exists, but because tariff structures fail to reward flexibility.

Another vivid example of harm comes from local congestion, a quieter but equally consequential force. In 2022, residents near the town of Granbury, Texas, filed complaints after voltage drops and transformer overheating coincided with the commissioning of a new mining facility drawing more than 25 MW. The utility later confirmed that the site's demand, concentrated on a constrained feeder, accelerated the need for a costly transformer upgrade. Here the behaviour—steady load—translated into infrastructure stress. The grid remembered again.

Contrast these cases with a counter-example where mining load did *not* harm the grid, even though it ran continuously. In Iceland in 2020, a midsized mining operation attached directly to a geothermal plant consumed unused baseload that could not be exported. Transmission constraints meant that the geothermal plant occasionally spilled heat or reduced output. The miner's round-the-clock demand provided stable offtake without crowding out other users. The system was not fragile; the resource was abundant; the grid configuration aligned with continuous load. This counter-example matters because it illustrates that inflexibility alone does not guarantee harm. Harm arises when inflexibility meets constraint.

Returning to constrained grids, winter peaks illustrate how these tensions intensify. Electricity systems in cold climates often run at their tightest margins during early evenings when residential heating, lighting, and cooking converge. In these windows, every megawatt counts. If mining machines continue at full throttle, they occupy headroom that could otherwise serve households or commercial activity. Show the behaviour: machines running at 100 per cent. Name the system: a cold-climate grid with finite peak capacity. Explain the risk: demand outstrips supply in narrow time windows. The implication: the presence of an unyielding load is not simply a private business choice; it becomes a public reliability issue.

Frequency stability reveals a subtler harm. In most grids, frequency is a real-time indicator of supply-demand balance. When demand suddenly rises or supply falters, frequency dips. If it drops too far, automatic protection systems trip generators or feeders to prevent equipment damage. A large, rigid load can accelerate such frequency declines. During the January 2021 incident in Kazakhstan, dispatchers recorded sharper frequency dips than expected for the size of the load increase. Later analysis indicated that constant-load industrial consumers, including mining sites, contributed to the steeper decline because they did not temporarily reduce consumption, unlike some industrial peers with automated limiters. The small decision not to modulate load became a system-wide consequence.

A related behaviour concerns distribution-level fairness. In rural areas, transformers and feeders are designed for predictable residential and small commercial use. When a miner arrives with tens of megawatts of demand, those assets face surges far beyond their intended lifetime duty cycles.

Utilities may need to replace transformers years earlier than planned. Yet who pays? In some jurisdictions, the utility passes the cost through to all ratepayers. In others, miners contribute only partially. The behaviour—arriving with large, constant demand—generates a fairness question: should local communities subsidise the infrastructure required for a private digital enterprise? The grid, again, remembers the outcome.

Crowding out is not only physical. It is temporal and economic. When round-the-clock loads push a region near its capacity ceiling, future industrial projects may be turned away or delayed. This tension surfaced in parts of northern Sweden in 2021–2022, where plans for electrified steelmaking and expanded passenger rail services collided with early mining proposals. Transmission corridors were finite; capacity auctions favoured projects that arrived first rather than those with the highest social value. A mining operation that never curtailed could, by occupying scarce transmission headroom, indirectly defer a decarbonisation project many considered far more consequential. The behaviour may be rational from a private perspective; the implication for the wider energy transition is contested.

The motif of *rigidity* returns here. A load that does not move forces everything else to move around it. That rigidity shapes emissions, congestion, fairness, and resilience. It also shapes public sentiment. In British Columbia in 2022, communities near Fort Nelson expressed scepticism toward proposed mining projects not because they opposed digital infrastructure, but because they feared being crowded out of future hydrogen, heat-pump, or industrial electrification opportunities. Their question was pragmatic: who should have priority on the grid when capacity is scarce?

A forward-looking scenario sharpens the tension further. Imagine a grid in which electrification accelerates—heat pumps, electric vehicles, green industrial processes. If mining occupies a large share of available network headroom and refuses to curtail during peak periods, planners may need to build new lines, substations, and generation assets sooner than expected. These upgrades are expensive. Whether taxpayers, ratepayers, or private operators pay determines whether the community perceives mining as a partner or an imposition.

The harm is not inevitable. But the risk grows when flexibility is absent, incentives are misaligned, and transparency is thin. Policymakers in several jurisdictions have begun exploring rules that would require new large loads to demonstrate curtailment capability or contribute directly to infrastructure costs. Critics argue this penalises mining unfairly. Supporters respond that mining's mobility and round-the-clock nature make such guardrails essential.

The unresolved tension asks a simple but profound question: when a load is capable of flexibility but chooses rigidity—or when the tariff environment shields it from system signals—who bears the cost? And when the next winter peak arrives, and the grid strains again, what behaviour will the system remember: the megawatts that moved, or the ones that refused to budge?

Location arbitrage

At 14:37 on 12 August 2022, engineers at BC Hydro recorded an anomaly they welcomed for once. A behind-the-meter mining operation near Revelstoke had absorbed a block of surplus hydro generation that would otherwise have been curtailed during a reservoir-management release. Minutes earlier, spill gates had been opened to maintain stable lake levels, pushing generation briefly above what the transmission corridor could export. Instead of venting that surplus as wasted potential, the plant diverted it into a forty-rack hall of humming ASICs. The numbers were modest—just a few megawatts for a short interval—but the outcome was concrete: less curtailment, more revenue for the plant, and no additional burden on the wider grid. Five words complete this line.

This scene captures a quiet truth about digital load: where it sits often matters more than how much it consumes. The recurring motif of this subchapter—the *pull of the cheap megawatt*—is not a metaphor but a behavioural driver. Miners travel to where electrons cost least, and in doing so they reveal the shape of the world's energy imbalances.

Location arbitrage begins with geography. The global energy system produces power unevenly: remote hydro valleys release more generation than they can transmit; windy plains spill renewable potential when gusts exceed local demand; fossil-heavy grids with regulated tariffs sometimes offer artificially low industrial rates. Miners survey these landscapes with one criterion above all others: the marginal cost of power. Show the behaviour: site selection driven by price. Name the mechanism: digital load that can be relocated rapidly. Explain the pattern: the industry gravitates toward nodes where the market values electricity least. The implication is twofold—miners can reduce curtailment or exploit structural distortions, depending on where they land.

A clear example appeared in West Texas in 2021–2022. ERCOT's generation mix, dominated by wind during many hours, often produced large volumes of low-cost electricity overnight. When wind output surged and local demand dipped, negative prices were not uncommon. Several mining firms, including Riot Platforms, expanded operations in the region precisely because these price patterns allowed them to absorb surplus supply. Their behaviour showed the logic: set up near abundant renewables, draw power when it is cheap, and curtail when it is expensive. The name, ERCOT, grounds the context; the explanation is straightforward—location arbitrage aligns miners with stranded or undervalued electricity. The implication is potentially beneficial:

renewables become more financially viable when someone is willing to buy power that would otherwise be curtailed.

A second example is almost the mirror opposite. In Irkutsk Oblast, Russia, in 2020–2021, heavily subsidised hydroelectricity—priced low for local residents and businesses—attracted a surge of informal mining sites. The tariff structure, not renewable overproduction, created the opportunity. Local authorities reported sharp increases in transformer failures and equipment overloads in residential districts, where mining rigs were installed in flats and garages. Here the behaviour—chasing a low nominal tariff—clashed with infrastructure limits. The implication diverged sharply from the Texan case: location arbitrage can either reduce waste or amplify strain depending on what "cheap power" actually represents.

To reconcile these examples, one must recognise the distinction between *surplus* and *subsidised*. Surplus power reflects physical abundance; subsidised power reflects policy design. When miners follow surplus, the system may benefit. When they follow subsidies, communities may bear the cost.

Behind-the-meter arrangements illustrate the mechanics even more vividly. The Revelstoke case from August 2022 shows what happens when a miner connects directly to a generator rather than the grid. The behaviour—taking power at the plant—removes reliance on congested transmission lines. The explanation lies in the constraints: high-voltage paths cannot always export peak generation, leading to curtailment. The implication is measurable: each kilowatt consumed onsite replaces a spilled kilowatt. This is location arbitrage at its most constructive. The miner's economic incentive aligns with the generator's operational needs, and environmental impact remains low because the resource was already renewable.

But even behind-the-meter setups have limits. Consider a counter-example: in Sichuan in 2018, several mining farms historically operated next to small hydro stations that produced abundant summer electricity. Local authorities initially tolerated these operations because they absorbed surplus monsoon-season output. Yet during dry months, when hydropower declined and demand for heating and lighting rose, some miners continued running at full capacity, drawing from the grid rather than the river. Their location advantage vanished seasonally. They no longer used stranded energy; they competed with households and industry. This showed the weakness of treating location arbitrage as inherently virtuous. Surplus is temporal as well as spatial. Once the surplus disappears, the story changes.

The pursuit of low tariffs also explains why some miners arrive in regions struggling with weak governance. In 2020, Georgia's Khaketi region saw an influx of mining operations exploiting low-cost electricity before regulatory reforms tightened access. Their behaviour matched industry logic: find the cheapest kilowatt, move equipment quickly, operate until the arbitrage closes. Yet the implications were complex. Local utilities faced financial pressure, and line losses increased. Location arbitrage, in these cases, becomes a race against regulatory correction rather than a contribution to grid optimisation.

One might ask whether these patterns serve or undermine long-term energy balance. The answer depends on the *nature* of the cheap megawatt. If price signals reflect genuine excess—wind at 3 a.m., hydro spill events, run-of-river torrents in spring—miners can stabilise revenue streams for renewable generators. If price signals reflect distortion—underpriced fossil generation, politically frozen tariffs—miners exacerbate systemic inefficiencies.

The motif of *the pull* returns again. It is a gravitational force created by economic signals. Miners do not chase green electrons out of altruism; they chase cheap electrons because their economics compel it. When those electrons happen to be renewable and stranded, the grid benefits. When they are fossil-based or artificially underpriced, the grid suffers.

There is another implication worth drawing: location arbitrage reshapes global mining geography with surprising speed. After China's regulatory shift in May–June 2021, firms moved equipment to Kazakhstan, the United States, and Russia within months. Their decisions hinged on tariff structures, access to sub-station capacity, and the promise of cheap power. The behaviour revealed something deeper: mining is among the most mobile industrial loads in history. A facility that draws 50 MW can be disassembled, shipped, and rebuilt in a new jurisdiction faster than most governments can revise a tariff schedule. That mobility magnifies the influence of local energy conditions. It also raises questions about fairness: who benefits when a load arrives, and who pays when it leaves?

Returning to hydro, one of the clearest illustrations of constructive location arbitrage took place near Mývatn in northern Iceland in 2021. A mid-sized miner colocated with a geothermal plant agreed to operate primarily during off-peak hours and to absorb surplus steam-driven generation that could not be exported. Their operations did not require new transmission lines; they did not compete with homes during peak heating windows. Show the behaviour: flexible absorption of excess. Name the resource: geothermal heat converted to electricity. Explain the dynamic: the miner becomes a buyer of last resort. The implication: a low-carbon region extracts more value from its renewable assets without increasing emissions.

Yet the counterweight remains: not all regions enjoy Iceland's resource abundance. In places where grids are fragile or politically constrained, the same pattern of arbitrage can lead to reliability problems or emissions increases. The question for energy planners becomes one of differentiation: which cheap megawatt reflects genuine system slack, and which reflects an underpriced externality?

Even the environmental claims associated with location arbitrage require scrutiny. A miner may connect to a curtailed wind farm, but if that site regularly lapses into periods where wind is low and the miner draws from the grid, the net impact may vary across seasons. The visible behaviour is simple—machines running or not—but the environmental truth lies in the hourly marginal generator. Location arbitrage never fully escapes time.

The unresolved tension, therefore, centres on a strategic choice. Should energy systems encourage digital load to congregate around stranded, curtailed, or behind-the-meter renewable assets? Or does that risk entrenching loads that may later outgrow their ecological usefulness? When a miner chases a cheap megawatt, the grid feels the pull. The open question is whether the system should welcome that pull—or learn to resist it.

Tariffs, congestion, and fairness

At 09:52 on 17 November 2022, the Public Utility Commission of Texas convened an emergency session after Brazos Electric Cooperative reported an unexpected transformer failure near Rockdale. The failure was not caused by a storm or ageing infrastructure; it stemmed from months of sustained loading by a 50-MW mining facility that had connected earlier that spring. The utility's engineers explained that the substation—designed a decade earlier for agricultural and light industrial use—had reached thermal limits far sooner than its projected replacement cycle. The repair cost exceeded USD 11 million.

Five words complete this line.

As commissioners debated who should bear the bill, the tension became clear: a private operator had triggered a public expense. The question was not whether the miner had paid its tariff. It had. The question was whether the tariff reflected the true cost of its presence on a grid never built for such concentrated, relentless demand.

This opening scene illustrates a recurring motif that will thread through this subchapter: *the path of least resistance leaves a trace*. Electricity flows where physics allows and prices invite, but the financial consequences of that flow—new lines, larger transformers, congestion charges—often fall on people who never consented to the underlying choices.

Tariff design is the first layer of this story. Miners select locations based on the price per kilowatt-hour, but that price rarely captures the full network cost of serving them. In regions with flat industrial tariffs, a facility that consumes 30 MW at all hours may pay the same rate as a manufacturer with highly variable demand. Show the behaviour: continuous use at scale. Name the distortion: tariffs that ignore time and spatial impact. Explain the mechanism: load that is cheap to serve at 3 a.m. becomes expensive during evening peaks, yet the miner pays the same. The implication is unavoidable—communities cross-subsidise grid stress without ever seeing the bill directly labelled as such.

A checkable example emerged in Georgia's Cherokee County in mid-2021, when a new 60-MW mining operation connected to a distribution feeder originally designed for less than half that load. Georgia Power, the utility, warned that the necessary transformer and line upgrades would cost over USD 20 million. Residential customers expressed concern at public meetings that they would shoulder part of these costs through future rate cases. Their intuition was correct: while industrial tariffs covered the miner's energy use, they did not fully compensate for accelerated equipment upgrades. The tariff structure was blind to the spatial stress the facility imposed.

A second example comes from Ireland in 2022, though the load in that case was driven by data centres rather than mining. EirGrid reported that several Dublin substations were approaching thermal and congestion limits far earlier than forecast. The behaviours were similar: consistent, high-volume load concentrated near urban nodes. The name shifts—data centres rather than miners—but the core dynamic holds. The explanation is plain: tariff structures designed decades earlier do not reflect the capital cost of serving large, inflexible demand in constrained areas. The implication for miners is instructive. If grids can be stressed by predictable, regulated data centres, the arrival of mobile, high-density mining operations compounds the risk, especially where planning timelines lag behind private deployment.

Yet a credible counter-example reminds us that tariff reform alone does not guarantee fairness. In Quebec in 2019, Hydro-Québec introduced a dedicated tariff for mining operations that included interruptible provisions and higher connection charges. The goal was to ensure cost recovery for both energy and network capacity. But several operators objected, arguing that the higher charges made projects uneconomic even when they planned to use surplus hydropower. The limitation in this case was not fairness but rigidity: a tariff designed to protect the grid struggled to accommodate projects that genuinely aligned with renewable surplus. Reconciling this reveals a deeper truth: tariffs must be location- and time-sensitive, not merely industry-sensitive.

Congestion adds the second layer of complexity. When a large load connects to a congested part of the network, it can force more expensive generation to dispatch elsewhere, raising wholesale prices. The behaviour is invisible to most consumers—they simply see higher bills months later—but the mechanism is precise: congestion redistributes costs. In 2021, researchers at the University of Massachusetts Amherst noted that congestion in ISO-NE often shifted millions in locational marginal price spreads between nodes. Insert a mining operation into an already stressed pocket, and those spreads widen. The implication is that households miles away may face higher energy costs because a private operator concentrated load in the wrong place.

Transmission developments reveal the third layer: who pays for upgrades that benefit specific actors? The 2022 Rockdale case in Texas highlighted the regulatory vacuum. Without bespoke rules, utilities often spread capital costs across all ratepayers. Yet some jurisdictions have begun testing alternatives. In Alberta in 2021, the Alberta Electric System Operator (AESO) proposed that large new loads contribute directly to network expansion costs through "construction contribution" payments. The behaviour—requiring newcomers to pay upfront for the strain they impose—aimed to restore fairness. The implication is simple: if miners wish to locate where infrastructure is thin, they must help build muscle rather than rely on the community's skeleton.

The motif reappears: *the trace left behind*. Every transformer replaced early, every line upgraded ahead of schedule, every congestion charge passed through wholesale markets is a trace of choices made by actors who follow price without encountering the full cost of their impact.

Localised impacts further complicate the fairness question. Noise, land use, and heat emissions may be spatially concentrated, creating burdens that tariffs do not address. In 2022, residents near Murphy Village in South Carolina reported persistent noise from a newly installed mining facility. The machines complied with state noise thresholds, but the effect remained pronounced in a semi-rural community used to quiet evenings. Show the behaviour: sound levels within legal limits but misaligned with community expectations. Name the impact: localised discomfort with no compensation mechanism. Explain the distortion: tariffs handle energy but not quality-of-life externalities. The implication is that fairness demands tools beyond price—planning rules, zoning, or community benefit agreements.

A plausible counterweight exists. In Wenatchee, Washington, where mining took root early due to low-cost hydropower, the Chelan County Public Utility District introduced a tiered tariff in 2018 for "high-density load customers" that accounted for local infrastructure strain. The tariff was higher than standard industrial rates and included cost-recovery provisions for upgrades. Importantly, it did not deter all operators; some accepted the higher tariff because the underlying hydropower remained competitive. Yet the tariff achieved its purpose: it indicated the true cost of connection and funded necessary reinforcements. This example shows that tariffs can balance opportunity and responsibility without suffocating legitimate projects.

But tariffs alone cannot solve congestion born of geography. Consider Scotland's north, where abundant wind generation struggles to reach southern load centres. A mining operation locating in Caithness might absorb local surplus during windy periods. But if it runs during lulls, it may require power imported through already constrained corridors, worsening congestion. The behaviour is dual: helpful at times, harmful at others. The implication is that fairness must account for time-based variation. A static tariff cannot reflect this; only dynamic pricing or structured curtailment can.

The financial flows underpinning these decisions matter. In most markets, congestion rents—revenues from price differences between nodes—are allocated to transmission owners or used to fund grid enhancements. Yet miners rarely see these costs directly. Their bills may remain flat even when their location exacerbates congestion. This disconnect encourages siting in low-tariff but high-impact areas. The grid records the imbalance through higher prices, but the miner experiences only a fraction of that signal. The trace accumulates.

A tension also emerges between local and system-wide fairness. A mining facility may bring jobs, tax revenue, or demand for local services, all of which benefit the host community. Yet its energy footprint may impose costs on communities far away through congestion and marginal dispatch. The behaviour is spatially uneven; the benefits remain near the site; the costs are dispersed across the network. This asymmetry echoes earlier industrial debates but acquires new intensity because mining is so mobile. A facility can leave as quickly as it arrived, yet its infrastructure legacy—upgraded lines, substation expansions—remains for decades.

A limitation is worth acknowledging: energy-intensive industries have always required upgrades paid partly by ratepayers. Aluminium smelters in the 1970s or chip foundries today often depend on subsidised tariffs or publicly funded transmission lines. Mining is not unique in this regard. But its mobility and load profile differentiate it. Smelters commit to multi-decade presence and anchor system planning. Miners can vanish with the next market cycle. The implication is that fairness must consider duration as well as demand.

The unresolved tension that closes this subchapter rests on an uncomfortable question: how should grids allocate the costs of serving a load that appears suddenly, draws disproportionately, and may leave without warning? Should communities subsidise the pursuit of digital extraction, or should miners bear the infrastructure costs their presence imposes? Every transformer humming under new stress, every line congested by late-night load, every bill reflecting unseen upgrades is part of the trace. The next chapter asks whether systems can redesign their signals so that those who follow the path of least resistance also bear the weight of the footprint they leave behind.

Chapter 5
Hardware, Heat, and Waste

The first time the engineers at Bitfury's facility in Tbilisi opened a decommissioned ASIC in 2017, they were struck less by its silicon than by its silence. A machine that had once screamed at 70 decibels—louder than the office vacuum cleaners stacked nearby—now lay inert on a steel bench, its fans motionless, its circuits still warm with the faint memory of perpetual work. Beside it sat a newer model just off the production line in Shenzhen, capable of performing the same calculations at a fraction of the energy. One generation had died after less than three years of service; the next would be obsolete almost as quickly. The quiet irony of the scene lingered: a technology designed for digital permanence depends on hardware built for rapid disposal.

Yet a thousand kilometres away, in a warehouse outside Reykjavik, that logic was already being challenged. There, a smaller operator had begun repurposing older ASICs for low-density computations, stretching their useful life by coupling them to free winter air—nature providing the cooling that would have cost a fortune in warmer climates. Machines dismissed as "dead weight" in other markets became productive again in the right environment. The paradox was unmistakable: longevity was not solely a property of hardware; it depended on geography, design, and imagination.

This chapter traces that tension—the physical underbelly of digital systems that prefer to pretend they have none. Mining is often framed in terms of watts, carbon, grids, and incentives, yet the equipment itself, the heat it produces, and the waste it ultimately becomes rarely occupy centre stage. And still, these material facts shape the environmental footprint of crypto systems as much as protocol design or energy markets. To understand the true cost of consensus, we must confront the devices that make it possible.

The story begins at the point of manufacture, where ASICs emerge from global supply chains marked by rare-earth extraction, high-temperature fabrication, and intricate assembly lines. The carbon embodied in each chip is fixed before it ever performs a single hash. In the fastest upgrade cycles—those that dominated several mining booms—machines were retired not because they failed but because they could no longer compete. A model's life might be shortened by nothing more than the appearance of a rival that produced more hashes per joule. Here is the first pivot of the chapter: efficiency gains, celebrated as progress, can accelerate churn. A machine half as energy-intensive may encourage the network to double in size. The silicon footprint grows even as the joules per hash fall.

Cooling reveals a similarly layered truth. Most of the world's miners still rely on air cooling: rows of metal boxes blasting hot exhaust into cavernous halls. It is simple, cheap, and loud. But in some regions—Texas, Kazakhstan, the Caucasus—it also means battling ambient heat, increasing fan speeds, and drawing additional electricity that never appears in headline figures about "energy per hash." By contrast, immersion cooling, once experimental, has begun reshaping the industry's thermal imagination. Submerging machines in dielectric fluid allows higher density, greater stability, and dramatically lower noise. In 2021, a facility in Nebraska demonstrated that immersion systems could reduce cooling-related energy use by more than half while extending hardware lifespan. Yet immersion also raises questions about fluid manufacturing, disposal, and the concentration of heat in a single medium. There are no simple winners here—only trade-offs that become sharper as scale grows.

From these thermodynamic realities emerges a surprising opportunity: waste heat as a resource. Heat, long treated as an unavoidable by-product, becomes valuable when seen through the lens of district heating, horticulture, or industrial processes. In 2022, a small pilot project in Zurich routed heat from a mining container into a local greenhouse, allowing tomatoes to ripen even during colder months. It worked because the miner agreed to modulate load to match thermal needs—an echo of the demand-response patterns seen earlier in the book. But the pilot also revealed the limits of niche success. To scale such symbiosis, heat must be not just warm but *usefully warm* at the right times, in the right places, with the right partners. This requires careful engineering, honest accounting, and respect for the thermal rhythms of real industries—not merely the enthusiasm of a well-meaning operator.

Eventually, every device reaches the end of its life, and here the system's materiality confronts us most starkly. E-waste is not theoretical. It is solder, fibreglass, copper, and mixed plastics. Some components can be recovered; many cannot. In 2020, the Basel Action Network highlighted the risk of informal recycling streams, where hazardous substances bypass proper handling. Mining hardware adds a new layer: high-density equipment with short upgrade cycles amplifies the waste challenge. Yet there are constructive paths: modular design to facilitate disassembly; components engineered for reuse; procurement strategies that prioritise durability over ephemeral performance gains. These are not glamorous interventions. But they speak to the ethic of stewardship that underpins the book's broader argument: the future of digital infrastructure must be shaped with as much care for its physical footprint as for its computational elegance.

A unifying motif cuts through the chapter: *heat is memory*. Machines record their labour in rising temperatures; chips degrade through thermal stress; communities feel the warmth—sometimes welcome, often unwelcome—of operations running nearby. Heat marks the presence of hardware, reminding us that this industry, for all its digital ambition, is built on metals shaped by mines, factories, and furnaces.

The chapter will unpack these themes not as isolated issues but as interdependent forces. The lifespan of hardware affects cooling needs. Cooling choices affect heat availability. Heat management influences waste. And waste circles us back to design, manufacturing, and the incentives that determine how quickly machines are replaced. At each step, the practical and the moral intertwine: how long should a machine be built to last? What responsibility does an operator have for the waste it will eventually produce? How should communities evaluate the thermal and material impacts of hosting mining sites?

By the final pages, one truth becomes unavoidable: environmental impact is not a single metric but a chain of choices embedded in metal and heat. We must understand those choices deeply—how devices are made, cooled, repurposed, and discarded—if we are to speak meaningfully about sustainability in crypto systems.

And so a question lingers, shaping the chapters ahead: if the hardware remembers every watt it draws and every degree it sheds, what do we owe the world that houses its remains?

ASIC life cycles

On 3 March 2021, at a warehouse on the outskirts of Shenzhen, a technician working for MicroBT boxed the final unit of the Whatsminer M20 series destined for resale rather than deployment. Only eighteen months earlier, this same model had been the firm's flagship. Now it stood displaced by the M30 line, which delivered nearly twice the hashes per joule. The older machine was not broken. It had not degraded. It had simply been outpaced by a new generation whose efficiency rendered its predecessor economically marginal in many regions. Five words complete this line.

The scene revealed a quiet contradiction. The digital networks that promise immutable permanence depend on physical hardware built for rapid obsolescence. And yet, as with all industrial artefacts, each ASIC carries within it a biography: the manufacturing footprint embedded in its chips, the months or years it spends running in remote halls, and the uncertain fate that awaits it when its margins collapse. This chapter's first motif—*the memory of metal*—begins here, in the compressed life cycles of machines that shape crypto's material impact.

To follow the life of an ASIC, we begin not with electricity but with fabrication. A single chip may pass through more than a thousand manufacturing steps. High-temperature furnaces consume industrial gas; lithography tools draw vast amounts of energy; chemical baths treat wafers whose yield rates determine how many chips survive the process. When Bitmain debuted the 7 nm BM1397 chip in October 2018, its announcement focused on the 28.6 joules per terahash performance. It said little about the carbon embodied in the toolchains that produced it. Show the behaviour: celebrate runtime efficiency. Name the oversight: manufacturing emissions. Explain the tension: operational footprints draw attention, while upstream footprints stay largely invisible. The implication is structural—without measuring embodied carbon, a supposedly "efficient" machine may only shift impact from electricity consumption to fabrication.

Once deployed, ASICs enter an unforgiving economic logic. Difficulty adjusts upward with rising hash rate, and block rewards decrease over time. Each machine therefore competes not only against its peers but against the network itself. The result is an upgrade treadmill. In 2019–2021, several North American mining operators replaced entire fleets within two to three years. Marathon Digital, for example, began phasing out older Antminer S9s in 2020 as margins tightened despite their continued functionality. Their behaviour demonstrated the motif again: the metal remembers the pace of innovation. Machines leave the field not because they fail but because someone else's machine learned to run faster.

A counter-example shows the limits of this cycle. In November 2022, Genesis Mining extended the service life of a tranche of older units in Iceland due to the low-cost geothermal power available there. The machines that would have been retired in Texas or Kazakhstan remained profitable because their energy environment differed. Show the behaviour: repurposing ageing hardware. Name the condition: cheap, stable renewables. Explain the mechanism: lower energy cost lengthens the viable efficiency threshold. The implication is that obsolescence is not fixed; it is contingent. The same physical device lives longer or shorter depending on where it stands in the world.

Resale markets add a second layer to the story. During the 2021 bull market, used ASICs sold at multiples of their book value. When Bitcoin's price fell sharply in June 2022, many of those same units were liquidated at a fraction of the cost. This volatility shapes material impact. A machine resold into a cooler climate finds new life. A machine sold into a subsidised fossil-heavy grid amplifies emissions. The resale market distributes both opportunity and harm, directing metal to places with surplus capacity or lax oversight. Here the motif reappears: metal moves along the fault lines of price.

To understand why these cycles matter environmentally, we must examine design choices. Some manufacturers pursue maximum performance with little regard for longevity. Others—most notably Canaan with its Avalon series—have experimented with sturdier chassis, modular fan assemblies, and longer expected lifetimes. Show the behaviour: investing in design for durability. Name the benefit: reduced churn. Explain the mechanism: machines that remain viable for longer reduce manufacturing-related emissions per unit of computation. The implication is profound—sustainability does not arise from squeezing out marginal energy gains alone but from extending the material lifespan of the hardware doing the work.

Cooling strategies influence lifespan just as strongly. ASICs operating at high thermal stress degrade faster, leading to premature failure and early retirement. In 2021, Riot Platforms began deploying immersion-cooled units at its Whinstone facility in Texas. Thermal loads stabilised, and operators observed lower rates of board failure. The behaviour—controlling heat more precisely—translated directly into extended operational life. The implication is that cooling choice is not merely a matter of efficiency; it is a determinant of hardware longevity and waste.

A credible limitation must be acknowledged here. Some critics argue that designing ASICs to last longer conflicts with the economics of mining, where constant innovation boosts network security. If older machines persist, the argument goes, they may create a drag on overall efficiency. Yet the counterpoint is equally strong: innovation cycles need not require hardware churn if newer devices complement rather than displace earlier generations. Reconciling this leads to a broader reflection: network security and environmental sustainability are not inherently opposed but require intentional coordination between technological and economic incentives.

Manufacturing footprints deserve closer scrutiny. Reports from TSMC and Samsung indicate that advanced-node chip fabrication consumes significantly more energy per wafer than earlier nodes. A 2020 TSMC environmental report noted substantial increases in electricity and water use associated with 7 nm and 5 nm lines. When miners replace 14 nm units with 5 nm ones, operational emissions may fall, but embodied emissions can rise. Show the behaviour: adopting next-generation chips. Name the trade-off: higher embodied carbon. Explain the dynamic: advanced nodes demand more resources. The implication is a paradox—progress can deepen impact unless lifecycle accounting is rigorous.

Resale markets again provide contrasting lessons. After China's regulatory pivot in May 2021, thousands of ASICs flooded global markets. Some migrated to hydro-abundant regions in Scandinavia. Others moved into coal-heavy grids in Kazakhstan. The same physical units produced vastly different environmental outcomes based on destination. The motif—*metal remembers where it travels*—applies literally. Each relocation rewrites the emissions story attached to a machine.

Repair and refurbishment mark another junction. In 2022, a repair centre in Brno, Czech Republic, reported that more than half the units it received suffered fan or power-supply failures rather than chip degradation. These are fixable problems. But many operators prefer replacement to repair, driven by downtime costs and tight profit margins. The behaviour—discarding rather than fixing—magnifies waste. The implication is that economic incentives often overshadow environmental considerations even when technical remedies exist.

A counter-example from Norway illustrates how incentives can be reshaped. A small mining cooperative in Bodø structured its operations around refurbished units purchased from Asian sellers. With access to low-cost hydro and a partnership with a local repair technician, they achieved multi-year lifetimes for machines that elsewhere would have been scrapped. Their model shows that refurbishment becomes viable when energy, labour, and community alignment interact favourably.

E-waste challenges loom at the end of every ASIC life. Unlike general-purpose computers, mining rigs contain highly specific boards, densely packed components, and solder compositions that complicate recycling. Informal recycling streams—particularly in parts of South Asia and West Africa—pose clear risks, as documented in a 2020 Basel Convention assessment. If miners dispose of units without proper oversight, environmental harm extends far beyond energy use. The implication is blunt: the life cycle of mining hardware is inseparable from global waste governance.

Throughout these examples, the subchapter's motif continues whispering: *metal remembers*. It remembers the fabrication energy that forged it. It remembers the climate of the warehouse where it hummed. It remembers the temperatures that strained it. It remembers the decisions that prolonged or ended its usefulness.

As network economics evolve, operators face a strategic question. Should the industry accept rapid obsolescence as the price of innovation, or commit to design principles and business models that extend hardware life, deepen refurbishment, and reduce material churn? The answer will determine not only the environmental footprint of mining but the ethics of its place in the world.

The unresolved tension remains: when the next efficiency leap arrives—more hashes, fewer joules—will the industry retire millions of kilograms of working metal, or will it choose a longer memory for its machines?

Cooling and climate

On a still morning in May 2021, engineers at Riot Platforms' Whinstone facility in Rockdale, Texas, lowered the first racks of Antminers into long steel tubs of clear dielectric fluid. Fans had been removed; instead of air screaming through metal cages, bubbles rose quietly as pumps began to circulate the liquid. Outside, the temperature would later climb past 30°C. Inside, the noise profile fell so sharply that one visiting analyst described the hall as "unnervingly calm" compared to the air-cooled buildings next door. The room sounded almost wrong. This small change in sound masked a deeper shift. With immersion cooling, the same footprint could host more machines. The operators measured lower chip temperatures, tighter thermal spreads, and fewer board failures. Air, once the only medium between silicon and Texas heat, had been replaced by a fluid that turned the entire tub into a heat exchanger. The physics were simple; the implications for energy use, water demand, and local climate were anything but.

Cooling is where mining's thermodynamics become visible. Every joule of electrical work ends up as heat. What differs is the path that heat takes from chip to sky—through air, through liquid, through towers that evaporate water into the atmosphere. Those paths decide how much extra electricity cooling consumes, how loudly facilities hum, how quickly hardware degrades and, in thirsty regions, how many litres of water vanish from rivers and aquifers each day. In a sector obsessed with hashes per joule, cooling is the quiet hinge that can either lighten or deepen the total footprint.

Start with what most people imagine when they think of mining: long rows of air-cooled machines blasting hot exhaust into cavernous sheds. Air cooling is the default because it is cheap, simple, and well understood. Fans bolt to the front and rear of units; louvres and shutters guide airflow; negative pressure pulls heat out through walls. In Inner Mongolia in 2019, before China restricted operations, some of the world's largest sites used little more than sheet-metal walls and high-capacity fans to keep ASICs within tolerable ranges. Show the behaviour: open-sided buildings, dust filtering in, fans labouring through summer. Name the limitation: as ambient temperatures rise, the gap between chip and air narrows, forcing ever-higher fan speeds and pushing cooling power consumption upward. The implication is clear—air cooling is inexpensive to install but costly in hot climates and noisy anywhere.

Noise is not just an annoyance; it is an external signal of inefficiency. A warehouse outside Norcross, Georgia, which housed a mid-sized mining facility in 2021, became a local flashpoint when residents complained about a constant roar "like a jet engine idling". The operator had done nothing illegal. The decibel levels skirted within regulatory limits. But the behaviour of the cooling system—fans running at near maximum for most of the day—made the environmental footprint literally audible. To maintain chip temperatures in humid summer air, the facility had little choice but to trade extra kilowatt hours for a few degrees of thermal headroom.

In cooler climates, the same air-cooled designs behave very differently. Icelandic sites near Keflavík or Húsavík can often rely on outside air for much of the year, with only minimal mechanical assistance. Louvered inlets and exhaust stacks turn winter wind into a natural chiller. Show the behaviour: machines running with fans at lower duty cycles, ventilation driven partly by pressure differences. Name the climate advantage: stable, low ambient temperatures and clean air. Explain the mechanism: less auxiliary power for cooling, lower fan wear, longer hardware lifetimes. The implication is that the environmental performance of air-cooled mining is not a constant; it is an interaction between design and weather.

Immersion cooling, by contrast, tries to decouple hardware from ambient swings. Submerging ASICs in a dielectric fluid with high thermal capacity allows heat to move away from chips far more efficiently than in air. At Whinstone, and later at facilities in Nebraska and North Dakota, operators reported the ability to increase power density—more machines per square metre—while keeping chip temperatures within tighter bands. The behaviour was observable: racks packed more closely, halls with fewer moving parts, a low hum from pumps instead of a roar from fans. The implication for energy use was twofold: some electricity once devoted to fans could be redeployed to hashing, and lower component stress reduced failure rates, extending hardware life.

Immersion, however, does not eliminate the need to reject heat to the environment. It changes where and how that rejection occurs. Many deployments pair immersion tanks with dry coolers on the roof—large radiators over which fans move outside air. In temperate and dry climates, these systems can operate without consuming water, pushing heat into the air through conduction and convection alone. In more extreme heat, some operators supplement with evaporative pads or chillers, reintroducing water or refrigeration into the loop. The motif emerges: *where does the heat go?* Air, fluid, water, sky—they are all links in the same chain.

Direct liquid cooling sits somewhere between these poles. Instead of immersing whole machines, cold plates or heat sinks attached to chips carry heat into water or glycol loops. High-performance computing and some data centres have used such systems for years. A handful of mining operations, particularly in China before 2021, experimented with plate-based liquid cooling to increase density in constrained spaces. The behaviour—piping coolant across racks, using pumps and heat exchangers—approaches immersion's thermal performance without fully submerging hardware. But water becomes central. Unless operators use dry coolers, they often rely on cooling towers that evaporate water to shed heat.

Water use is where cooling choices intersect most sharply with climate. Air cooling in a dry system can be water-free; immersion paired with dry coolers can be similarly frugal. Once evaporative cooling or cooling towers enter the picture, every kilowatt of waste heat implies ongoing water withdrawals. A data-centre study by Lawrence Berkeley National Laboratory in 2021 highlighted how some US facilities consumed significant volumes of water for cooling, often in regions already facing stress. Mining facilities using similar tower designs would face the same trade-offs. Show the behaviour: water vapour rising from towers on a hot afternoon. Name the resource at stake: local freshwater. Explain the risk: concentrating water-intensive cooling in arid regions amplifies existing scarcity. The implication is that choosing a cooling technology is also choosing a relationship with local hydrology.

A counter-example reminds us that water use is not inherently a flaw. In northern Sweden, district-heating networks have long used large heat exchangers and, in some cases, water-based systems to distribute warmth. A mining facility integrated into such a network could, in principle, use water loops to move heat into homes and businesses, displacing fossil-fuelled boilers. Here the behaviour—channeling heat into a productive system—recasts water as a carrier of value rather than a mere sink. The question then is not whether water is used, but how, and to what downstream effect.

Cooling also reshapes how we think about climate zones as hosts for mining. A warehouse in Phoenix trying to maintain chip temperatures through air-based systems will struggle, drawing heavy auxiliary power and potentially consuming water in evaporative systems. A similar facility in Tromsø can often treat outside air as a free resource, using modest fan power to keep temperatures stable. An immersion-cooled hall in Texas can, with enough rooftop heat-exchange capacity, maintain acceptable chip temperatures with lower fan noise and reduced sensitivity to heatwaves. Show the behaviour: different cooling architectures responding to the same thermodynamic imperative. Name the motif: *where does the heat go, and at what cost?* Explain the pattern: climate and design co-determine both energy efficiency and local impact. The implication is that environmental assessments must weigh cooling strategies and local climates, not simply tally nameplate efficiencies.

The noise dimension, briefly glimpsed at Rockdale, deserves a second look. When immersion systems remove fans from individual machines, they replace thousands of small acoustic sources with a handful of larger ones—pumps and external fans. The overall sound pressure level can drop substantially. For communities, the difference between a constant 70-

decibel roar and a lower, steadier hum matters. Noise shapes acceptance. It also signals underlying efficiency: fewer fans often mean less wasted energy. A facility in the Netherlands that converted one hall to immersion in 2022 reported both lower noise and a measurable improvement in the ratio of cooling power to hashing power. Behaviour at the mechanical level translated into social and environmental gains.

Yet immersion is not a cure-all. Fluids must be manufactured, transported, and ultimately replaced or disposed of. Some are derived from petrochemical feedstocks; others from engineered synthetics. If leaks occur, fires or contamination are possible. Operators must ensure compatibility between fluids and components, avoid swelling gaskets or corroding metals, and plan for end-of-life fluid handling. In other words, moving heat from air to liquid introduces new responsibilities. The motif repeats: shifting the path of heat means shifting the locus of care.

In regions where water is scarce and ambient temperatures high, the lessons converge. Air cooling alone will produce noise and high fan power. Evaporative systems will consume water. Immersion with dry coolers may offer the best compromise, but only if rooftop space, capital, and maintenance capacity exist. Each choice is a negotiation between energy, water, hardware longevity, and community tolerance. There is no neutral option; each design writes a different story into the local climate.

The unresolved question that closes this subchapter is therefore a practical one. As mining matures and regulatory scrutiny intensifies, what should count as responsible cooling? Is it enough to minimise electricity used by fans, or should operators be judged on water withdrawals, hardware lifetime, and the fate of the heat they shed into their surroundings? Put bluntly: when every joule becomes warmth somewhere, how far does the industry's duty extend in deciding *where* that warmth goes—and what it leaves behind?

Waste heat as a resource

In February 2018, residents of Lyngseidet, a small town in Troms, Norway, watched as technicians connected a cluster of modest mining rigs to the district heating loop serving a municipal workshop. The air outside hovered around -6°C. Inside, a set of insulated pipes delivered warm water generated not by boilers but by waste heat from machines hashing in a nearby shed. The output was small—around 30 kilowatts of thermal energy—but it replaced a meaningful share of the workshop's electric heating load during some of the coldest days of the year. The project, run by the company KryptoVault, was a pilot rather than a revolution. Yet it demonstrated something important: the warmth that mining machines shed as a by-product could slot into real community infrastructure, offsetting both cost and carbon at the margin. Heat, long dismissed as an unavoidable nuisance, became a material input.

Such scenes reveal a simple truth. All computational work becomes heat. The question is what happens to that heat next. It can dissipate into the sky through fans; it can evaporate water through towers; or it can be captured and pushed back into homes, greenhouses, and industrial circuits. That movement—from waste to resource—demands engineering discipline, local coordination, and a willingness to treat thermal energy with the same seriousness usually reserved for megawatt-hours. The motif recurs quietly throughout this subchapter: *where can the heat go?*

Begin with the baseline. A mining facility consumes electrical power with near-perfect conversion to thermal energy. A 1-megawatt site produces roughly 1 megawatt of heat continuously, hour after hour. Show the behaviour: racks of ASICs exhaling air at 60–80°C, fans fighting to maintain airflow. Name the opportunity: these steady streams of warmth are predictable and controllable. Explain the physics: stable thermal output makes mining an unusually reliable candidate for heat reuse, much more consistent than data centres that throttle workloads. The implication is that any community or industrial process needing low to medium temperature heat—say, 30–80°C—could, in principle, integrate mining heat into its existing system if distance, timing, and costs align.

Greenhouses offer the clearest example of such alignment. In 2020, a horticultural pilot in Boden, Sweden, placed air-cooled miners adjacent to a small greenhouse used for testing cold-climate crop growth. Warm exhaust was ducted directly into the growing space. Behaviour first: fans moved heated air through simple filters, pushing it into the greenhouse at a rate tuned to the plants' tolerance. Name the entity: the Boden Business Park testbed, known for its earlier "Boden Type DC One" experiments in data-centre efficiency. Explain the mechanism: horticultural heating demands stable, moderate temperatures, making it compatible with mining waste heat. The implication was notable—thermal energy that would have risen uselessly into the subarctic air instead accelerated crop maturation and cut facility heating costs. Yet the same example hints at a limitation. Greenhouses need heat at specific times. Seasonal and diurnal variations matter. A greenhouse in northern Sweden demands heat for long stretches of the year. One in southern Spain might need cooling instead. Waste heat is constant; agricultural demand is not. Reconciling this mismatch requires storage—thermal tanks, insulated pipes, or even seasonal boreholes. Those systems cost money and space. The motif returns: *where can the heat go, and when?* Not every location can answer both questions well.

District heating networks come closer to ideal off-takers. Unlike greenhouses, they tend to operate continuously across large customer bases. Towns in Finland, Denmark, and Sweden maintain loops that distribute 60–120°C water through insulated pipes, feeding radiators and domestic hot water systems. If a mining site can deliver heat at appropriate temperatures, integration becomes a matter of plumbing and contractual alignment. A 2022 project by HIVE Blockchain in Boden, Sweden, routed immersion-cooled waste heat into a local system, raising water temperatures with heat exchangers to feed parts of the network. Show the behaviour: hot immersion fluid flowing through plate exchangers, transferring energy without mixing. Name the infrastructure: municipal district heating networks with established metering and control systems. Explain the attraction: these networks already demand large amounts of heat, smoothing out variability and reducing the need for storage. The implication is that mining could become a flexible, low-carbon thermal contributor—if sited close enough to existing loops. But proximity is non-negotiable. District heating pipes are expensive to extend. Even a few hundred metres can impose significant capital costs. This is the first major constraint: heat does not travel cheaply. Moving electrons is simple; moving warm water or air is not. As a result, many promising heat-reuse concepts die at the feasibility stage once engineers calculate pipe runs, trenching, and required temperature lifts.

Industrial processes present a different avenue. Some food-processing facilities, indoor aquaculture systems, or drying operations demand moderate, stable heat. Mineral drying plants, for example, often require 60–100°C air for continuous operations. If a mining facility sits adjacent to such an industry, the pairing seems natural. In Quebec in 2021, a small aquaculture pilot used mining heat to maintain tank temperatures for fish breeding. Show the behaviour: ducting warm air from miners into heat exchangers that warmed water baths. Name the sector: aquaculture, with its strict thermal tolerances. Explain the constraint: reliability is paramount. If miners stop unexpectedly due to price swings or curtailment events, biological systems may suffer. The implication is that industrial off-takers need assurances—backup heating, contracts, and predictable power-to-heat conversion. Waste heat is valuable only if it is dependable.

Reliability, then, becomes the quiet fulcrum of the entire field. Mining heat is constant *as long as machines run*. In markets with volatile electricity prices or curtailment obligations, thermal output can fluctuate. For mining facilities participating in demand response—ramping down during price spikes—heat availability collapses at precisely the moments some systems need it most. The tension is visible: a miner that helps the grid by curtailing may disrupt its heat customers. A miner that commits to heat customers may lose revenue opportunities during price events. The motif once more: *where can the heat go, and at what operational cost?*

The small-scale pilot in Lyngseidet helps clarify both the promise and the limits. Its outcome was measurable. The workshop reduced its winter electricity consumption, saving money and lowering emissions in a region where heating loads mattered. But the heat output was modest, and scaling it to town-wide loops would require far more mining capacity, new pipes, and robust heat-exchange infrastructure. The pilot proved feasibility, not scalability. Its central lesson was that mining heat fits best into micro-scale or modular thermal systems: district heating spurs, remote facilities with singular heating needs, or industrial niches where heat demand is constant and local.

Two larger examples reveal the spectrum of possibilities. In 2021, Heatbit, a consumer-facing company, began marketing compact mining heaters to households in Europe and North America. These units embed ASICs in insulated casings, delivering warmth while performing computational work that offsets running costs. Show the behaviour: a heater that earns while it warms. Name the company and year. Explain the trade-off: household integration works only at very small scales and produces noise and heat profiles suitable for single rooms, not whole-building systems. The implication is that household mining heat is charming but marginal—technically real, socially limited.

At the opposite end stands the concept of large-scale immersion-cooled farms feeding district heating, as explored in Denmark and Sweden. Operators there experimented with returning high-grade heat—often between 50 and 70°C—to municipal systems. Behaviour: heat exchangers linking mining loops to district networks. Metrics: thermal flows measured in hundreds of kilowatts. Explanation: immersion enables higher and more stable outlet temperatures than air-cooled systems. The implication is clearer—immersion-cooled operations, when located close to thermal loads, offer the most credible path to meaningful heat reuse.

A counter-example tempers the enthusiasm. In parts of Texas, some immersion-cooled mining sites explored waste-heat capture during winter months but found little local demand. The climate was too mild; the distances too great; the infrastructure nonexistent. Here, the behaviour—abundant heat—met no viable off-taker. Reconcile the contrast: heat reuse thrives where the built environment already values and distributes thermal energy. Where heating demand is low or infrastructure sparse, waste heat remains just that.

The promise, however, remains substantial, especially when framed against mining's broader sustainability challenges. Waste heat reuse does not erase the electrical footprint of mining. It does not neutralise emissions from upstream energy sources. But it changes the calculus of local impact. A 1-megawatt mining facility feeding 800 kilowatts of thermal energy into a district loop effectively displaces heat that might otherwise come from natural gas or electric resistance systems. That displacement, if quantified accurately, becomes part of the environmental story.

Scaling this vision demands three conditions. First, spatial alignment: mining sites must stand close enough to thermal loads to avoid excessive infrastructure costs. Second, temporal alignment: heat demand must be sufficiently steady to match mining's constant output. Third, institutional alignment:

operators and municipalities need contracts, guarantees, and controls that manage volatility in both mining profitability and local heating needs. Without those three pillars, heat reuse is reduced to anecdotes rather than infrastructure.

And so the unresolved tension emerges. Waste heat promises to turn mining into a thermal ally—an industry whose by-product becomes a service. Yet heat reuse depends on geography, networks, and markets that vary immensely from region to region. The key question, then, is simple but stubborn: can an industry built for global fluidity commit to the local anchoring that meaningful heat reuse requires?

E-waste realities

In May 2016, investigators from the Basel Action Network (BAN) placed GPS trackers inside a batch of discarded computer equipment collected at municipal recycling points in Seattle. The devices were meant for responsible processing within the United States. Instead, by July, several trackers pinged their location from Hong Kong's New Territories, in yards where workers dismantled electronics by hand, surrounded by piles of circuit boards and burnt insulation. One unit travelled more than 10,000 kilometres before ending its life in a workshop that lacked proper ventilation or protective gear. The journey exposed an awkward fact: even in jurisdictions with formal e-waste pathways, valuable components often slip into opaque secondary markets, where environmental controls weaken and toxic materials disperse into soil, water, and air.

That disquieting trail offers a frame for mining hardware. ASICs do not follow the same routes as discarded household equipment, but their afterlives can pass through similarly unregulated spaces when upgrade cycles accelerate and resale markets globalise. When a 14 terahash-per-second machine becomes uneconomic in Quebec or Arkansas, it does not disappear. It moves—sold on secondary exchanges, shipped to regions with cheaper power, and dismantled when no longer viable. The question, recurring quietly through this subchapter, is simple: *where does the hardware go when the hash rate moves on?*

Begin with the behaviour that triggers the problem. Mining machines have finite operational lifetimes, not because they stop working but because their efficiency—measured in joules per terahash—loses competitiveness as new models arrive. A device still functional after five years may burn twice the electricity per unit of computation compared with its successors. Show that in action: Bitmain's Antminer S9, launched in 2016, consumed around 90 joules per terahash. By 2021, leading-edge models such as the Antminer S19 Pro delivered performance closer to 30 joules per terahash. Name the pattern: rapid efficiency gain. Explain the consequence: as electricity costs rise or network difficulty increases, older models fall out of profitable operation. The implication is that obsolescence becomes an economic outcome long before it becomes a technical one.

This dynamic produces waves of displaced hardware. In 2018, during the downturn following Bitcoin's late-2017 price surge, Chinese miners offloaded thousands of S9 units through Shenzhen brokers at steep discounts. The behaviour was visible in trade flows—pallets of used ASICs shipped to Kazakhstan and parts of Siberia where electricity was cheaper. Here, older machines found temporary economic refuge. But the implication remains: each migration delays but does not erase the waste problem. These units eventually age out, leaving operators with metal frames, aluminium heat sinks, plastic fan housings, power supplies, and boards dotted with solder containing lead or other hazardous substances.

At this point, one counter-example often arises: that ASICs are "fully recyclable" because they contain metals of high value. It is a comforting claim, but incomplete. Show the reality first. A circuit board contains copper traces, small volumes of gold and silver in connectors, tin-lead or lead-free solder, epoxy resin, and various flame retardants. Reclaiming the precious materials requires shredding, smelting, or chemical leaching—all processes that generate emissions, effluents, or toxic residues. Name the barrier: downstream capacity. In many countries, sophisticated e-waste facilities operate well below the scale required to process large volumes of mining hardware. Explain the issue: unless operators commit to certified recycling chains, used ASICs often disappear into informal channels where recovery methods are rudimentary. The implication is that high metal content does not guarantee responsible recycling; it merely ensures economic incentive for extraction, whether clean or not.

Two specific examples illustrate the poles of current practice. In 2021, the Norwegian company KryptoVault partnered with a certified recycler in Oslo to process decommissioned boards under strict environmental standards, recovering metals through controlled smelting with proper filtration. Behaviour here is concrete: pallets logged, boards shredded in enclosed systems, emissions monitored. Named entities, named practices. The implication is that high-standard recycling is technically feasible when operators pay for it. Contrast that with a 2019 observation documented by BAN, tracking laptop boards—not ASICs specifically—entering informal yards in Guiyu, China. There, open-air acid baths and uncontrolled burning were common. Although Guiyu has since formalised parts of its recycling sector, pockets of informal processing persist across Asia and West Africa. Reconcile the contrast: the underlying physics of component recovery do not care whether a board came from a miner or a laptop. Both require structured processes to avoid toxic exposure. Without those structures, environmental harm follows. The motif returns: *where does the hardware go, and through which hands?*

Component reuse tempers the problem but does not eliminate it. Power supply units (PSUs) often survive beyond a miner's operational lifetime and can be redeployed in other computing or industrial contexts. Aluminium heat sinks can be melted and re-formed with minimal contamination. Fans—usually 120 mm or 140 mm units—find secondary life in server racks or specialised ventilation setups. Yet the ASIC chips themselves have little reuse potential outside mining; they are too application-specific. When their hashing performance no longer matches economic conditions, no alternative workload can save them. This asymmetry drives the bulk of e-waste volume: the very property that makes ASICs efficient—tight specialisation—makes them difficult to repurpose.

A second constraint deserves attention: geographic mismatch between where e-waste arises and where compliant recycling capacity resides. North America and parts of Europe operate well-regulated facilities, though often focused on general electronics rather than high-density mining hardware. Kazakhstan, a major destination for secondhand ASICs after China's 2021 mining restrictions, had—at that time—limited capacity for processing complex circuit boards safely. The behaviour is observable: used rigs arriving en masse where electricity is cheap but recycling infrastructure is thin. The implication is unsettling. When those rigs break or age out, their disposal depends on local capacity that may not exist, increasing the likelihood of informal dismantling or export to other regions.

Balancing this, one credible limitation tempers the worry. ASIC lifetimes have lengthened in periods of high crypto prices or slow efficiency gains. During parts of 2020–2021, secondary markets remained surprisingly strong, keeping older units in operation rather than in scrap channels. High utilisation delays e-waste generation. But reconcile it: delay is not avoidance. When eventual scrapping occurs, the same questions of handling and toxicity apply, simply shifted forward in time.

Toxicity, often downplayed, deserves direct treatment. Lead solder persists in older units. Brominated flame retardants appear in PCB substrates. Capacitors and batteries, although small, contain electrolytes that require controlled disposal. When boards are shredded without filtration, fine particulates enter soil and water. When casings or wires are burnt, dioxins and other hazardous compounds form. Naming these materials is necessary because they shape policy debates. They also shape the design questions at the core of this subchapter: *how can hardware be built to reduce the burden of its eventual disposal?*

Several design principles emerge from practice rather than theory. First, modularity. Manufacturers that adopt chassis designs with easily separable components enable cleaner end-of-life handling. Show the behaviour: a miner whose fans, power supply, and heat sinks detach with standard screws rather than soldered or glued joints. Name its consequence: disassembly becomes faster, cheaper, and safer. The implication is that recyclers can extract valuable metals with fewer mixed-material hazards.

Second, durability. A shift towards components that can withstand longer operational cycles—higher-quality capacitors, thicker heat sinks, and cooling systems designed for lower thermal stress—extends functional lifetimes. When an ASIC can operate efficiently for seven years rather than three, total waste declines even as the network grows. Third, transparency. Operators who publish decommissioning records and commit units to certified recycling channels create verifiable chains of custody. Behaviours such as serial-number logging, third-party audits, and disposal attestations reduce the chance of leakage into informal markets.

A fourth, subtler principle is thermal management. Cooling systems influence e-waste by determining operational stress and failure rates. Immersion cooling, for example, can extend component lifetimes by reducing dust ingress and temperature swings, slowing degradation of solder joints and capacitors. This is visible in immersion facilities in Iceland after 2020, where some operators reported fewer fan and power supply failures compared with air-cooled equivalents. While immersion does not eliminate the e-waste problem, it shifts its tempo, easing the churn of spare parts.

A counterpoint is necessary. Some design recommendations—such as "fully recyclable" ASICs or "zero-waste mining"—overclaim. They turn a complex story into marketing. Even the best designs must contend with the inherent limitations of mixed-material boards and globalised waste channels. Perfect circularity remains improbable. The goal is not to pretend otherwise but to close the gap between current practice and responsible disposal—incrementally, measurably, and verifiably.

The motif sharpens as we approach the end: *where does the hardware go?* Every decision—manufacturing, procurement, operation, resale, decommissioning—nudges the answer in one direction or another. The unresolved tension lies precisely there. Mining thrives on rapid iteration and opportunistic mobility; responsible e-waste management thrives on stability, documentation, and local infrastructure. Can an industry built on speed and global arbitrage accept the friction required to manage its physical footprint responsibly?

Chapter 6
Carbon-Neutral or Carbon-Neat?

At the height of the European energy squeeze in January 2022, a wind farm in Jutland curtailed its output for the third night in a row. Not because the breeze had faltered—it was blowing steadily across the Limfjord—but because the local grid could not carry any more power southward. Turbines spun freely, blades carving the winter air while megawatts went untapped. A few kilometres away, a data-centre operator proudly announced it had purchased enough renewable certificates to declare its operations "100 per cent green". The paradox was impossible to miss: electricity that could have displaced fossil generation elsewhere was stranded, while claims of environmental purity travelled across borders through paperwork rather than physics. The scene distilled a question that now shadows every industry engaging with energy markets, crypto mining included: what does it mean to be clean when electrons do not obey marketing? The language of carbon neutrality has become deceptively smooth. Over the past decade, companies have learned to assemble impressive narratives from offsets in Peru, certificates from Texas wind farms, or contracts pledged against solar arrays yet to be built. Some of these instruments drive real decarbonisation. Others do little more than shuffle accounting columns. The ambiguity is deliberate. When environmental virtue can be signalled cheaply, the temptation to signal rather than transform grows strong. For sectors like mining—whose energy use is both visible and contested—the distinction between genuine mitigation and aesthetic neatness matters as much ethically as it does environmentally.

This chapter begins by peeling apart the mechanisms behind those claims. Offsets differ fundamentally from renewable energy certificates. Power purchase agreements with new-build projects do not resemble the purchase of surplus certificates from long-amortised wind farms. Each tool carries its own logic, incentives, and risks of misuse. Yet debates often collapse these distinctions into a single question: *is the operation carbon-neutral?* The motif that threads through these pages—*paper versus power*—helps resist that collapse. Certificates exist on paper; emissions and avoided emissions are questions of power flows, grid physics, and marginal generation. Only by keeping those domains separate can we assess any claim with honesty.

A necessary starting point is to examine offsets themselves. Whether through forest preservation, reforestation, or methane capture, offsets promise to compensate for emissions by reducing or removing greenhouse gases elsewhere. But compensation is not creation. The central problem, explored through real cases, is additionality: would the beneficial action have occurred without the offset purchase? A forest protected by law in 2005 cannot credibly offset a megawatt-hour consumed in 2023. The book does not ask the reader to become a carbon accountant, only to adopt a simple test: if the claimed benefit would likely have happened anyway, the offset belongs in the category of neatness rather than neutrality. Mining companies, keen to project responsibility, have leaned heavily on offsets in the past few years. For some, this reflects genuine attempts to cover unavoidable operational emissions. For others, it masks an unwillingness to confront siting decisions and electricity contracts that lock them into fossil-intensive grids.

A contrasting set of instruments—renewable energy certificates—functions differently. They track attributes of electricity generation, allowing organisations to claim a share of renewable output even when the electrons that power their machines come from a mixed grid. The certificates are tradable and often inexpensive, which makes them accessible. Yet their environmental effect depends almost entirely on the state of the market they operate in. In a region overflowing with mature wind and hydro, certificate purchases may do little to alter the build-out of new renewable capacity. They prove demand, but not necessarily *new* demand. In other regions, structured properly, they can help close financing gaps for projects that genuinely require revenue certainty. The chapter will examine these nuances, not to overwhelm but to clarify the difference between participating in a functioning market mechanism and merely acquiring a credential.

Then comes a more direct route: on-site and behind-the-meter renewables. Some miners have chosen to colocate with hydro plants in British Columbia or Norway, where water spillage in rainy seasons can render surplus energy effectively free. Others have built operations adjacent to wind farms in West Texas to absorb curtailed output during low-demand nights. These examples matter because they show mining acting as an absorber of waste, not a competitor for scarce resources. Yet even here, vigilance is required. Locating beside a renewable asset does not in itself guarantee low emissions. What matters is whether the operation reduces curtailment or displaces fossil-fired generation. Siting next to hydro in a region with a fully saturated grid may simply divert energy from other users rather than recover lost potential. The subtlety lies in the counterfactual: *what would happen to the electrons if mining were not present?*

Temporal matching sharpens this analysis further. Annual balancing—the idea that consuming fossil-intensive electricity at one hour can be offset by purchasing renewable certificates on an annual basis—has dominated corporate claims for decades. Yet this form of matching ignores the hourly variation of carbon intensity. The difference between a wind-heavy midnight and a gas-heavy afternoon can be measured in hundreds of grams of CO_2 per kilowatt-hour. Hourly matching, by contrast, forces purchasers to align their consumption with clean generation in time, not merely in aggregate. For miners with flexible loads, especially those capable of operating opportunistically, this approach offers a path to genuine reductions rather than symbolic neutrality. The complexity is real, but so is the reward: a mining facility that draws power only when the grid is clean can become a stabilising force rather than an environmental liability.

Accountability anchors the final section of the chapter. Claims about carbon neutrality are only as credible as the methods and assumptions behind them. Selective accounting—counting only operational emissions, ignoring upstream impacts, or relying on certificate markets with weak additionality—turns sustainability into performance rather than practice. The chapter proposes a rubric rooted in transparency. What electricity was consumed, where, and when? What instruments were used to mitigate emissions, and with what evidence of additionality? What uncertainties remain? Mining companies often fear that disclosing such details invites criticism. In fact, transparency invites trust. Without it, even sincerely green operations risk being dismissed as mere branding.

The stakes cannot be understated. As energy systems restructure worldwide, industries that use significant power must decide whether they will lead or follow. For crypto mining—an activity often caricatured as wasteful—the opportunity to redefine its environmental profile lies not in polished announcements but in physical decisions: siting, timing, contracts, and verification. The narrative arc that emerges from this chapter is forward-tilted, not fatalistic. Carbon-neutrality is not a static label but a practice, one that requires constant alignment with the evolving physics of grids and the social expectations of credibility.

The chapter closes with a tension that will carry the reader onward. Every organisation claims to want sustainability. Fewer are willing to subject their claims to scrutiny. Fewer still are prepared to change their operations to match their rhetoric. Mining's environmental story will be written by the choices it makes along this narrow line between neutrality and neatness. The chapter's promise is to illuminate that line so clearly that the reader will never mistake the two again.

Offsets and certificates

In September 2021, the Dutch Authority for Consumers and Markets ordered the energy supplier Greenchoice to amend its advertising after investigators found that a tranche of "100% green electricity" certificates used in its consumer plans came from Norwegian hydropower plants built long before 2000. The electrons lighting Dutch kitchens had not changed; what had changed was the story told about them. The episode sharpened a broader question that has troubled energy regulators from Brussels to California: when a company claims carbon neutrality, what exactly has happened in the physical world? A shift in atmospheric emissions—or merely a shift in accounting? The answer depends on instruments whose names have become familiar yet whose workings remain obscure: offsets, renewable energy certificates (RECs), and power purchase agreements (PPAs).

The tension revealed by the Greenchoice case provides the motif for this subchapter: *what does the paper say, and what does the power do?* That motif surfaces repeatedly because the distinction matters. A certificate may travel hundreds of kilometres and several years. An electron travels only as far as the grid allows, and only when demanded. The credibility of any climate claim turns on understanding this gap. Offsets form the first part of the landscape. They promise to counterbalance emissions by reducing or removing greenhouse gases elsewhere. The promise is seductive: plant trees in Panama to offset a gas-heavy hour in Pennsylvania; preserve peatland in Indonesia to compensate for a diesel generator in Inner Mongolia. Yet the mechanism depends on additionality—a term that becomes real only when tied to behaviour. Additionality asks a simple question: *would this activity have happened without the payment?* If the answer is yes, the offset has generated no new climate benefit. The Clean Development Mechanism, created under the Kyoto Protocol, wrestled with this problem for years. In 2016, a review commissioned by the European Commission found that around 85 per cent of surveyed projects were "unlikely" to be fully additional. The implication was uncomfortable: millions of tonnes of claimed carbon savings rested on counterfactuals that did not hold.

A mining operator that purchases offsets must therefore examine the underlying activity, its timing, and its dependency on offset revenue. A reforestation project launched in 1998 with community support and external grants does not suddenly become additional because a mining firm buys a certificate in 2024. By contrast, a carefully audited methane capture project at a landfill in Maharashtra, commissioned in 2023 and financed partly through advance credit purchases, has a clearer link between revenue and outcome. The visible behaviour—installation of new capture equipment—anchors the abstraction of "emissions reduction" in something that can be checked, measured, and monitored.

RECs, known in Europe as Guarantees of Origin, take the argument in a different direction. They track the environmental attributes of renewable electricity generation, allowing buyers to claim the *character* of clean energy without receiving the electrons themselves. In 2019, Google announced that it had matched 100 per cent of its annual electricity consumption with renewable purchases, largely through these certificates. The claim was accurate in accounting terms. But as critiques from the Regulatory Assistance Project (2020) noted, many of the certificates originated from long-established hydro and wind facilities unlikely to be influenced by corporate demand. The project's output was real; the environmental *impact* of the purchase was minimal. This reveals the key limitation of RECs: unless they directly cause new renewable generation to be built—by providing financing certainty—they serve as labels rather than levers.

And yet there are cases where certificates do shift the system. In 2020, Colorado's Tri-State Generation and Transmission

Association signed a structured REC-backed agreement with a new solar project in Montrose County. The contract ensured revenue sufficient to unlock construction financing. The behaviour linked to the certificate purchase—ground-breaking on previously uncertain generation—demonstrated additionality in practice. The contrast with legacy hydropower certificates is instructive. What matters is not the certificate itself but the causal chain connecting money and megawatts.

PPAs offer the most direct route through this thicket. These long-term contracts commit buyers to purchasing electricity from a new renewable project at a fixed price. When Microsoft signed a 15-year PPA in the Netherlands in 2020 with the Vattenfall Wieringermeer wind farm, the financial commitment was integral to the project's expansion. Unlike RECs, which circulate detached from physical flows, a PPA ties a buyer to a generator, aligning their interests in a measurable way. For mining companies with significant and predictable demand, PPAs represent a path toward genuine additionality. The implication is clear: if you want new renewable capacity to exist because of you, sign a contract that makes it bankable.

A counter-example sharpens the point. Some miners, particularly during the 2021 North American build-out, signed contracts nominally linked to renewable assets but structured as virtual PPAs—financial hedges rather than physical commitments. While these arrangements may stabilise prices, they do not necessarily alter generation on the grid. They are financial products, not climate instruments. The limitation does not invalidate them; it simply means they should not be used to claim a reduction in real-world emissions. Reconciling this limitation with the industry's appetite for clean narratives requires discipline: describe financial hedges as hedges, not decarbonisation.

The interplay among offsets, RECs, and PPAs reveals a simple diagnostic that readers can apply without specialist training. Ask three questions: *Did my action cause a new physical change? Did it change the behaviour of a generator or landholder? Would this outcome have occurred without my involvement?* If the answer to all three is yes, you have likely contributed to real mitigation. If not, you may have engaged in carbon neatness: tidy accounting that feels responsible but leaves atmospheric concentrations unchanged.

Throughout this landscape, a quiet motif persists: *paper follows power poorly*. Claims that float far from physical systems lose credibility. Mining, with its conspicuous energy use, cannot rely on opacity. Operators who make bold environmental statements without disclosing procurement details, additionality assumptions, or verification methods invite scepticism. By contrast, those who subject their claims to scrutiny—publishing contract terms, revealing the age and financing structure of certificate-linked generators—strengthen trust through candour. The visible behaviour here is transparency itself: open ledgers of environmental data, not only of hashes.

Two examples illuminate the stakes. In 2022, a Canadian mining company partnered with BC Hydro to absorb surplus run-of-river output during snowmelt peaks. The electricity would otherwise have been curtailed. The causal chain was direct and measurable. The grid operator reported reduced spill events, and the mining firm publicly disclosed its hourly consumption patterns. The environmental claim rested not on paper instruments but observable changes in power flow. Contrast this with a US operator that purchased RECs from an Iowa wind farm commissioned in 2008. The certificates were inexpensive; the marketing impact was large. Yet the wind farm's output and revenue were stable long before the mining purchase. Nothing in the physical world changed. The environmental benefit was therefore nil. The two cases do not indict RECs universally—they simply illustrate that provenance matters.

As the subchapter closes, the unresolved tension sharpens: if every mechanism can be used well or poorly, how should companies choose? The test is not philosophical but practical: commit to actions that change what is built, what runs, or what is preserved. Avoid actions that change only what is claimed. The gap between these two realms—paper and power—remains the defining fault line of carbon markets.

On-site renewables

In February 2020, the Danish grid operator Energinet reported an unusual pattern at the Horns Rev 3 wind farm off the coast of Jutland. On several windy nights, turbines capable of generating more than 400 MW of clean electricity were instructed to curtail output because local transmission routes were saturated. The power existed; the grid could not carry it. Two months later, a small mining consortium colocated a mobile data centre near a cluster of West Jutland turbines facing similar curtailment pressures. By drawing power only when output exceeded export capacity, the miners reduced curtailment hours and secured electricity at prices that dipped below €15 per MWh. The outcome was measurable: more wind delivered to productive use, fewer megawatt-hours wasted, and mining economics decoupled from national peak prices. What began as an opportunistic experiment revealed a deeper truth—siting matters as much as technology.

The motif that threads through this subchapter—*use what would otherwise be lost*—emerges strongly in such cases. The logic is simple, but not simplistic. Where renewable generation outpaces local demand or exceeds grid capacity, additional flexible load can reduce spillage. Where demand already pushes a region's clean generation to its limits, new consumption may quietly pull electrons away from users who would have relied on them. The distinction between those two conditions is not semantic but physical, and crypto mining, with its relocatable infrastructure and interruptible loads, straddles that line more visibly than many industries.

Solar, wind, and hydro each offer distinct opportunities and constraints for on-site integration. Solar's rhythm is predictable: it rises and falls daily, varies with season, and pairs well with loads that can throttle or pause. A mining facility adjacent to a solar farm in Kern County, California, demonstrated this in 2021 by running at full capacity during midday surplus hours when the California Independent System Operator (CAISO) prices frequently plunged towards zero. During these hours, when solar oversupply would otherwise force curtailment or depress market prices below operating costs, the miners converted electrons into hashes with minimal incremental emissions. The visible behaviour was clear: rigs ramped up when the grid was flushed with sunlight, then idled as prices climbed in the evening. That pattern anchored abstractions like "alignment" and "grid-friendliness" in the hourly physics of generation and demand.

Wind produces a different profile. Its variability is less predictable, yet in some regions—especially Texas, Denmark, and northern Germany—it generates long stretches of night-time surplus. In 2022, the Electric Reliability Council of Texas (ERCOT) reported several instances where West Texas wind output exceeded 20 GW while transmission bottlenecks limited export. A mining operator colocated near Sweetwater ran its machines only when local nodal prices fell close to zero or dipped negative. Again, the behaviour was observable: rigs switched off automatically when prices rose, freeing capacity during high-emission peak periods. The implication was straightforward. By absorbing surplus and exiting during scarcity, the miners reduced both curtailment and peak stress, while their environmental footprint closely tracked the marginal intensity of the grid.

Hydro, however, reveals the most intricate interplay between location and impact. Northern Québec and British Columbia offer classic cases: abundant hydropower, low marginal emissions, and constraints in long-distance transmission. When a mining firm in British Columbia in 2019 secured a behind-the-meter agreement with a run-of-river hydro operator during snowmelt season, the arrangement made operational sense. Run-of-river plants lack storage and often face brief but intense seasonal surges when meltwater overwhelms turbines. Diverting a portion of this seasonal surplus to flexible loads reduced spillage. Yet hydro also exposes a limitation: when demand is already steady and transmission unconstrained, behind-the-meter arrangements can deprive the grid of renewable electricity that would have served other users. The distinction between reducing waste and simply reallocating supply is central, and only rigorous energy accounting—not sentiment—can determine which side a project falls on.

Two contrasting examples illuminate the stakes. In 2021, a mining facility in Sichuan attempted to rely on monsoon-season hydro surplus. For four months, when reservoirs overflowed, the operation ran almost entirely on spill-avoiding electricity. But outside the monsoon period, the facility drew from a mixed grid that included coal-fired generation from the Sichuan Basin. The operator marketed its output as "hydro-powered mining". The claim was technically accurate for part of the year and misleading when viewed over the full load cycle. The behaviour—year-round consumption without year-round surplus—revealed the flaw. Good intentions could not substitute for temporal fidelity.

A counter-example—this time constructive—emerged in 2022 in Finnmark, Norway, where a mining site colocated with a small hydro station on the Repparfjord River. Unlike the Sichuan arrangement, this Nordic facility entered a contract requiring automatic curtailment whenever reservoir levels fell below threshold. The miners operated fully only when water was plentiful and marginal emissions near zero. During dry spells, the rigs stood still. The operational discipline—measured in hours rather than narratives—anchored the environmental claim in enforceable constraints rather than aspiration.

Economic implications are inseparable from environmental ones. On-site renewables reduce transport losses and can unlock long-term price stability through PPAs that guarantee fixed supply. They also require capital, engineering, and trust between energy producers and miners. The trust manifests in visible decisions: permitting miners to curtail automatically; sharing operational data; structuring tariffs to reflect real costs. Each act reinforces or erodes confidence in the partnership. The reverse is also true. A mining operation that consumes during scarcity hours or hides behind generic "green" labels risks undermining public support for colocated models entirely.

The quiet motif—*use what would otherwise be lost*—returns here. Solar overproduction, wind curtailment, and hydro spill are the clearest candidates. But the motif encourages deeper thinking. A facility that installs a modest battery alongside its rigs can shift consumption by minutes rather than hours, smoothing ramp-up behaviour and reducing reliance on fossil-fired peakers used in many grids to stabilise frequency. A site that integrates thermal reuse, directing the heat from miners to greenhouses or community buildings, gains more value from every unit of renewable electricity it consumes. These refinements transform a simple colocation into a platform for resource efficiency, not merely a price arbitrage.

Yet the model has boundaries. A credible counter-example arises when a miner colocates with a solar array in a region where the grid is already clean and undersupplied. In parts of Norway or Tasmania, for example, incremental renewable generation may be limited. In such places, dedicating solar or hydro output to mining may deny clean electricity to other sectors struggling to decarbonise. The contradiction is real. But it can be reconciled by returning to the counterfactual: *what would the electrons have done otherwise?* If they would have displaced higher-emission generation, mining worsens the grid. If they would have been curtailed or unused, mining improves it.

The subchapter's arc converges on a forward-looking question. Every mining company that contemplates on-site renewables faces a choice between aligning with the surplus of the system or competing with essential loads. Will it measure its impact against the hourly, locational reality of the grid—or rely on the aesthetic neatness of proximity to a wind turbine or solar array?

The tension remains open, and intentionally so. On-site renewables can anchor mining within a cleaner energy future. They can also camouflage impacts behind pleasing imagery. The difference lies in physics, not rhetoric.

Temporal matching

On 14 September 2020, Google announced from its headquarters in Mountain View that it would move from "100% renewable" electricity on an annual basis to matching its consumption with carbon-free power *every hour* in every grid where it operates by 2030. Only three years earlier, the company had celebrated reaching its long-stated 100% renewable target by buying enough wind and solar output, in aggregate, to cover its yearly demand. The spreadsheet said they were. Yet engineers inside the company knew something awkward: servers in Dublin and Iowa still ran on coal- and gas-heavy power during many evenings and winter peaks. Annual accounting said "green"; hourly grid data said otherwise. That dissonance, made explicit by Google's shift, captures the central problem temporal matching seeks to address. It is not about buying more renewable electricity *in total*. It is about buying the right kind of electricity at the right times. For crypto miners operating almost continuously, often at industrial scale, this difference is not a technical nuance. It is the hinge that separates a credible claim of climate benefit from a neat story assembled out of accounting devices.

The motif that runs through this subchapter is disarmingly simple: *what hour are we talking about?* Ask that question of any environmental claim tied to electricity use, and the mask of annual averages begins to slip. A miner that consumes heavily during the most carbon-intensive hours of the day cannot meaningfully declare itself "clean" by purchasing certificates from wind farms that produce their output at other times of the year. Physics does not recognise yearly balance sheets; grids operate minute by minute.

Temporal matching starts from a fact already established earlier in the book: carbon intensity on a grid can swing dramatically over a single day. In Great Britain, National Grid ESO's data in 2021 showed hourly carbon intensity ranging from below 50 gCO_2/kWh during blustery spring nights to more than 300 gCO_2/kWh during calm, dark winter evenings. The same kilowatt-hour drawn at different times carries very different climate consequences. Show the behaviour: a miner runs flat-out, 24/7, on a British node. Name the effect: its average annual emissions may obscure the fact that a disproportionate share arises from a few hundred hours when gas plants dominate the stack. Explain the implication: to cut real emissions, one must address *which* hours are being served, not just how many megawatt-hours are bought from renewables in aggregate.

Annual balancing—book-and-claim accounting—ignores this dimension. A company consumes grid electricity whenever it needs it, but buys enough renewable energy over the course of a year to equal that consumption. The electrons from its wind farms and solar arrays may be produced at different times, even in different regions, yet the ledger declares success. Google's pre-2020 regime looked like this; so did many corporate "100% renewable" claims. For mining, such an approach can be particularly misleading because the load is often flat and round-the-clock. A facility might happily burn coal-heavy power at 18:00, then assert environmental virtue using certificates from a wind farm whose peak output occurs at 02:00.

Hourly matching flips the question. Instead of asking, "Did we buy enough green megawatt-hours over the year?", it asks, "For every hour we consumed power, did a matching quantity of low-carbon generation occur in the same grid?" This is a much more demanding standard. It requires granular data, more complex contracts, and often a willingness to curtail or shift load in response to system conditions. But the payoff is real: if done honestly, hourly matching ensures that a miner does not hide its dirtiest hours behind someone else's windy spring.

Google's 24/7 commitments are one well-known example. Microsoft has articulated a similar 100/100/0 goal: 100% of electricity consumption, 100% of the time, from zero-carbon sources by 2030. These are not mining companies, but their actions shape the benchmark by which other digital industries, including miners, will be judged. The behaviour is concrete: signing PPAs tied to specific projects, integrating grid carbon-intensity data into operational decisions, and publishing hourly matching statistics. The implication for miners is clear. If large technology firms can expose their hourly profiles to scrutiny, claims of "green mining" resting solely on annual REC purchases will look increasingly thin.

Mining does, however, have one structural advantage over traditional data centres: flexibility. Many proof-of-work operations can ramp down within minutes without compromising service-level commitments, and proof-of-stake validators, while less energy intensive, can choose providers in grids with cleaner or more predictable profiles. Hourly matching for mining need not be purely contractual; it can be operational. A facility in West Texas, for instance, might choose to mine only when ERCOT's real-time carbon intensity falls below a defined threshold. The behaviour is visible: rigs shut off during gas-heavy evening peaks, then resume during windy nights. The motif surfaces again: *what hour are we talking about?* Here, the answer changes emissions in the real world.

A mining example from practice helps tie this down. In 2022, a mid-sized operator near Lubbock integrated WattTime-style marginal emissions signals into its dispatch software. It measured hourly carbon intensity from ERCOT's nodal data and set thresholds for operation. During hours when marginal emissions exceeded a set value, machines throttled or shut down. Over a year, the facility ran fewer hours but at much lower average marginal intensity. The result was quantifiable: lower effective emissions per bitcoin mined, even though aggregate electricity use fell less than one might expect. The behaviour—time-selective operation—produced genuine environmental benefit without relying solely on certificates.

Now set that beside a counter-example. A different operator in the same state ran continuously but claimed "100% renewable" status by purchasing annual volumes of RECs from wind farms scattered across the Panhandle. Its marketing materials highlighted the total megawatt-hours of wind it had bought. Yet grid data showed that the facility's peak consumption coincided with constrained hours when gas plants carried the marginal load. No attempt was made to match consumption to renewable production in time. Nothing in the physical system changed because of the REC purchases. The environmental effect, beyond transferring some money to wind-farm owners, was marginal. Reconciling these cases illustrates the core point: annual balancing can be environmentally hollow unless combined with attention to hourly patterns.

Temporal matching does not require perfection to be useful. Even moving from annual to monthly or daily matching reduces the gap between claims and reality. But as measurement technologies and data access improve, the frontier has shifted. System operators in Europe and North America now publish detailed carbon-intensity data at hourly or even five-minute granularity. Software tools can ingest those signals and align load accordingly. For miners, whose business model already depends on sophisticated monitoring of network difficulty and price, integrating carbon data is an incremental rather than revolutionary step.

The difficulties are not trivial, and they deserve honesty. Hourly matching can increase procurement complexity. It may require a portfolio of renewable assets—solar for daytime, wind for nights, hydro for seasonal balancing—to approach round-the-clock coverage. It can expose operators to residual grid emissions during hours when clean generation is scarce, forcing either residual offset purchases or acceptance of non-zero footprints. For miners tethered to locations with rigid tariffs and no access to granular grid data, implementation may be more aspirational than immediate.

Moreover, temporal matching interacts with location. An operator in Iceland, drawing on near-constant geothermal and hydro, can approach 24/7 low-carbon supply with relatively simple contracts. A miner in Poland or India faces grids where coal remains dominant for many hours; even aggressive contracting cannot conjure non-existent renewables. Here, temporal matching reveals a harsher truth: in some grids, the only honest way to cut emissions is to reduce load or help build new clean capacity. Book-and-claim approaches can paper over this reality; hourly matching exposes it.

This exposure is precisely why temporal matching matters beyond accounting. It forces operators to confront marginal emissions in specific hours and places. It invites a different conversation with regulators and communities. A miner that can show, with data, that it curtails during the dirtiest hours and runs when the grid is clean, offers a more compelling case for its social licence than one brandishing annual certificates. Behaviour replaces narrative as the primary evidence.

The motif surfaces one last time: *what hour are we talking about?* For a grid engineer, the answer is obvious. For a marketing department, it is inconvenient. For a miner seeking to align profit, security, and climate responsibility, it must become central. Temporal matching does not promise moral purity. It offers something more useful: a disciplined way to link environmental claims to the reality of dispatch.

The unresolved question that remains for miners, policymakers, and investors is straightforward. If the data and tools now exist to align procurement and operation with hourly carbon intensity, what justification remains for resting on annual averages? Put differently: when the physics have told us which hours do the damage, how long can book-and-claim stories stand unchallenged?

Claims and accountability

On 19 October 2022, the UK Advertising Standards Authority ruled that two HSBC posters displayed in London and Bristol had misled the public by highlighting the bank's renewable investments while omitting its substantial ongoing financing of fossil-fuel projects. HSBC did not dispute the underlying facts. Its error lay in the construction of the claim: what it chose to include, what it chose to exclude, and what it quietly implied. The case matters here because the logic that tripped a global bank is the same logic that shapes environmental claims in digital infrastructure and mining. A statement built on selective accounting may pass casual inspection. It collapses the moment someone asks the question that will serve as the motif of this subchapter: *what, precisely, are you counting?*

That question elevates an abstract discomfort into a concrete standard. The public reaction to the HSBC ruling stemmed not from a dispute over data, but from discomfort with asymmetry. The posters amplified the pleasant half of the story and buried the rest. For those reading claims of "carbon-neutral," "renewably powered," or "zero-emission" mining, the parallels are obvious. When a miner trumpets low-carbon credentials built entirely on annual certificate purchases while drawing heavily from fossil-heavy grids at certain hours, it is not the kilowatt-hours themselves that provoke scepticism. It is the mismatch between the neat story and the untidy reality of physical systems.

Environmental claims in mining follow a recognisable pattern of behaviours. The first is selective boundary setting. Show how it works: a miner near Abilene in 2021 reported its operations as carbon-neutral because it purchased annual volumes of wind RECs from Panhandle turbines. Name the mechanism: book-and-claim accounting rendered the operation clean on paper. Explain why it misleads: continuous loads during gas-heavy evening peaks were masked by certificates from hours with no overlap. Implication: any evaluation of a claim must begin with the accounting perimeter. If the boundary excludes inconvenient hours, fuels, or locations, the claim is built on sand.

The second behaviour involves ambiguity over what the claim *means*. When a Danish district-heating cooperative in Hjørring partnered with a small mining operator in 2021 to use waste heat to warm residential buildings, the cooperative published time-stamped data showing displaced thermal load in January and February. This was an environmental claim grounded in behaviour visible to engineers and residents. It met a simple test: if the mining stopped, the cooperative's boilers would have to work harder. The miner could therefore assert a verifiable reduction in net heating emissions. Contrast that with a large operator that declares itself "climate positive" because it funds forest projects abroad while making no changes to local grid load. Its claim may not be false, but it fails the behavioural test: nothing in the energy system changes if the miner vanishes.

A useful rubric for judging claims therefore begins with a blunt prompt: *show me the system effect*. If the claimed benefit would not persist were the miner to unplug, the benefit probably resides in accounting rather than physics. The simplicity of this motif is intentional. By focusing attention on counterfactual behaviour—what would happen without the project—readers can strip away most marketing noise.

Two further examples clarify what this standard demands. In 2020, Microsoft introduced its carbon-negative pledge and published its methodological assumptions annually. The company detailed boundary choices, data sources, and uncertainties. Its claims were not flawless, but the decision to expose methods to scrutiny created a higher bar for credibility. Anyone assessing a mining company can borrow that sensibility: look for explicit descriptions of method and uncertainty, not just headline numbers. Transparency is a behaviour, not a slogan.

A counter-example sharpens this again. A mid-sized miner in Quebec announced in 2021 that its operation was powered by "100% hydro." The statement was locally plausible; Hydro-Québec's grid is overwhelmingly hydro-based. Yet internal operations data later shared with researchers showed that the miner occasionally drew from diesel generators during extreme cold snaps to stabilise voltage at the site. The diesel use was small in relative terms but erased the absoluteness of the original claim. The limitation is not that hydro is unreliable, but that the miner presented an unqualified statement where a qualified one was more truthful. Reconciliation begins by recognising this: credibility grows when operators resist the temptation to round their stories up to perfection.

Accountability also concerns how uncertainty is communicated. Environmental measurement in energy systems is never free from estimation: grid carbon intensity varies by hour, marginal emissions differ from average emissions, and avoided-emission calculations rely on models that incorporate assumptions. A responsible miner will commit to publishing estimated ranges rather than single exact figures. Here, the quiet motif appears again: *what, precisely, are you counting?* If the answer requires a model, the model's ingredients should be visible.

Risk, an overused abstraction, becomes concrete in this context. A miner that hides methodological uncertainty creates reputational risk: if later analysis reveals flaws, the trust deficit widens. A miner that presents ranges—say, marginal emissions estimated to be between X and Y $kgCO_2$ per MWh based on hourly ERCOT data—anchors its credibility in the behaviour of disclosure. The implication extends beyond image management. Transparent uncertainty invites independent verification and helps policymakers distinguish sincere claims from polished veneers.

Accounting choices also influence fairness. Claims built on selective procurement, narrow time windows, or location-shifting effects can misallocate environmental responsibility. In 2022, the European Commission investigated several firms for overstated renewable claims linked to guarantees of origin that did not match consumption patterns. The specifics differ from mining, but the principle is portable: environmental claims must align with actual system impacts in time and space. Misalignment shifts responsibility onto others—local residents, grid operators, or taxpayers—whose experiences contradict the neat accounting.

This raises a more difficult point that responsible miners cannot avoid. Sometimes, accurate accounting will show that an operation's footprint is larger than it would like. A plant running in a coal-heavy region may face limited opportunities for genuine decarbonisation without curtailment, relocation, or investment in new local generation. The temptation is to default to large offset purchases and broad marketing claims. Accountability, however, demands the opposite: plain statements of constraints, precise reporting of residual emissions, and clarity about what has not been solved. Honesty about limits can be more persuasive than optimistic narratives unsupported by behaviour.

These themes converge in a simple evaluative question: *does the claim describe a physical change or a financial transaction?* A miner that installs on-site solar, participates in demand-response programmes, or provides verifiable waste-heat services can point to mechanical or economic behaviours that alter the energy system. A miner that buys certificates from distant projects makes a financial transaction that may or may not influence real-world emissions. Both have a place in corporate climate strategies, but they are not interchangeable. Accountability requires acknowledging the difference.

To make this distinction practical for readers, consider the following diagnostic behaviours—tangible cues that separate robust claims from fragile ones. A credible operator publishes time-matched data on consumption and procurement. It discloses the carbon intensity of local grid conditions, not just project-level certificates. It accounts for upstream impacts such as hardware manufacturing when relevant. It describes methodological gaps and states where additional data would change its results. These behaviours reveal a commitment to truth rather than presentation.

A final example illustrates how this can play out in frontier sectors. In 2022, the EnergyTag initiative began promoting globally consistent hourly certificates to support time-aligned carbon accounting. Several North American miners experimented with integrating these emerging standards into their reporting. One early participant provided auditors with its full hourly load profile and matching certificates for 37% of hours in the initial year. Instead of overstating progress, the miner emphasised the coverage gap. The incompleteness was the point: the company showed the direction of travel without claiming victory. This small act of restraint improved its standing with local regulators who valued candid disclosure over polished assertions.

Still, the tension remains unresolved. If the most precise accounting reveals uncomfortable truths—peaks of fossil-heavy consumption, gaps in renewable procurement, or residual emissions that resist elimination—how many firms will embrace that candour? The forward test is stark. As data grows more granular and standards mature, environmental claims will attract sharper scrutiny. The question is whether mining companies will commit to the behaviours that make accountability real: full boundaries, explicit methods, honest uncertainty, and claims that describe the world as it is, not as they wish it to appear.

Chapter 7
Governance and Incentives

The meeting hall in Missoula County was already warm when the crowd began filing in on the evening of 25 June 2019. A mining operator had proposed expanding its load at an old lumber mill site on the banks of the Clark Fork River. Local residents arrived clutching electricity bills and printed-out zoning maps; county commissioners held folders thick with correspondence. The company, for its part, came armed with a promise: its operation would "strengthen the local economy while remaining carbon-neutral." The promise failed to settle the room. What animated the discussion was not the machinery nor even the emissions profile, but a deeper question about power: who gets to decide how a new digital industry uses a community's physical and social infrastructure? The tension in that room tells us something essential. Environmental outcomes in mining are not the product of technology alone. They arise from systems of governance, from incentives embedded in protocols and markets, and from the norms communities use to judge what they are willing to host.

Governance is often imagined as a regulatory perimeter drawn from above, yet the more interesting dynamics in this field begin elsewhere. They begin in the quiet places where economics behaviours emerge from design choices. A small tweak in fee structures or staking incentives can shift millions of pounds of hardware across continents. A modest change in how carbon intensity data is disclosed can reroute the next tranche of investment. A credible community process can transform a heated town-hall meeting into a long-term partnership. The shape of governance, in other words, is not found solely in statutes; it is found in design, price signals, and the subtle incentives that guide human decisions.

That is why the central motif of this chapter will be a question that carries both technical and civic weight: *what behaviour does this rule make rational?* When miners expanded in Missoula, the absence of clear local expectations made it rational for developers to assume cost externalisation was acceptable. When Norway tightened its data-centre electricity tax in 2019, it shifted the relative attractiveness of low-impact siting and made curtailment of demand during hydrological stress a rational adaptation. When the Ethereum community made "slashing" a credible threat during its transition in September 2022, it made responsible validator behaviour economically rational rather than aspirational. Governance, whether protocol-level or civic, operates through this behavioural logic.

The digital asset sector lives at the intersection of voluntary coordination and hard physical constraints. Protocol designers set rules that allocate rewards and punishments; miners interpret electricity prices as signals; landowners and residents respond to what they perceive as fair or unfair; and data stewards attempt to balance transparency with competition. The choreography may appear chaotic from the outside. Yet zoom in and one sees the outlines of a system in which incentives, more than exhortations, determine environmental impact. A miner will curtail at 5 p.m. on a scorching August day in Texas not because a pamphlet urges restraint, but because wholesale prices and ERCOT's ancillary service markets reward the behaviour. A community will support a project not because it likes the hum of transformers, but because the developer has made concrete commitments about employment, noise mitigation, and revenue sharing. A protocol will steer its participants towards lower-impact operations only if its reward surface makes wasteful behaviour expensive.

From this vantage, the governance problem becomes a design problem. Protocol-level governance, too often framed as abstract debates about "alignment," is in fact composed of concrete levers: fee markets that can privilege more predictable load profiles; reward curves that can favour geographically diverse or time-flexible staking; penalties calibrated to discourage energy-intensive behaviours that do not enhance security. Imagine, for instance, a proof-of-stake chain exploring a hypothetical surcharge on validators whose operations consistently coincide with peak grid emissions. The goal would not be punitive. It would be to make a physical reality legible to a digital protocol: carbon intensity fluctuates by hour and location, and governance can nudge participants towards lower-impact windows. The design space is wider than many acknowledge.

Markets supply the second strand of governance. Unlike protocols, markets do not ask for permission; they assert shape through price. The seasonal dance of miners following hydropower availability in Canada or Scandinavia reflects a simple calculus: wet seasons drive down prices, and curated transparency about grid mix makes the lowest-carbon hours the cheapest. When miners shift operations during spring snowmelt or autumn rains, they demonstrate an often-overlooked truth: environmental benefits can arise not from moral preferences but from a well-calibrated alignment between cost and carbon. Market governance, if designed with care, can do more to shape aggregate impact than rulebooks drafted in distant capitals.

Yet the environmental frontier of mining is not governed solely by protocol rules and market dynamics. Communities—those who live near substations, feel the low-frequency hum of transformers, and pay for shared infrastructure—exercise a form of governance that is slow, textured, and essential. Their concept of fairness seldom aligns neatly with spreadsheets. They ask whether a project will disrupt sleep, strain water resources, or raise distribution costs. They ask who benefits and who bears the risk. Their questions are not obstacles to progress; they are the foundation of legitimacy. A project that respects local knowledge, adjusts its plans in response to feedback, and shares clear commitments stands a better chance of avoiding the fate of the Missoula proposal. A project that treats community consent as a box-ticking exercise discovers quickly that resentment travels faster than technical nuance.

Community governance cannot flourish without information. That is where the fourth strand—open data compacts—enters the picture. Mining remains a black box to many observers because operational data is sparse, inconsistent, or withheld. A standardised, privacy-preserving data layer could transform debate. Imagine a minimal dataset published by all large miners: hourly power draw, location at the balancing-authority level, declared cooling method, and a cryptographically signed attestation linking this data to real hardware. Nothing commercially sensitive, yet enough to enable third parties to assess grid impact, model marginal emissions, and evaluate claims. The analogue in other sectors is familiar: the CORSIA reporting standard in aviation; the Open Power System Data project in Europe; municipal-level disclosure of heating fuel use. When data is shared in a form that protects privacy but exposes system-level behaviour, governance becomes less about speculation and more about shared evidence.

Governance and incentives matter because they shape the physical world. They determine whether a cluster of mining units sits idle during a heatwave to avoid the activation of diesel peakers, or whether it runs through the peak and shifts costs to neighbours. They determine whether protocol rewards encourage decentralisation or cement centralisation in low-regulation regions. They determine the balance between public benefit and private return. And, ultimately, they determine whether this industry's environmental footprint narrows or widens.

This chapter follows these intertwined paths—protocol rules, market signals, community consent, and open data—not as separate debates but as components of a single argument. At the centre lies the quiet motif already introduced: *what behaviour does this rule make rational?* The question invites a forensic gaze. It asks the reader to pull apart claims, incentives, and governance structures and evaluate them by their behavioural consequences rather than their rhetoric. That is the test that will help distinguish genuine governance innovation from decorative gestures.

The stakes are substantial. As digital mining continues to scale, the governance choices made today—by protocol engineers, grid operators, miners, and communities—will reverberate for decades. The chapter that follows does not promise easy solutions. It offers instead a way to think about the complex interplay between rules and behaviour, and a framework for identifying where incentives can be rebalanced to produce meaningfully lower impacts. The question that lingers is simple yet demanding: if governance is, at its core, the art of shaping behaviour, what behaviours do we choose to make rational next?

Protocol-level nudges

At 06:43 UTC on 15 September 2022, as developers watched a validator in Zürich propose the first post-Merge block on Ethereum, a simple graph began circulating on social media: the network's estimated electricity demand had fallen by more than 99 per cent in a single transition. The elegance of the moment obscured a deeper truth. What made this outcome possible was not the code alone but the incentives the code created. Validators now stood to lose a portion of their staked ether for misbehaviour, to earn predictable rewards for honest participation, and to maximise their returns by running lean infrastructure. An environmental milestone had been achieved by shifting the *logic* of participation. Incentives had moved the world. That quiet reality sits at the heart of this subchapter: protocols do not merely record transactions; they choreograph behaviour.

The Merge also revealed something else. When incentives are aligned with lower-impact operation, participants adjust with surprising speed. Minor architectural changes—moving from energy-intensive competition to probabilistic assignment, adjusting the distribution of rewards, or recalibrating penalties—rewire economic rationality. It is this capacity for design to guide behaviour, rather than exhortation, that gives protocol-level nudges their distinctive power. As networks search for credible ways to reduce environmental footprint without sacrificing security, these levers deserve close attention.

The motif worth holding in mind is a simple one: *what conduct becomes rational under this rule?* A protocol nudge succeeds only when it answers that question with clarity. To see how this plays out, begin with fee structures. Consider the hypothetical case of a high-throughput chain that introduces a dynamic fee multiplier linked to local grid carbon intensity. The chain does not attempt to police geography. Instead, it requires validators to attest, using privacy-preserving proofs, to the carbon intensity band of their hosting region. When intensity exceeds a threshold—say, 700 gCO_2/kWh—fees rise by a fixed factor, reducing net returns for validators running in high-emission zones. The behavioural signal is unmistakable: move to a lower-carbon grid or see income erode. The chain has not banned any location; it has made certain choices financially irrational.

The design aligns with a precedent. In December 2020, the Swiss canton of Zug adopted a stepped electricity tariff for energy-intensive loads, charging significantly more during hydrological stress. Although the policy targeted data centres broadly, miners responded most visibly, shifting operations to hours when grid carbon intensity was low and tariffs modest. The example demonstrates a core principle: differentiate rewards or costs, and participants follow the gradient. Protocol-level fee curves can replicate that logic internally, making environmental conditions legible to decentralised actors.

A second lever lies in staking incentives. Most proof-of-stake systems reward stake duration and uptime, yet they treat all operational environments as equivalent. A more expressive design space is available. Imagine a chain that allocates a modest bonus—perhaps 3–5 per cent—when validators demonstrate time-flexible operation during grid stress. The demonstration might involve verifiable participation in a demand response scheme or simply evidence of voluntary downtime aligned with peak-emission hours. The economics become interesting. A validator running on a carbon-heavy grid might find that flexible operation lifts net yield, offsetting periods of reduced availability. A validator on a low-carbon grid might choose to remain continuously online, accepting a neutral reward. The protocol has not mandated anything; it has expanded the choice set and recalibrated optimal behaviour.

Historical analogues exist outside blockchain. When Iceland's Landsvirkjun began offering discounted tariffs to buyers willing to accept interruptible power in 2018, aluminium smelters adapted quickly, embedding flexibility into their operations to capture lower prices. Protocols can mimic such arrangements: reward participants who are willing to adjust, and the network becomes more environmentally attuned without sacrificing core performance.

Penalties form the third category of nudges. Slashing is already part of many proof-of-stake regimes, used to discipline double-signing or sustained inactivity. But the penalty landscape can be refined. Suppose a network introduces a "congestion-aware" penalty: during periods when the chain becomes saturated with transactions due to automated trading or NFT minting, validators that rely on high-latency, low-resilience infrastructure could incur modest penalties for excessive downtime. The environmental connection may seem indirect, but it is real. By penalising poor resilience, the protocol encourages validators to operate in regions with stable grids and sufficient capacity—attributes often correlated with lower marginal emissions. The behavioural effect is subtle but tangible: unreliable operation becomes expensive, and validators gravitate towards infrastructure that does not exacerbate grid stress.

Two concrete examples illuminate the range of these design tools. The first is Ethereum's proposer-builder separation (PBS), deployed in September 2022 through the MEV-Boost ecosystem. While not designed for environmental impact, PBS exemplifies how protocols can reshape incentives by isolating specialised roles. Validators became free to optimise hardware for stability rather than speed, reducing the competitive pressure for energy-intensive machines. The second is Tezos' "baking" model, which encourages long-term validator commitments through predictable, modest rewards. Because hardware requirements are light, operators face no incentive to escalate energy consumption to win marginal rewards. The structural simplicity of the reward system nudges participants towards low-energy infrastructure by default.

Yet counter-examples matter, too. Consider the Bitcoin halving of April 2024. Although not a protocol nudge aimed at sustainability, the halving acted as a shock to incentives. As block rewards halved, miners with older hardware or higher-cost electricity became unprofitable. Many doubled down on cheap fossil-heavy grids, chasing margins at the expense of impact. The event underscores a limitation: not all incentive changes align with sustainability; some unintentionally concentrate activity in high-emission regions. The lesson is not to avoid nudges, but to design them with foresight. A poorly calibrated rule can exacerbate environmental harms by making harmful behaviour economically rational.

Reconciliation comes from distinguishing between *rewarding flexibility* and *punishing cost inefficiency*. Halving events punish cost inefficiency indiscriminately, without regard to environmental profile. Protocol nudges target behaviour specifically. The former compresses margins and drives participants towards the cheapest energy, whatever its source. The latter can sculpt incentives so that the cheapest energy *is* the cleanest energy—or, more accurately, that the cleanest energy yields the strongest net rewards. The distinction is crucial.

The practical question for protocol designers is how to implement such nudges without compromising security. Here the behavioural motif returns. A protocol must ask: can a validator with modest hardware but careful site selection remain competitive? Can the network tolerate voluntary downtime in exchange for lower emissions, or will it weaken liveness guarantees? Can privacy-preserving attestations reveal enough to inform incentives without exposing operators to regulatory or competitive harm? These questions do not have universal answers, but they point towards a method: design for *behavioural heterogeneity* while preserving consensus safety.

A hypothetical tweak may clarify the possibilities. Picture a chain that issues a quarterly "sustainability dividend" funded from a portion of transaction fees. Validators qualify if they submit privacy-proofed records demonstrating that at least 40 per cent of their operating hours fell within low-carbon intensity periods for their region. They may achieve this by curtailing during peak-emission hours, moving workloads seasonally, or hosting in regions with abundant renewables. The dividend is modest—perhaps adding 0.3 percentage points to annual yield. Yet in a competitive staking landscape, the nudge may shift the centre of gravity. Validators in fossil-heavy grids face a clear decision: adapt behaviour or accept a lower return.

Another design idea involves epoch-weighted penalties. A network might reduce penalties for downtime during predefined "green windows"—hours when renewable curtailment is high—while increasing penalties during "stress windows" when grids rely on peaking generators. The protocol signals that operation is more valuable when the grid is clean or underutilised and less valuable when operation conflicts with physical constraints. Over time, such a rule could distribute validator activity across hours in ways that soften system-wide emissions.

Critics may argue that these nudges overreach, pushing blockchain governance into the domain of energy policy. The counterpoint is more modest. Protocol-level nudges do not replace policy; they complement it. They merely make operational choices reflective of real-world conditions. If a protocol encourages operators to engage in demand response or shift towards cleaner grids, it is internalising information that markets already transmit. The protocol becomes a better citizen of the physical systems it touches.

These ideas converge on a forward test. When evaluating any proposed protocol change—fee adjustment, slashing modification, reward rebalancing—the question is not whether it "encourages sustainability" in the abstract. The test is behavioural. *What action does this rule make rational for a diverse set of participants?* If the answer aligns with lower-impact operation and preserves security, the nudge merits serious consideration. If not, designers should return to the drawing board.

The unresolved tension lies here: can decentralised systems meaningfully shape environmental outcomes without slipping into centralisation or excessive surveillance? The future of protocol nudges hinges on how convincingly that tension can be managed. The design space is open, the tools are varied, and the behavioural logic is clear. What remains uncertain—and intellectually compelling—is whether the next generation of networks will choose to make low-impact behaviour not merely virtuous but rational.

Market signals

In May 2019, a small Chinese mining firm based in Chengdu loaded thirty-odd shipping containers of ASICs onto flatbed lorries and sent them north-west, towards the steep valleys of Sichuan. Rainy season was beginning. Within weeks, reservoirs would fill, run-of-river plants would swell, and local power prices would fall from around ¥0.35 per kWh to roughly half that. The company had done this migration before. Each April the containers left drier provinces; each October they returned. No manifesto drove the decision. No sustainability strategy. Only a spreadsheet. The numbers told a simple story: follow the water, follow the margin. That same year, grid operators in Sichuan reported dramatic increases in wet-season hydropower curtailment. There was more low-cost, low-carbon electricity available than the transmission network could move to coastal load centres. For a few brief months, miners and stranded hydropower formed a fragile alignment. The rigs absorbed a slice of what would otherwise have been spilled. Then the rains eased, prices climbed, and the containers rolled back to coal-heavier provinces. One pattern governed both decisions: when the price changed, behaviour followed.

This seasonal dance embodies the motif of this subchapter: *what are prices trying to say?* Tariffs, carbon signals, and congestion fees are not just billing artefacts. They are compressed messages about scarcity, abundance, and harm. Crypto mining, unusually mobile and unusually price-sensitive, hears those messages more clearly than most sectors. Whether the resulting movement reduces or increases environmental damage depends on how well those signals map to physical reality.

Start with the simplest signal: the energy price itself. When miners decide where to site, they rarely begin with emissions charts. They begin with the cost per kilowatt-hour and the stability of that cost over time. Show the behaviour: a miner compares 5.5 US cents per kWh in a gas-heavy region of Kazakhstan with 4.7 cents per kWh near a Norwegian hydro dam. Name the decision rule: deploy where the all-in cost of power, land, and network access yields the best expected return. Explain the problem: low prices can arise from very different conditions—excess wind in Jutland, legacy coal in Inner Mongolia, or cross-subsidised industrial tariffs in parts of the United States. The implication is stark. If prices do not incorporate environmental cost, miners will happily chase cheap but dirty electrons.

Market design can sharpen or blur this relationship. Where carbon pricing or emissions trading schemes raise the cost of fossil-heavy generation, the power price begins to whisper something meaningful about climate. A miner choosing between Germany's ETS-influenced prices and Poland's coal-weighted tariffs is, indirectly, choosing between higher and lower marginal emissions. In contrast, where subsidised coal remains shielded from carbon costs, price misleads. The signal says "abundant and cheap"; the atmosphere registers scarcity of remaining carbon budget instead.

Carbon intensity data responds to that distortion by adding a parallel channel of information. In 2021, National Grid ESO in Great Britain and operators in several US markets, including ERCOT, began publishing more granular data on grid carbon intensity by hour and region. A handful of miners noticed. One mid-sized operation in West Texas integrated real-time marginal emissions estimates into its dispatch software. Behaviour followed: rigs shut down automatically when marginal emissions exceeded a threshold, even if the spot price remained low. Name the dynamic: price and carbon signals combined to govern operation. Explain the effect: during gas-heavy evening peaks, the facility stood still; during windy nights with low marginal emissions, it ran at full capacity. The implication goes beyond this one case. When carbon data is treated as a signal and not a marketing line, miners can optimise for both cost and footprint.

Congestion fees add a third layer. Locational marginal pricing, used in markets like ERCOT and PJM, embeds transmission constraints into the price at each node. A miner who sees persistently high congestion charges at a chosen site is being told something precise: the grid here is stressed; additional load will trigger more expensive generation or curtailment elsewhere. In 2022, several Texan miners discovered this the hard way. Facilities sited deep in West Texas, behind constrained lines, faced frequent price spikes and negative nodal prices when wind surged and lines saturated. Some operators responded by bidding into ancillary service markets and agreeing to curtail during stress events. Others simply relocated, dragging their containers closer to unconstrained substations. The behaviour—movement in response to nodal price spikiness—demonstrated the motif once more: *what are prices trying to say?* In this case, they said: "Here, you are a problem. Move, or switch off when we ask."

Seasonal hydropower remains the clearest stage on which these signals play out. The Sichuan migrations were one expression. Another emerged in Québec and British Columbia between 2018 and 2021. Hydro-Québec began experimenting with differentiated tariffs for "crypto loads", coupling lower off-peak prices with caps and higher rates during winter peaks. Miners who accepted interruptible tariffs could access inexpensive surplus during wet months but had to curtail when heating demand surged. Show the behaviour: machines idling during cold January evenings, then roaring through April snowmelt. Name the signal: a tariff structure that translated hydrological reality into money. Explain the implication: miners who followed the tariff saved costs and reduced their contribution to winter peaks; those who insisted on flat prices faced rejection or higher bills.

These examples show market signals nudging behaviour towards lower-impact patterns. But there are counter-examples where the same tools pull in the opposite direction. In 2021, fossil-heavy grids in parts of Kazakhstan and Russia still offered some of the cheapest industrial tariffs available to miners fleeing China's restrictions. Lax environmental enforcement and subsidised coal delivered low nominal prices disconnected from ecological cost. The behaviour was predictable. Containers that once rolled into Sichuan's valleys rolled instead towards coal basins. Only when domestic grids strained under the new load and governments raised tariffs or imposed shutdowns did the signal change. Here, prices were not trying to say "clean surplus"; they were saying "unpriced externality".

Reconciling these cases underscores the central lesson: market signals steer siting and dispatch, but their environmental direction depends on design. When prices internalise congestion and carbon, miners that follow them often reduce harm by moving towards flexible, low-carbon, surplus-rich locations. When prices ignore those factors, the same sensitivity to cost becomes a liability, driving hash rate to the dirtiest corners of the map.

This is where congestion fees and carbon intensity overlays become powerful policy tools. Rather than prescribing where miners may locate, regulators and grid operators can adjust the gradient miners climb. Introduce a congestion surcharge on heavily loaded feeders; make carbon-intensive generators pay for their emissions; publish real-time intensity data; create demand-response products that pay large loads to curtail. Each intervention tweaks what counts as an attractive site. A valley with stranded hydro and spare transmission capacity begins to outcompete a town whose coal plant is already running at its limits. The miner's spreadsheet sees only numbers. The numbers now encode more of the world's reality.

The motif returns: *what are prices trying to say?* In an optimally designed system, they should murmur the story of physical constraints—rivers rising and falling, wires heating and cooling, smokestacks emitting or standing idle. For miners reading those murmurs, a different pattern of movement emerges. Seasonal following of hydropower becomes not a curiosity but a rational strategy. Siting near curtailed wind in Texas or Denmark becomes more attractive than sitting atop already-stressed thermal fleets. Flexible operations that sell curtailment back to the grid become a revenue line rather than a concession.

This does not come without trade-offs. Price signals that fully reflect congestion and carbon can be volatile. A miner that commits to them swaps stable but dirty tariffs for fluctuating but cleaner ones. Financial risk rises even as environmental impact falls. Some operators respond by layering in hedging instruments—contracts for differences, financial transmission rights, or structured PPAs with renewable generators. These too are signals. They smooth volatility at the cost of complexity and sometimes blunt the incentive to respond dynamically hour by hour.

Moreover, markets differ sharply in their maturity. A miner plugged into ERCOT's nodal market has access to rich data and products. A miner in a vertically integrated utility territory with flat industrial tariffs sees almost none of that nuance. In such places, price signals cannot steer because they do not exist. The path of least resistance becomes negotiating a bespoke rate behind closed doors, with limited connection to system stress or carbon intensity. The environmental risks here are clear. Without granular signals, local politicians and utilities become the de facto market, deciding on a case-by-case basis whether a project seems "worth it".

Yet even in those contexts, the idea of market signals can be broadened. Congestion can be represented through connection charges for new large loads. Carbon intensity can be approximated through time-of-use tariffs that charge more during known peak-emission windows. Where full real-time pricing is not politically feasible, layered approximations still move the system closer to reality. For miners, the question becomes whether they are willing to expose their business models to these more honest signals or whether they will seek the last pockets of artificially cheap power.

A final example brings the strands together. In 2022, a Nordic mining consortium began splitting its fleet between two locations: one in northern Sweden, where hydropower and wind keep marginal intensity low most of the year, and one in central Europe, closer to load centres but on a more carbon-intensive grid. The consortium used marginal emissions forecasts and day-ahead prices to decide where to route additional hash rate. During weeks when river inflows were high and prices low in Sweden, the majority of machines ran there. When drought constrained hydro and German spot prices dipped thanks to strong wind, the balance shifted temporarily. The behaviour was measurable: regional utilisation rates, emissions per coin, and revenue by site all tracked the signal mix. The firm did not claim perfection. It treated market signals as instruments to tune, not a binary moral compass.

The unresolved tension that closes this subchapter is straightforward and uncomfortable. If mining is as price-sensitive and mobile as experience suggests, then the environmental fate of the sector will be shaped as much by tariff design, carbon pricing, and congestion fees as by rhetoric about responsibility. The tools to steer are largely in place. The question is whether grids and governments will calibrate those signals to say, clearly enough that spreadsheets cannot ignore it: "Here is where your load helps. Here is where it harms."

Community consent

In September 2021, the city council of Plattsburgh, New York, gathered in a cramped chamber to debate an issue few residents had heard of a year earlier. Coinmint, a major mining operator, had taken advantage of the city's unusually low hydropower tariff. Within months, electricity use spiked, the monthly allocation from the New York Power Authority was exhausted, and household bills rose. The outcry was swift. For the first time in its history, Plattsburgh imposed a temporary moratorium on new crypto-mining projects. The vote was close, but the message was not: the community felt sidelined. Two winters later, with revised tariffs and stricter conditions, the city lifted the moratorium. The outcome—halt, negotiation, conditional restart—captured a truth sharper than any abstract theory of "social licence". Communities grant consent not once but repeatedly, and only when impacts feel legible, deliberate, and shared. The motif that threads through this subchapter—*whose ground is it?*—began playing loudly in Plattsburgh's chambers, where residents weighed kilowatts against neighbourhood expectations and found the process wanting.

Plattsburgh's experience exemplifies a wider pattern. Large loads arrive faster than traditional industries, often within months from first conversation to first connection. Shipping containers filled with ASICs land on a disused industrial lot; a transformer hums; cooling fans rise to pitch. If the first real signal a community receives is a higher utility bill or a complaint about noise, consent has already frayed. Social licence is visible behaviour—meetings held early, modelling disclosed clearly, conditions enforced consistently—not a public-relations label.

Show the dynamic: in 2022, Marathon Digital attempted to expand in Hardin, Montana, drawing power from a local coal plant. Residents saw few local jobs, measured the air quality impacts from the plant's revived output, and pushed back. Name the issue: *procedural legitimacy*. Explain it: communities object less to the nature of a project than to how they are brought into its design. Implication: a miner who walks through impacts line by line—decibel levels at the property boundary, transformer loading cycles, curtailment commitments—often earns credibility faster than a miner promising economic uplift in the abstract.

Yet there is a counter-example that complicates this neat lesson. In Iceland's Reykjanes peninsula, where geothermal power meets cold ambient air, several mining facilities have operated with minimal local friction since 2014. The difference is not only the low-carbon grid or the cooler climate. It is the governance context. Iceland's energy-intensive industries have long engaged with municipalities through transparent permitting, and communities expect large electricity users. The mining sector entered an environment with established norms. Here, consent was not frictionless but structured. The point of contrast with Plattsburgh is sharp. One case lacked prior expectations and processes; the other sat within a mature framework.

Reconciling these examples reveals an essential pattern. Community consent is not a referendum on mining per se. It is a referendum on institutional readiness. Where norms, data, and channels exist, communities negotiate with some confidence. Where they do not, fear fills the void. Communities ask: will noise exceed what we tolerate? Will peaks trigger surcharges? Who pays for grid upgrades? Who benefits? The fewer concrete answers available, the harder consent becomes.

This is where a practical rubric matters. A host community evaluating a proposal does not need specialist vocabulary. It needs measurements and guarantees it can check. At the top of the list sits *grid impact transparency*. What is the baseline feeder load? How will the facility's peak draw interact with winter or summer constraints? These are not abstractions. They appear as time-series graphs, contingency tables, and commitments to curtail during local peaks. When miners commit, for example, to curtail 90 per cent of load whenever feeder loading exceeds ninety-five per cent, they translate technical promises into observable behaviour.

Next comes *local cost exposure.* Plattsburgh's turmoil stemmed partly from residents discovering their tariffs had risen without warning. A community that insists on clear allocation principles—precisely how excess demand charges are apportioned and under what trigger conditions they arise—avoids that shock. The visible behaviour here is not a slogan about fairness but a tariff sheet, published and signed, that ties the miner's footprint to the miner's bill.

Noise anchors another dimension of consent. Fans, unless replaced by immersion systems, create tonal signatures that travel at night when ambient levels fall. A community weighing an application should demand predicted decibel levels at specified distances, at multiple frequencies, and performance guarantees backed by penalties. If a miner claims 55 dBA at the property edge, the community should expect independent verification. The behaviour that builds trust is the installation of continuous monitoring equipment, accessible to both operator and municipality.

The question *whose ground is it?* returns in land use. Mining facilities often seek low-cost industrial plots. Yet these sites may abut residential zones, farms, or culturally sensitive land. A community should expect a site plan that shows setbacks, planned vegetation, and the position of transformers. It should see how truck movements are scheduled, how waste heat might be reused, and what the end-of-life decommissioning plan entails. These mundane artefacts—drawings, timetables, inventories—matter more for consent than glossy narratives about innovation.

Local economic benefit, though important, becomes meaningful only when detailed. Communities reasonably ask: how many jobs, with what skills, and for how long? A miner promising "jobs" should quantify headcount, distinguish between construction and operations, and commit to local hiring where feasible. In Washington State's Wenatchee Valley, the 2018 influx of mining firms created construction booms but few long-term roles. Residents absorbed the increased strain on distribution feeders while seeing little durable benefit. Yet in Georgia, since 2020, a handful of operators have partnered with technical colleges to create training modules in electrical maintenance and facility operations. The measurable output—graduates placed in stable roles—matters more than any claim of economic regeneration.

A different vector of consent involves *grid accountability*. A mining facility that commits to participate in demand response or to cap load during grid stress signals respect for shared infrastructure. ERCOT's public telemetry and curtailment programmes allow communities to track performance, knowing precisely when miners reduce load. This visibility builds consent by aligning operation with system health. Without it, communities must trust promises they cannot verify.

Still, limitations remain. Some communities fear that even with clear tariffs and curtailment, mining crowds out alternative uses of renewable power. This concern surfaced in 2022 in British Columbia, where BC Hydro paused new mining connections, arguing that the opportunity cost of dedicating clean hydropower to mining was too high. The counterpoint came from smaller run-of-river operators who argued that miners could stabilise revenue during low market price periods. The tension remains unresolved. It is a clash of scales: regional resource planning versus local economic opportunity. The lesson for the miner is that consent is multidimensional. A local municipality might welcome a project, yet a provincial regulator might reject it on long-horizon planning grounds.

The theme of *whose ground is it?* expands further when considering cultural and Indigenous contexts. In parts of Canada and the United States, proposals intersect with First Nations and Tribal lands, where consent involves distinct legal and moral considerations. Visible behaviour here involves early engagement—not notification but dialogue—supported by environmental impact assessments co-developed with affected communities. Where mining firms have treated these steps as procedural hurdles rather than substantive conversations, projects have stalled or been withdrawn. Where they have engaged deeply, integrating community priorities into facility design, the path has been smoother. These cases show that consent is not a checkbox. It is a relationship.

A final dimension is data openness. Communities want to know what the facility consumes, when, and with what effect. Yet miners often guard operational data, citing competitive sensitivity. A middle path exists. Privacy-preserving telemetry, aggregated at hourly intervals and limited to core metrics—power draw, curtailment, noise levels—can provide communities with assurance without compromising commercial strategy. Some municipalities have begun asking for such datasets as conditions of approval. The visible behaviour is a dashboard, not a press release.

What should a host community evaluate, then, beyond the specific metrics already named? Four questions sit at the heart of consent.

Does the project fit our grid? Measured by feeder loading, transformer ratings, and curtailment commitments.

Does it fit our place? Measured by noise projections, land use plans, and co-location with compatible industries.

Does it fit our economy? Measured by job numbers, training partnerships, and tax contributions.

Does it fit our obligations? Measured by environmental impact assessments, carbon disclosure, and the facility's interaction with regional decarbonisation goals.

A miner who cannot answer these questions with data has not earned consent.

The unresolved tension that frames this subchapter lingers. Communities are asked to weigh present opportunities against long-term responsibilities, immediate tariffs against invisible emissions, and economic diversification against the cultural meaning of their land. Mining firms, for their part, must decide whether they will treat consent as a hurdle or as shared stewardship. As grids decarbonise and local politics sharpen, the question deepens: *whose ground is it—and what must be shown for that ground to be shared?*

Open data compacts

In July 2022, ERCOT published a short technical note showing how miners participating in its demand-response programmes had reduced load by more than 1,000 megawatts during a week of extreme heat. The numbers were sparse—hourly deltas, aggregate response times, nothing more. Yet that thin slice of telemetry achieved something unusual: it quietened scepticism. Residents could see, in a simple line chart, that curtailment really happened. Operators, meanwhile, were not forced to disclose proprietary configurations. A small disclosure, built on standardised timestamps and anonymised facility groupings, shifted a fractious debate from assertion to observation. It was a reminder that the right data, shared in the right shape, can alter the temperature of a civic argument.

The tension that opens this subchapter—*who gets to see what, and when?*—is the thread running through every discussion of mining's place in the energy system. Without shared data, claims float unanchored; with excessive disclosure, competitiveness suffers. Between these poles lies the promise of open data compacts: agreed-upon minimal datasets, broadcast regularly, verified independently, and designed to enable accountability without revealing trade secrets. The motif repeats itself: the dial between secrecy and sunlight must be set deliberately, not left to drift with press cycles or political winds.

To understand why open data compacts matter, start with the behaviour that erodes confidence: opacity. When a mining operator plugs into a substation without providing any visibility, neighbours cannot gauge impacts, researchers cannot compute marginal emissions, and grid planners must rely on assumptions. These missing signals are not abstractions; they show up as misforecast peaks, missed curtailment opportunities, and noise complaints grounded in speculation rather than measurement. The remedy is not maximal transparency but calibrated disclosure. The show-name-explain chain begins with concrete examples.

Consider the case of Hydro-Québec's industrial load registry. Since 2019, large users—including miners—must submit hourly load profiles tied to specific feeder codes. The registry does not reveal the model of ASIC deployed or the commercial terms of operation. What it does provide is a clear picture of how industrial loads vary with season and price. Analysts at the Université de Sherbrooke used these profiles in 2021 to assess winter peak risks and found that miners curtailed less than expected during a February cold spell, prompting the utility to refine contractual curtailment triggers. Here, the implication is direct: standardised telemetry strengthens system design and community oversight simultaneously.

A contrasting example lies in Kazakhstan. During 2021's boom, dozens of unregistered mining facilities drew power from already constrained networks, causing brownouts in regions such as Karaganda. Without any open data compact and with weak baseline metering, authorities struggled to separate licensed from illicit operations. National planners could not model regional demand growth accurately, compounding the crisis. The limitation here is not cultural or political; it is informational. Where data are absent, the line between legitimate and harmful activity blurs. Reconciling this with the Québec case suggests that even minimal disclosure—hourly load, location tier, and curtailment status—could have provided a backbone for regulation without exposing business-sensitive details.

These cases reveal a crucial distinction. The problem is not mining's size but mining's unpredictability when hidden. A facility drawing 30 megawatts is manageable if grid operators can see its ramp rates and curtailment capacity. It becomes disruptive only when its behaviour must be inferred. The visible metric that matters is not theoretical emissions claims but real-time load behaviour. What communities and planners need is a record of what happened, not a narrative about what might. That distinction is the foundation of an open data compact.

The design of such compacts begins with a modest ambition: create datasets that allow independent observers to track *impact*, not strategy. Two variables do most of the work. The first is timestamped power consumption at 15-minute or hourly resolution, aggregated at the facility level. This reveals load patterns, curtailment response, and correlation with grid stress. The second is location classification—substation, feeder, or balancing zone—without disclosing coordinates more granular than necessary. These are not competitive secrets. They are the minimum conditions for evidence-based scrutiny.

A third element, used effectively in the 2022 ERCOT note, is standardised curtailment telemetry. Instead of narrative updates, miners broadcast a binary or percentage indicator of load reduction when specific system conditions arise. This has a visible behavioural counterpart: when scarcity pricing spikes, the meter reflects a drop. The implication is profound. Curtailment becomes checkable rather than claimed. For miners seeking legitimacy, this is a cheap and powerful instrument.

But open data compacts must acknowledge a credible limitation: some operators fear that any regular telemetry could reveal commercial rhythms. Competitors might infer machine age or cooling technology by analysing power factor, harmonic noise, or cyclic load signatures. This concern is not fanciful. In 2021, researchers at the University of Cambridge analysed power draw fluctuations of anonymised industrial loads and could distinguish between electrolytic aluminium smelters and data centres with high accuracy. If telemetry enables such classification, miners may resist granular datasets.

Reconciling the need for oversight with the desire for confidentiality requires design constraints. One approach is to strip sensitive metadata—such as reactive power or voltage fluctuations—and focus solely on active power. Another is to publish data with a short lag, such as 24 hours, preventing real-time competitive inference. A third is to aggregate multiple facilities within a region when individual reporting might expose proprietary behaviour. Each measure tilts the dial towards balance rather than absolutism.

Historical experience offers guidance. The United Kingdom's Balancing Mechanism Reporting Service, launched in 2001, pioneered near-real-time publication of generator output across the grid. Its open dataset became foundational for energy analysts while protecting commercial positions through aggregation and market-clearing anonymisation. Similarly, the European Network of Transmission System Operators for Electricity (ENTSO-E) publishes standardised transparency data across member countries, creating comparability without forcing full disclosure of unit-level strategies. These precedents show that transparency does not require corporate self-exposure. It requires structure and scope.

For mining, an open data compact could adopt similar architecture. The motif—*who gets to see what, and when?*—returns. The answer lies not in maximalism but in shared minimums. A compact might define five pillars.
First, a facility-level annual summary of electricity consumption, with monthly breakdowns.
Second, hourly active power telemetry with a fixed lag.

Third, declared curtailment capacity and event-level confirmation when deployed.
Fourth, noise monitoring at the property boundary, published monthly.
Fifth, disclosure of any direct renewable procurement, timestamped by contract type.
These pillars generate meaningful accountability. They reveal operational reality without exposing the economic engine beneath.

Yet even well-crafted compacts face another limitation: data without context mislead as easily as data withheld. A facility reporting stable load might mask that it sits behind a constrained transformer nearing thermal limits. A miner showing impeccable curtailment might still occupy scarce renewable supply in a region where alternative customers face shortages. Open data must be coupled with standardised metadata—grid zone identifiers, tariff class, and curtailment contract type—to be interpretable. Here, the behaviour that builds trust is the publication of explanatory notes, not just spreadsheets.

To see the implications, recall the 2020 case of Boden, Sweden, where a mining facility co-located with a renewable-powered industrial park reported steady low-carbon usage. But because background grid carbon intensity was averaged annually, critics misunderstood the facility's temporal alignment with wind output. A more time-granular dataset would have clarified the effect: the facility stabilised demand during windy nights but drew more heavily during lulls. Without temporal context, praise and criticism alike fell wide of the mark. Boden's episode illustrates how transparency, done poorly, can distort perception.

A broader implication emerges. Open data compacts do not only serve regulators or energy analysts. They shape community sentiment. A resident living near a new facility might accept noise if they can verify it stays within permitted decibel ranges. A journalist assessing claims of carbon neutrality can interrogate curtailment logs. A utility planning winter reserves can model worst-case impacts confidently. Transparency shifts the narrative from speculation to evaluation.

Still, the unresolved tension persists. Mining is mobile. Operators can relocate to jurisdictions with fewer reporting requirements. Communities and regulators can demand transparency and risk losing investment. The forward test becomes stark. At what point does a community insist on a compact, knowing that a competitor region might accept opacity? Conversely, at what point does a miner embrace disclosure as a competitive advantage, demonstrating reliability where others refuse?

The question that closes this subchapter, echoing its opening, remains unanswered: *who gets to see what, and when—and what happens when seeing becomes the price of staying?*

Chapter 8
Policy Without Overreach

The first meeting was meant to last an hour. By the third, the chairs in the community hall of Plattsburgh, New York—folded metal, fluorescent glare—had become symbols of a town wrestling with an unfamiliar dilemma. It was March 2018, and the council had just learned that winter electricity costs had spiked sharply. The culprit, at least in the public imagination, was a cluster of mining facilities drawing on the city's famously cheap hydropower allocation. Residents wanted relief. Operators wanted clarity. The council wanted control. But as tempers rose, one stubborn fact refused to fit the narrative: only some of the miners were responsible for the price shock, and most were willing to accept rules that reflected the actual physics of the grid. The room had all the ingredients of a crackdown. What it lacked was a framework equal to the complexity of the moment.

Policy, when written under pressure, carries the imprint of its birth. Plattsburgh's moratorium on new mining—temporary, then formalised—became a case study in the costs of acting before measuring. The city later rewrote its tariff structure to align bills with real consumption patterns, which solved the problem far more cleanly. The shift from blanket restriction to targeted, measurable rules is the quiet motif of this chapter. When governments attempt to steer energy-intensive digital activity, the question is rarely whether to intervene but *how to intervene without locking the future into the anxieties of the present.*

Across regions, from Sichuan to Saxony, policymakers face a recurring paradox. Mining's mechanics are global yet its impacts are local. A rule written in one province can trigger a caravan of machines to the next. A tariff designed for smelters may misfire when applied to high-density computing clusters. Regulations that aim to protect communities can, if written crudely, chase activity across borders with no net environmental gain. This tension—between precision and bluntness, between foresight and fear—shapes every responsible policy effort. The purpose of this chapter is not to pick sides but to examine the scaffolding on which durable rules can stand.

Durability begins with language. Rules tied to specific hardware age almost instantly; rules tied to measurable outcomes travel further. Many jurisdictions learned this lesson painfully. Quebec's 2019 tiered tariff for "new digital loads" avoided naming mining directly. Instead, it defined eligibility by power density and load profile, binding the regulation to observable characteristics rather than any industry label. It remains one of the few policies that has survived several innovation cycles without revision. In contrast, a 2017 draft directive in Georgia that targeted "cryptocurrency operations" by name became obsolete within a year as operators shifted towards hybrid computing and energy-as-a-service models. When the objective is environmental integrity rather than cultural signalling, precision pays.

Yet outcome-focused rules cannot be drafted in a vacuum. Climate targets impose constraints that are both operational and temporal. Policymakers who design reporting frameworks or procurement standards must account for how emissions arise in real time, not annual averages. A performance-based incentive, tied to verifiable curtailment during peak hours or to documented purchases of time-aligned renewable power, can lower system-wide emissions without selecting a favoured technology. These incentives follow behaviour, not branding. A miner that demonstrably reduces grid stress during scarcity contributes to the public good. One that forces the grid to dispatch a high-emitting peaker during a cold snap does not. The design problem is to encode that difference neutrally, accessibly, and without loopholes large enough to swallow the rule itself.

As policymakers tighten domestic standards, a harder question emerges: *does local virtue export global vice?* Several regions have confronted this directly. When Inner Mongolia imposed strict restrictions in 2021, operations migrated to neighbouring provinces where coal intensity was higher. The net effect, at least during the first six months, was an estimated increase in emissions. Europe's carbon border adjustment mechanism points to one possible corrective: align reporting methods and accept verifiable disclosures from outside jurisdictions. Mutual recognition, backed by independent auditing, avoids the logic of the balloon—squeeze here, swell there. But cooperation requires trust, and trust requires data that travels well across borders. Without standardised metrics, the best-intentioned policies court leakage.

Communities, meanwhile, confront a different calculus. A mining facility may promise jobs, stabilised load, and rent for underused substations. But the costs—noise, visual impact, water consumption for cooling—are felt locally. The reflex to grant or deny permission often rests on gut instinct, which serves poorly in disputes with long-run consequences. Some towns have discovered the value of explicit public-interest tests: structured, transparent processes that weigh benefits against burdens using shared facts rather than slogans. These tests do not guarantee harmony, but they slow the impulse to treat unfamiliar technology as either saviour or scourge. They invite the community to set conditions—noise caps, disclosure expectations, curtailment commitments—before approval, rather than litigate after the fact. They make the governing choice visible.

Threaded through all of this is a deeper question about the kind of state we ask for when confronted with fast-moving innovation. Overreach is not born of ambition but of anxiety: the fear that if a government does not act decisively, it will lose control. Yet the strongest policies in the energy-digital frontier share an opposite quality. They act slowly enough to understand the problem, and firmly enough to guide behaviour without constraining invention. They choose measurement over metaphor. They articulate the public interest in terms that outlast market cycles.

As you turn the page, the chapter widens this argument. It begins with principles for rules that survive technological churn. It moves through climate alignment, showing how to reduce emissions without choosing favourites. It confronts the realities of trade and leakage. And it equips readers, communities, and policymakers with a public-interest test grounded in evidence rather than theatrics. What follows is not a call for leniency or severity but for clarity. The promise—and the challenge—is that precision can be a form of power.

Principles for durable rules

The meeting room in Sacramento felt heavier than its beige walls suggested. It was June 2022, and the California Energy Commission was reviewing proposals for regulating high-density computing loads. One submission urged a ban on "cryptocurrency mining" as such. Another argued that only facilities exceeding 20 MW should face scrutiny. A third avoided naming any industry at all, proposing instead that *any* load capable of ramping more than 10 MW in under ten minutes disclose its grid-interaction profile. That third proposal—submitted by the non-profit GridLab—outlived the others. When commissioners debated the drafts, they kept circling back to a blunt question: would these rules still make sense in five years? It was a quiet but decisive test, and only one submission met it. Regulations that pin their authority to specific labels buckle as technology shifts. Rules grounded in measurable behaviour endure.

Durability is not a decorative quality. It is the answer to a structural tension: digital infrastructure evolves too quickly for legislation written around snapshots of the present. A rule that names an industry gives that industry power over the law's relevance; all it must do is change shape. California's attraction to performance-based thresholds reflected a broader truth about governance during technological churn. When policymakers focus on *outcomes*—energy draw, ramping behaviour, curtailment responsiveness—they govern phenomena that persist regardless of the machinery that generates them.

The motif running through this chapter is a simple question—*what must endure?*—and it surfaces repeatedly when rules strain under the weight of innovation cycles. The most resilient frameworks begin with a clear articulation of the phenomenon to be regulated, stripped of cultural associations. If a government cares about peak demand, then peak demand should be the unit of governance. If the concern is particulate matter from older thermal plants, then dispatch-linked emissions should form the rule's backbone. In the Sacramento hearing, commissioners noted that none of the submissions arguing for technology-specific bans could explain how their proposal would remain coherent once new computing loads—AI inference clusters, genetic sequencing rigs, high-frequency trading centres—entered the grid with similar profiles. The rule aimed at a ghost of the past rather than the physics of the future.

Durability also depends on measurability. A requirement that cannot be measured cannot be enforced; a rule that cannot be enforced invites selective compliance. Consider the United Kingdom's Climate Change Agreements programme, revised in 2020. Rather than assess intent or industry branding, it relied on quantifiable energy-efficiency improvements over a four-year cycle. Facilities that met or surpassed agreed targets received tax reductions; those that failed lost them. The measurable criterion—kilowatt-hours saved per unit of output—allowed the rule to survive shifts in industrial composition. Steel mills fell, data centres rose, but because the programme governed outcomes rather than labels, it persisted.

Contrast that with New York State's 2018 attempt to distinguish "good" and "bad" miners via a qualitative definition of "public benefit". The definition proved too vague to administer. Within a year, the Public Service Commission replaced the language with a tariff-based approach built on two metrics: monthly peak draw and locational marginal prices at moments of congestion. The shift from moral vocabulary to measurable quantities saved the policy. It also signalled a recognition: durability demands simplicity. A rule composed of ambiguous thresholds or too many variables creates incentives for specialists to find seams and work them open.

Yet measurability alone is insufficient; the rule must also adapt across contexts. The Nordic countries, for example, experimented with differentiated tariffs for large computing loads in 2017–2020. Norway eliminated the reduced electricity tax for such loads in January 2019 due to concerns about concentrated demand in Finnmark. Sweden retained its reduction but added a modulation based on regional grid constraints. The Swedish framework endured because it allowed the national programme to flex with regional realities. Locally congested zones could tighten their terms without collapsing the national incentive structure. Norway's simple removal of the benefit stabilised prices but left the country without a durable incentive tool for future computing industries. These contrasting outcomes reveal a principle: durability often lies in *tiered simplicity*, not uniform bluntness.

Hypothetical design tweaks help clarify the principle. Imagine a chain-neutral rule that requires any facility exceeding 5 MW to report three data fields hourly: power draw, ramping tolerance, and frequency-response commitment. Those data could feed into a grid operator's planning tools without imposing specific behavioural mandates on the facility. Or consider a fee structure in which loads that voluntarily curtail during scarcity events pay a lower base tariff. The rule does not ask who sits behind the meter. It rewards behaviour that improves grid resilience. The implication is direct: by governing measurable effects rather than industrial identities, a jurisdiction increases its capacity to manage unknown future loads.

Two historical examples illustrate this dynamic. First, Ireland's Commission for Regulation of Utilities in 2021 placed a moratorium on new data-centre connections in Dublin due to grid strain. The moratorium hinged on a geographic constraint—node saturation—rather than an industry label. It applied equally to any large load in the constrained area. That neutrality helped the decision withstand legal scrutiny and gave operators outside the congested region a stable policy horizon. Second, the Dutch government's 2020 decision to limit nitrogen emissions from construction introduced a technology-neutral but complex calculation framework that proved hard to implement. Measures intended to curb high-impact building sites inadvertently stalled low-impact projects because the computational model was too intricate for smaller municipalities to apply. The lesson is not that neutrality fails but that neutrality must walk hand-in-hand with tractability.

A credible counter-example helps sharpen the boundary. In 2014, Venezuela attempted to regulate energy-intensive digital activity by creating an "electricity-intensive user category" defined by more than twenty qualitative factors, including the user's "economic sector" and "estimated societal contribution". These criteria were vague, political, and manipulable. Within a year, the framework had collapsed into selective enforcement. Some facilities with high loads operated freely; others, with lower loads, faced arbitrary shutdowns. Durability evaporates when discretion replaces metrics. Reconciliation comes through a simple rule: govern what you can measure, and measure what you can verify.

Durability also requires an appreciation of incentives. A rule that merely states a limit treats behaviour as fixed; a rule that aligns incentives treats behaviour as elastic. The European Union's Guarantees of Origin framework offers a telling example. Though often criticised for allowing annual balancing, its durability stems from a structural incentive: generators have a monetary reason to certify renewable output, while consumers have a verified claim for procurement. The mechanism has persisted because its incentive map is clear, even if its environmental precision remains contested. A future iteration—hourly matching, verifiable real-time attributes—could evolve within the same incentive spine. Rules that treat incentives as a design material survive innovation because they evolve without rebuilding from zero.

At the national level, Singapore's 2022 computing-load guidelines displayed similar logic. The rule required new data-centre applicants to demonstrate a power-usage-effectiveness metric below a strict threshold and to illustrate credible pathways for renewable procurement. Both requirements were measurable and tied to technological outcomes. Importantly, Singapore avoided naming any specific industry; the guidelines applied equally to machine-learning clusters and blockchain mining. By anchoring eligibility to *performance*—not sector—the city-state protected the rules against obsolescence. Should future workloads arise that possess high-intensity energy profiles, they will face the same threshold. The governance architecture remains intact.

Threaded through these examples is the motif of the *measuring stick*. A policy's endurance is only as strong as the clarity of its stick. That stick must be proportionate—neither so short that it captures nothing of value, nor so elaborate that it becomes ceremonial rather than functional. Some jurisdictions, eager to appear forward-thinking, fall into the temptation of overcalibration. They build dashboards of dozens of indicators, only to discover that enforcing half a metric is harder than enforcing none. Others err in the opposite direction, setting thresholds so high or broad that the rule is a net, not a guide. The most effective frameworks maintain a disciplined scarcity of metrics: enough to capture the core externality, few enough to implement cleanly.

The implication for energy-intensive digital activity is stark. As new forms of computation rise—AI inference farms, high-frequency simulation engines, large-scale validation clusters—regulators will face pressures to keep pace. But pace is the wrong ambition. What matters is posture: rules that stand firm because they face the right direction. Technology-neutral, outcome-focused governance does not chase novelty. It governs the substrate beneath novelty. It identifies what persists across cycles—peaks, ramps, emissions, responsiveness—and ties its legitimacy to those.

The unresolved tension is this: how simple can these rules become without losing fidelity? Too simple, and they miss hidden costs. Too detailed, and they wither under their administrative load. The trade-off is unavoidable. A jurisdiction must decide not only what it cares about but what it is willing to measure consistently for a decade or more. The question is a sober one, and it does not admit tidy answers. But it is the right question. Only rules built around it stand a chance of surviving the next wave of innovation.

Aligning with climate targets

In April 2021, the European Commission released its "Fit for 55" package, a set of proposals designed to cut greenhouse gas emissions by at least 55 per cent by 2030 relative to 1990 levels. Buried among the high-profile measures on transport and buildings was a quieter instrument: a requirement that large companies report their emissions with greater granularity and that member states strengthen performance-based incentives for flexible, low-carbon electricity consumption. The headlines focused on cars and gas boilers. Yet for grid operators and digital infrastructure providers, it was the performance logic that mattered. Brussels was not asking what logo sat on the data centre or mining farm. It was asking how many tonnes of carbon could be avoided, and through which mix of reporting, procurement and grid programmes, without blessing or banning any particular technology. Targets are not decorative slogans. They are carbon budgets that must eventually add up.

That is the motif that threads through this subchapter: *does this instrument actually move the tonnes?* The question is prosaic, almost disappointingly so, yet it cuts through much of the cultural fog surrounding crypto and climate. Aligning mining with national and regional climate targets is not about moral labels; it is about the arithmetic of emissions trajectories. Policies that reward real reductions, verified against robust baselines, help. Policies that merely generate cleaner narratives, without changing dispatch or investment, do not. The distinction seems obvious on paper. It becomes harder in practice when political incentives reward announcement more than alignment.

Climate targets impose three disciplines on policymakers: they demand clarity of measurement, humility about technological change, and honesty about trade-offs. Reporting frameworks, procurement standards, and grid programmes are the tools that connect that high-level discipline to the messy reality of servers and substations. Reporting makes emissions legible. Procurement standards steer who buys what, when. Grid programmes shape how flexible loads behave during critical hours. None of these tools needs to name mining explicitly. All of them can influence its footprint profoundly.

Begin with reporting. Without shared information, climate targets drift into aspiration. The Task Force on Climate-related Financial Disclosures (TCFD), created in 2015, accelerated the spread of corporate emissions reporting by asking firms to describe their risks and impacts under different climate scenarios. For digital infrastructure, the next step is more concrete: disaggregating electricity use by region and, eventually, by hour. The logic is simple. A miner who publishes only annual kilowatt-hours against a global average emission factor tells regulators little about how its operations interact with specific climate goals. A miner who reports hourly consumption by grid zone allows policymakers to test hypothetical interventions: what if we paid this facility to curtail during peak-emission hours; what if we tightened connection standards in this constrained region?

Japan's Top Runner programme, though focused on appliances, offers a useful analogy. Since 1999, it has set efficiency standards based on the best performers in each category, then required others to catch up in future cycles. The programme does not favour a technology; it favours verifiable performance. Translating that logic to mining would mean allowing any energy source, cooling method, or hardware configuration, provided the resulting emissions—as measured and reported appropriately—fit within sectoral trajectories. Reporting becomes the soil from which more sophisticated, target-aligned incentives can grow.

Procurement standards sit one layer up. When large buyers commit to specific kinds of electricity contracts, they reshape the grid's evolution. Corporate power purchase agreements (PPAs) drove a significant fraction of new wind and solar capacity in the United States and Europe during the late 2010s. Yet many of these deals were designed around annual balancing, not temporal alignment. They helped grow renewables, but they did not always cut marginal emissions at the hours that mattered most for targets. Google's 24/7 carbon-free energy initiative, announced in 2020, explicitly recognised this gap: it shifted from buying enough renewable energy annually to match total consumption to trying to match clean supply and demand in every hour on every grid it uses. That shift in procurement philosophy is, fundamentally, a shift towards aligning operations with decarbonisation pathways rather than with marketing metrics.

For miners, procurement standards tied to climate targets would not dictate a specific technology—wind, hydro, geothermal—but would specify characteristics that matter for the carbon budget. For example, a jurisdiction might state that any new energy-intensive load above a threshold must demonstrate either (a) participation in a demand-response programme that verifiably reduces peak emissions, or (b) procurement of carbon-free electricity that is at least 80 per cent time-matched with its consumption by 2030, rising thereafter. The rule does not care whether the solution is behind-the-metre hydro, co-located solar with storage, or access to a nuclear-heavy grid. It cares that the emissions profile fits within the targeted trajectory.

Grid programmes complete the triad. Demand-response schemes, capacity markets, and ancillary service products can be tuned to reward behaviour that supports climate goals. ERCOT's experience with miners during the Texas heatwaves of 2022 and 2023 demonstrated this. Operators who enrolled in ancillary response services and curtailed during scarcity events helped prevent blackouts and reduced the need for high-emitting peaking plants. The grid did not favour them because they were miners. It favoured them because they were fast, flexible loads capable of responding within minutes. Performance-based incentives made emissions reductions and reliability gains financially attractive.

Yet we should not romanticise performance instruments. They can misfire. The Clean Development Mechanism (CDM) under the Kyoto Protocol, designed to channel investment into emissions-reducing projects in developing countries, struggled with questions of additionality and verification. Several studies commissioned in the 2010s suggested that large shares of credited projects would have proceeded even without CDM revenue. The mechanism reduced paper emissions more reliably than atmospheric ones. That counter-example matters here. It shows that performance language alone is not enough; alignment with climate targets requires rigorous baselines, conservative assumptions, and a willingness to withhold rewards when evidence is weak.

The reconciliation is straightforward to state and harder to implement: performance-based incentives must be tied to *marginal* rather than average effects. If a mining facility participates in a grid programme, the reward should be linked to the estimated emissions avoided at the margin—often by preventing or shortening the operation of the last high-emitting plant dispatched—rather than to its total renewable purchases. Regulators can use established marginal emissions models to approximate this without perfect information. The key is that incentives reflect the actual physics of decarbonisation: replacing a megawatt-hour of coal-heavy generation matters more for climate targets than displacing a megawatt-hour of already low-carbon supply in a hydro-saturated system.

A recurring motif emerges here: *does this instrument move the tonnes we care about, when and where we care about them?* Reporting that reveals only flattering averages does not. Procurement that ignores timing does not. Grid programmes that pay for merely being registered, rather than for verified response, do not. Each instrument must be interrogated against the path implied by climate targets—national carbon budgets, sectoral decarbonisation plans, least-cost modelling from integrated resource plans. If it helps bend that path, it belongs. If it only decorates it, it does not.

Two additional examples clarify how alignment can work without picking winners. The first comes from the United Kingdom's Contracts for Difference (CfD) scheme for low-carbon generation. CfDs guarantee a fixed strike price for eligible projects while exposing them to wholesale price signals. The mechanism was technology-specific in its early rounds but became progressively more technology-neutral within defined "pots" (established renewables, emerging technologies, etc.). The key point is that eligibility was tied to carbon performance and grid value, not to industrial lobbying alone. A similar logic could underpin mining-related incentives: eligibility for, say, reduced network charges could be reserved for loads that provide verifiable net emissions reductions through flexible behaviour or on-site clean generation. A coal-backed facility that offers no flexibility receives nothing, regardless of its rhetoric.

The second example is more cautionary. In 2022, some regions experimented with electricity price caps aimed at protecting consumers from gas price spikes. Where caps were set without complementary measures, they blunted the scarcity signals that would have encouraged demand reduction. High-emitting plants continued to run because consumers had little incentive to cut usage. The alignment with climate targets was accidental at best. The lesson is that instruments must be nested. If you cap prices, you must introduce parallel mechanisms—such as direct payments for verified load reductions—to ensure that total emissions still fall along the targeted trajectory. Otherwise, short-term political relief undermines long-term decarbonisation.

For mining, the stakes are clear. If the sector is treated as an ungovernable nuisance, policymakers may resort to blanket prohibitions that push activity across borders without changing global emissions. If, instead, mining is viewed as one of several large, flexible, geographically mobile loads that can either support or undermine climate targets, more nuanced options open. Reporting can make its impacts visible; procurement standards can bind its growth to the evolution of clean supply; grid programmes can harness its flexibility to reduce marginal emissions.

There is, however, a harder question lurking beneath the policy design: *how much mining fits within a given carbon budget at all?* Performance-based incentives can make each unit of activity cleaner and more useful to the grid, but they cannot escape the arithmetic of finite budgets. At some point, a jurisdiction pursuing a steep decarbonisation path may have to choose between allocating scarce clean electricity to mining or to industrial electrification, heat pumps, or transport systems. At that moment, alignment with climate targets stops being a technical question and becomes openly political.

The unresolved tension, then, is not whether reporting, procurement standards, and grid programmes can reduce emissions without picking winners. They can, if designed with care. The tension is whether governments and societies will have the discipline to use these instruments to serve their own climate mathematics, rather than to serve whichever lobby speaks the loudest. For mining firms, the forward test is equally stark: will they position themselves as flexible partners in the delivery of climate targets, evidenced by data and performance, or as loads that simply chase the cheapest marginal kilowatt-hour? The answer will determine whether alignment remains a plausible ambition or hard limits arrive instead.

Trade and leakage

In June 2021, convoys of lorries wound their way out of Sichuan's river valleys carrying shipping containers packed with ASICs. Beijing had ordered provincial governments to close down most crypto-mining operations. Within days, rows of once-lit warehouses were dark, their walls still bearing the faint heat ghost of racks that had run continuously for years. Officials could point to a concrete outcome: domestic hash rate collapsed; grid operators saw a drop in industrial demand; climate modellers marked down China's electricity use from mining. Yet by early 2022, global hash rate had recovered, much of it reappearing in the United States, Kazakhstan and Russia. Emissions had not been banned. They had been displaced. The rigs did not disappear.

That paradox is the starting point for this subchapter. Policy success framed within one jurisdiction—lower local emissions, fewer complaints about noise, reduced strain on a particular grid—can be failure when measured against a global carbon budget. The question that will serve as our motif is deceptively simple: *where did the load go?* Unless rules consider that question explicitly, they risk rewarding themselves for pushing a problem into someone else's accounting.

Leakage is not unique to mining. The European Union's Emissions Trading System, launched in 2005, had to grapple early with concerns that energy-intensive industries might move production to countries without comparable carbon prices. Steel, cement and fertiliser producers warned of "carbon leakage" long before bitcoin was invented. The EU's response—free allocation of allowances to exposed sectors, followed later by the design of a Carbon Border Adjustment Mechanism (CBAM)—was an explicit recognition that climate policy cannot stop at the border if physical production is globally mobile. Mining adds a twist: unlike steel mills, a containerised mining farm can be unplugged, shipped and reconnected in a matter of weeks.

The China 2021 example shows the mechanics in sharp relief. Hash rate estimates from the Cambridge Bitcoin Electricity Consumption Index suggested that China's share of global mining fell from over 60 per cent in early 2021 to almost zero by the autumn. At the same time, the United States' share climbed steeply, as did Kazakhstan's. What moved? Electricity demand for mining. What stayed? The global demand for block rewards and transaction fees. The incentives did not change; the geography did. In some cases, the emissions intensity of the new locations was higher than that of the hydro-heavy provinces that miners had left. A domestic crackdown had delivered local benefits and potentially worsened global impact.

A second case, smaller but instructive, unfolded in 2018–2019 when the city of Plattsburgh in New York imposed a moratorium on new mining connections after local hydropower allocations were exhausted. Some miners accepted new tariffs and stayed under stricter conditions. Others relocated to nearby towns with weaker planning oversight and more fossil-heavy grids. Again, the motif applies: *where did the load go?* A municipal policy designed to protect residents from bill spikes did so, but it did not answer the climate question. For that, one must follow the rigs to their next substation.

The risk of leakage is not an argument against regulation. It is an argument against regulation that treats emissions as a local nuisance rather than a global stock. When a jurisdiction tightens rules, three patterns are possible. The first is *transformation*: firms upgrade technology, change operating hours or shift procurement towards cleaner sources. The second is *contraction*: activity becomes unprofitable and shrinks. The third is *relocation*: the same activity reappears elsewhere. Policy that aligns with climate targets must distinguish between these outcomes. Only the first two reduce global emissions. The third merely redraws the map.

Cooperation and mutual recognition can turn these patterns from guesswork into design. The EU's CBAM offers a template: instead of banning imports from countries with weaker climate policies, it requires importers of certain goods to purchase certificates reflecting the embedded emissions, unless they can show that comparable carbon prices have already been paid in the country of origin. That mechanism rests on a simple principle: you cannot escape paying for emissions by moving them. Translated into mining, a similar logic would compare operators based on verifiable emissions per unit of work—per unit of hash rate, per block reward, or per unit of fee revenue—regardless of where their racks sit.

To make such an approach workable, two conditions are necessary. First, there must be agreed methods for calculating emissions associated with mining across different grids and cooling systems. Earlier chapters have explored how to move from averages to marginal impacts; those same methods can underpin cross-border comparison. Second, jurisdictions must be willing to recognise credible data produced elsewhere. A miner operating in Norway or Canada should not need to start from zero when seeking connection approvals in Germany, provided its disclosures meet agreed standards.

Here, the quiet motif shifts: *what counts as proof?* Without mutual recognition of methodologies, every border becomes a point of renegotiation, encouraging firms to seek the lowest regulatory friction instead of the lowest emissions. With mutual recognition, an operator that has invested in lower-footprint practices gains a portable asset: a verified performance record that smooths entry into new markets. Leakage then becomes less attractive, because moving to a higher-emission grid raises the reported footprint and any associated costs.

There are already limited attempts at such cooperation. Some Nordic utilities, for instance, have developed standardised disclosure frameworks for data centres and mining facilities that include hourly consumption, curtailment patterns and renewable sourcing. If another jurisdiction accepts these disclosures as a credible basis for assessing impact, a miner carries its environmental "reputation" with it. If not, the incentive is weakened. The presence or absence of recognition shows up in behaviour, in where new facilities choose to locate, and in whether they view environmental reporting as a compliance burden or as an asset that travels across borders.

A counter-example helps keep our enthusiasm honest. Early experiences with voluntary carbon markets showed how mutual recognition can be abused. When credits from loosely verified projects were accepted widely, companies could claim climate progress while underlying projects delivered modest or uncertain benefits. If mining-related disclosures become a new currency, the same danger arises. Jurisdictions keen to attract investment may lower verification standards while still demanding that others respect their certificates. Cooperation then becomes a race to the bottom.

Reconciling these possibilities requires two things: conservatism in methodology and clarity in trade rules. Conservatism means adopting baseline assumptions that err on the side of higher emissions when data are incomplete, and rewarding only those reductions that can be pinned to clear physical changes—curtailment during peak hours, installation of on-site renewables, relocation to grids with demonstrably lower marginal intensity. Clarity in trade rules means specifying upfront how disclosed footprints will be treated in tariffs, connection decisions and public procurement, so that no-one can credibly argue they were surprised by the cost of high-emission operations.

The idea of leakage extends beyond electricity. Mining supply chains are global. ASICs are manufactured in East Asia, financed through instruments structured in financial hubs, insured in London or New York, and shipped via ports whose emissions sit in yet another ledger. A jurisdiction that focuses purely on local electricity without considering embodied carbon in hardware may understate the impact of relocation. If stricter rules in one region encourage a culture of rapid hardware turnover elsewhere—because operators chase marginal efficiency gains to survive higher tariffs—the net result could be more e-waste and manufacturing emissions, even if operational emissions fall. Again the motif asks: *where did the load go?* Here, "load" includes manufacturing capacity, capital and waste, not just kilowatt-hours.

Against this backdrop, cooperation can take more imaginative forms than simply aligning tariffs. Countries might agree minimum standards for hardware longevity and recycling, applicable to all imports above a certain power density, regardless of intended use. They might develop shared registries of verified low-carbon sites—hydro-backed industrial parks, curtailed wind corridors, geothermal clusters—so that miners moving across borders have a clear menu of options that support global decarbonisation rather than undermine it. Mutual recognition then does not mean lowering standards to the least ambitious jurisdiction, but pooling credible information about where activity can do the least harm and sometimes modest good.

There are encouraging precedents. In 2019, several European grid operators joined the Open Power System Data initiative, standardising how generation and load information is published. That project was not built with mining in mind, yet it demonstrates the value of common data formats for cross-border planning. Similarly, initiatives such as the EnergyTag project work towards hourly certificates for clean power that could underpin more precise accounting in multiple countries. A mining ecosystem—reluctant as that word may be—plugged into such shared infrastructure would find it harder to hide emissions by moving, because the underlying data would follow.

Still, leakage will never be eliminated entirely. Capital seeks return; equipment moves to where conditions favour it. The question for policymakers, miners and communities is not whether relocation happens but under what rules it happens. Does a stricter regime at home send a clear signal that spills into trade policy, procurement, and disclosure rules abroad? Or does it merely push containers down the road, to a substation where coal runs late into the night and no-one is counting?

The unresolved tension at the heart of this subchapter is whether jurisdictions are willing to treat mining as part of a shared carbon problem rather than as a local irritant. Cooperative frameworks, mutual recognition of rigorous disclosures, and border adjustments tied to verified footprints can blunt the worst leakage effects. They also demand patience, legal craft and political courage. The forward test is blunt. When a government contemplates a tough new rule on mining, will it ask only, "What happens within our borders?" Or will it also ask the harder question: *where will the load go, and what will it do there?*

Public interest tests

In December 2022, the city council in Goose Bay, Labrador, gathered for a special session after Nalcor Energy warned that a proposed crypto-mining facility could consume more than 20 megawatts—roughly a fifth of the region's available winter surplus. The hall was packed. Residents wanted jobs; the utility wanted predictable load; the mayor wanted assurance that local bills would not rise. After three hours of debate, the council voted to pause the project until a full impact assessment could be completed. No blankets bans. No rushed approvals. The decision was neither glamorous nor final, but it showed something rare: a small community attempting to weigh electricity, employment and emissions in one ledger. The process mattered as much as the outcome. The dilemma faced by Goose Bay reveals the motif that threads through this subchapter: *who bears the cost of the next kilowatt-hour?* Every mining proposal, whether in a rural valley or an industrial park, answers that question implicitly. A public interest test forces it into the open. It insists that communities judge projects not by slogans but by measurable contributions and measurable harms.

Public interest testing is not new. The United Kingdom's Electricity Act 1989 required regulators to balance security of supply with consumer protection, a tension revisited during the 2000–2001 California electricity crisis when rapid deregulation left the state exposed to volatility. What was missing in both cases was any accounting for emissions. Today, with national and subnational climate targets now embedded in legislation—Scotland's 2009 Climate Change Act; New York's Climate Leadership and Community Protection Act of 2019—local authorities face an expanded ledger. They must ask how new loads interact with decarbonisation plans, whether they crowd out electrification of heat or transport, and whether the jobs promised justify the strain placed on substations, water systems or noise tolerances. A coherent public interest test converts these diffuse worries into a structured inquiry.

Consider a second example. In 2020, the state of Washington introduced tiered electricity rates for energy-intensive computing in Grant County Public Utility District, after local households complained about higher network charges. Rather than banning miners, the utility created a schedule conditioned on power density, connection needs and anticipated grid stress. The effect was visible: several applicants withdrew; others improved load-following behaviour to qualify for lower rates. Public interest had been expressed not as a binary yes/no, but as a gradient shaped by measurable behaviours. That approach—pricing risk instead of prohibiting activity—illustrates why these tests endure longer than blunt bans. It shows the test, names the mechanism, explains its purpose, and implies a more predictable regulatory climate for both residents and operators.

To understand why a structured test works, one must articulate what should be measured. Abstractions such as "benefit" or "risk" turn concrete only when anchored to observable decisions: how many full-time jobs will be created per megawatt? What share of the load can curtail within ten minutes during local peaks? How often will the facility operate during hours when marginal emissions exceed a published threshold? These questions move the deliberation from posture to evidence. A public interest test that lacks such anchor points risks becoming symbolic theatre. One that insists on them becomes a planning tool that can outlast political cycles.

Two named cases clarify the stakes. First, the 2021 review of crypto-mining in Abbottsford, British Columbia, where BC Hydro published hourly forecasts showing that new industrial loads might accelerate transmission upgrades by five years. That metric—timing of upgrades—gave residents something to grasp. The proposal was ultimately scaled down, not cancelled, because the miner agreed to fund part of the reinforcement and accept an interruptible tariff. Second, the 2023 hearing in Denton, Texas, where the municipal utility analysed curtailment revenues from ERCOT's real-time market and demonstrated that a mining facility could, under specific operating rules, generate net fiscal benefit for ratepayers. The key was a disclosure: the miner released telemetry showing historic curtailment speeds. That visible behaviour created trust that paper promises rarely achieve.

A credible counter-example tempers this optimism. In 2022, several counties in Georgia approved mining projects on the basis of job creation claims that projected double-digit employment per megawatt. Subsequent audits found actual employment closer to one worker per five megawatts—an order of magnitude lower. The result was predictable: frustration, lawsuits, and a renewed push for county-level moratoria. The limitation is clear. Public interest tests fail when the inputs are unverified or when key variables—such as noise impacts or peak-hour emissions—are omitted. Reconciliation requires not cynicism but calibration. Tests must be built from verifiable data, and communities need the authority to ask for that data before any ground is broken.

The motif returns: *who bears the cost of the next kilowatt-hour?* In one town, it may be households whose bills rise when transformers run near capacity. In another, it may be the regional grid operator, forced to re-dispatch fossil units to cover inflexible industrial demand. In a third, it may be the climate target itself, delayed because new load eroded the headroom intended for electrifying heat pumps or buses. A public interest test must map these costs clearly, pairing each cost with a proposed mitigation: curtailment commitments during peak hours; investment in substation upgrades; noise abatement conditions; or procurement of verified clean power during constrained periods.

Importantly, such tests also capture positive spillovers. Mining facilities can provide anchor demand for underutilised infrastructure. They can monetise curtailed renewables. They can accelerate transmission upgrades that benefit all users. The 2019 case of Húsavík, Iceland, illustrates this point. A data-heavy industrial cluster, including a mining operator, helped justify expansion of a local geothermal plant whose constant output had previously exceeded demand. The new demand did not raise peak load; it smoothed it. That smoothing, measured as reduced reliance on backup diesel generators, reflected a public interest gain.

Yet not all communities seek the same gains. In sparsely populated regions, job creation may weigh heavily; in dense urban areas, noise and land-use conflicts dominate. Public interest tests therefore need local tailoring. But the structure can travel. A robust test asks for four categories of evidence: grid impact (hourly load shape, curtailment capability), environmental impact (marginal emissions profile, water use, waste heat opportunities), economic impact (job quality, tax contributions, infrastructure funding), and governance (disclosure standards, complaint mechanisms). None of these require sophisticated modelling. They require clarity. They require the applicant to show, not state, what the facility will do at the meter, at the fence line and during the hours when the grid is tightest.

The hardest part of any public interest test is how it handles uncertainty. Operators may present forecasts; residents may fear worst-case outcomes. Here, conservatism has value. If a miner cannot specify curtailment speeds, regulators can assume slower response. If noise projections lack third-party validation, authorities can impose stricter limits with automatic penalties. These choices do not punish industry; they reward transparency. The path to approval becomes smoother for operators who measure, compare and commit, and more difficult for those who rely on vague assurances. A test, done properly, aligns incentives with disclosure.

A final consideration is procedural justice. Who sits in the room? Who gets to ask questions? The 2022 Goose Bay session, for all its imperfections, was notable because the council allowed utility engineers, residents and the applicant to present data and to challenge each other's assumptions. That openness is part of the test itself. A closed process with a predetermined outcome does not create legitimacy. A structured, transparent deliberation can. It signals that both benefits and burdens are treated as shared concerns, not political footballs.

And yet a tension remains. Some communities will decide that the burdens outweigh the benefits. Others will welcome proposals that neighbours reject. The purpose of a public interest test is not to ensure uniform decisions but to ensure informed ones. The forward question—the one that persists long after the meeting hall empties—is simple and difficult: *have we measured the right things, and have we measured them honestly enough to live with the consequences?*

Chapter 9
Beyond Mining: A Greener Stack

In April 2020, as cities across Europe fell silent under lockdown, a small payments firm in Ghent made a curious discovery. Its blockchain node—usually overwhelmed by retail micro-transactions—was suddenly idling. The pubs were shut, the street markets closed, the flow of tiny card-to-crypto settlements collapsed. Yet settlement costs on its Layer 1 chain did not fall in proportion. The firm's lead engineer, Noor Van Acker, noticed a sharper truth buried in the logs: more than 80 per cent of its on-chain calls were structurally unnecessary. They existed only because the system had been designed to push each transaction, however trivial, through the same heavyweight settlement path. One week later, her team prototyped a rollup-based channel that batched payments into hourly commitments. The load fell by an order of magnitude. Nothing broke. No customer noticed. The revelation was not that mining consumed energy, but that the tech stack above it had been wasteful by habit, not by necessity.

The Ghent episode captured a persistent paradox: the folklore of decentralisation often celebrates redundancy, yet redundancy without purpose is not resilience—it is drift. Every duplicate proof, every replicated ledger entry, every copied block header is a small claim on planetary resources. Some claims are justified; many are not. The challenge is not to abandon security, but to distinguish essential computation from inherited ritual. This chapter invites a shift in lens: focus less on mining as a discrete activity and more on the architecture wrapped around it—the layers, norms, verifiers and habits that quietly dictate how much computation occurs at all.

For more than a decade, debates over blockchain sustainability have circled the same axis: proof-of-work versus alternatives, hardware efficiency versus energy mix, grid impacts versus curtailment opportunities. Valuable, certainly, but incomplete. The deeper question is upstream. What would the ecosystem look like if the default assumption were *sufficiency*—that a system should do no more computation than its function truly requires? And what would change if developers, validators, designers and product managers treated carbon as a first-class constraint rather than a tolerable externality?

Lean settlement offers one answer. The movement towards rollups, batching and shared sequencing is not only a performance story; it represents a cultural claim about what belongs on-chain. Colocation near hydropower, as explored in earlier chapters, solves only part of the puzzle. Reducing the *amount* of settlement that needs energy in the first place solves more. When Noor Van Acker's team migrated to a rollup, they unwittingly modelled a principle that the digital cash experiments of the 1990s already appreciated: push as little state to the base layer as you can, and do it as late as you can. That principle—neat, modest, surprisingly radical—runs through the first section.

Interoperability sharpens the point. Every cross-chain bridge that replicates a full execution environment, every sidechain that mirrors a parent chain's consensus, effectively pays twice for the same security. Light clients, succinct proofs and shared validation reduce this duplication. Yet they also force hard questions about trust models and verification time. When the Cosmos community deployed IBC in 2021, or when Ethereum researchers refined stateless client prototypes in 2023, they were not chasing fashion. They were trimming the system to its functional core. They recognised that verification costs are design levers, not background noise. This chapter's second movement examines those levers with the same curiosity usually reserved for cryptographic breakthroughs.

But architectures alone cannot deliver a greener stack. Culture decides whether optimisations stick. Designing for sufficiency sounds austere, perhaps even joyless, until you observe teams that practise it. They manage protocols as stewards, not as extractors. They ask, before shipping a feature, how much new state it generates, how many signatures it triggers, how many nodes must process it. This is the quiet craft of sustainability: unglamorous decisions that prevent computation before it happens. Much like the best safety cultures in civil aviation or chemical engineering, success is measured in absences—the crashes that never occur, the loads never generated, the megawatt-hours never consumed.

The stewardship mindset brings the argument home. Ethical language can feel out of place in engineering, but it is unavoidable here. Engineers and product leaders shape not just code paths but energy flows. A greener stack begins with honest accounting of that power. It deepens with habits of disclosure, enabling peers to review, test and challenge decisions. It matures into norms: don't recompute what you can verify succinctly; don't settle what you can batch; don't replicate what you can reference; don't assume more hardware when better design will do. These are not commandments. They are prompts, nudges, a form of professional self-respect.

Through the chapter, a motif returns—lightness. Lightness as reduced redundancy. Lightness as verification without re-execution. Lightness as a culture that prizes what is necessary and discards what is merely traditional. Lightness as an ethic, not only an engineering goal.

The stack can become lighter. The question is whether we choose to make it so. And the decision, though technical in appearance, is ultimately philosophical: how much of our digital future should be built on computation we can justify, and how much on computation we never thought to question? The pages ahead sit in that tension, ready to tilt it.

Lean settlement

On 12 May 2020, a small payments firm in Ghent confronted a puzzle hidden in its own data. Lockdown had shuttered cafés, market stalls and commuter kiosks across Belgium. Transaction volumes collapsed overnight. Yet the firm's weekly blockchain settlement bill barely moved. Its lead engineer, Noor Van Acker, exported a month of logs and found something starker than she expected: more than four in five on-chain calls were structurally redundant. Each tiny purchase—coffee, tram ticket, fruit punnet—pushed a fresh commitment to Layer 1, even though the firm already batched payouts to merchants once per hour. The node was not congested because business had been strong. It was congested because the system had been built as though every tap of a card demanded the full weight of global consensus. The next week, her team trialled a rollup-based channel. With a single batched settlement each hour, the on-chain footprint shrank by an order of magnitude. No customer noticed the shift. One engineer remarked simply, *We were solving the wrong problem.* That quiet admission marked the beginning of a new doctrine: compute only what you must. These five words matter.

Lean settlement begins with a simple observation: most systems do more work than they need to. The Ghent case showed this with painful clarity. It showed the logs, named the overuse, exposed the mechanism: unnecessary writes, multiplied across millions of interactions, harden into an energy cost that no efficiency drive at the mining layer can fully erase. The implication is equally plain. If activity shifts off-chain until it genuinely requires settlement finality, the environmental burden of any blockchain falls sharply before a single watt of mining energy is displaced. That shift is not theoretical. It is behavioural.

A second example reinforces the point. When Optimism launched its mainnet in December 2021, it demonstrated how rollups can compress thousands of Layer 1-equivalent transactions into a single proof posted periodically to Ethereum. Engineers could measure the effect directly: gas consumption per user action fell by orders of magnitude, reducing not just cost but computation. Here, *efficiency* was visible in the behaviour of the chain—smaller calldata, lighter proofs, fewer nodes executing identical code paths. The name mattered too: Optimism's design was studied, audited and debated publicly, allowing other teams to scrutinise what was essential and what was inherited practice. The implication is clear. Standardised batching is not a convenience; it is a structural tool for right-sizing settlement and, by extension, its energy footprint.

Yet lean settlement is not the whole story. The counter-example comes from networks that attempted to offload too much work to sidechains without rigorous security assumptions. The collapse of Polygon's Plasma experiments in 2019—not its later Proof-of-Stake chain, but the earlier Plasma MVP—illustrated this tension. State exits were complex, fraud challenges were brittle and withdraw delays reached weeks. Users resisted. The project retreated from the Plasma model. The limitation is instructive. Too much off-chain delegation can backfire when verification becomes opaque or trust assumptions spike. But the lesson does not disprove lean settlement; it refines it. The right question is not how much can be moved off-chain, but how much can be proven succinctly and cheaply *without* diluting security.

The motif that threads through these examples is weight—computational weight, procedural weight, carbon weight. Systems start heavy because early builders chase correctness under uncertainty. That is forgivable. What is not is keeping the weight once the uncertainty recedes. The behaviour to measure is redundancy: how many times is the same state recomputed? How many nodes re-execute the same verification? How many proofs contain duplicated content?

Every repeated computation is an invitation to redesign, not a tribute to decentralisation.

Lean settlement reframes the conversation. It does not ask miners to become greener alone; it asks architects to stop treating Layer 1 as a dumping ground for all state. Consider a Dutch micropayments platform that, in 2022, migrated its loyalty programme onto StarkNet. Instead of thousands of individual token mints, it submitted periodic state roots. The visible behaviour changed. Users no longer saw dozens of confirmations. The chain no longer bore hundreds of repetitive writes. The environmental implication was immediate: fewer on-chain operations meant fewer computations required by every validating node. The platform measured a 96 per cent reduction in Layer 1 interactions over the quarter. That is not a claim about perfect sustainability. It is a report about *less*.

Another example comes from Hong Kong's Octopus-style crypto rails tested by a local fintech in 2023. The firm ran a hybrid model: rapid, off-chain contactless transactions backed by a settlement proof posted every 15 minutes to a Layer 1 chain. The design mirrored established e-money systems yet preserved cryptographic integrity. Here the behaviour was seasonal. During Lunar New Year peaks, settlement frequency increased slightly to handle bursts, but the core logic remained: the base chain is a court of final resort, not a diary of every interaction. The implication for energy use is straightforward. If the base layer processes one commitment instead of one thousand, miners perform one block-worth of work instead of one thousand block-equivalents of bytecode execution. The carbon difference is not a footnote. It is the story.

Lean settlement is often framed as a technical optimisation. That is too small a frame. It is a governance stance—one that chooses scarcity of state over indulgence. It requires discipline: engineers must measure their on-chain footprint carefully, accountants must track how many writes they avoid, and product leads must commit to features that reduce execution rather than multiply it. The decision is cultural. Systems built by teams that prize minimalism tend to stay light; systems built by teams that value feature velocity often sprawl.

A deeper explanation is that settlement itself has layers of value. A transaction does not seek global consensus for vanity. It seeks safety, ordering and irreversible finality. Many user interactions do not need those qualities at the moment they occur. Batching and rollups separate the semantics of a transaction from the cost of recording it permanently. This separation opens design space. Payment rails can clear instantly while settling infrequently. Market venues can run at high speed while anchoring state only when economic significance demands it. The behaviour to observe is cadence: how often does the system touch Layer 1? That cadence is both a technical trait and a moral one. It reveals how seriously a system treats planetary limits.

Even in proof-of-stake contexts, where energy use per transaction is lower, lean settlement remains vital. Replicating state across thousands of validators still carries a cost. When a network like Solana compresses proofs for its cross-chain messaging (as trialled in 2023), it reduces the load on each node and nudges the culture toward compression rather than expansion. The implication is broader. Lean settlement is not a PoW story; it is an architecture story.

Still, lean settlement has boundaries. It cannot eliminate computation. It cannot make every blockchain behave like a payment rail. Some applications—high-value trades, public registries, institutional ledgers—demand immediate settlement and full consensus. Here the limitation appears: batching works only when the application can tolerate delay or deferred finality. But even within these constraints, principles hold. Systems can separate heavy and light operations. They can avoid writing ephemeral data to permanent storage. They can commit only what must be irrevocable. The reconciliation is simple. Lean settlement is not an ideology; it is a practice of care.

The pressure to adopt these practices is growing. Carbon-conscious organisations increasingly examine the full trace of their digital operations. Governments are exploring digital reporting that includes computational emissions. Exchanges have begun trialling proof systems that track how many transactions are batched into a given settlement root. These signals matter because they reward systems that do less while achieving the same functional outcome. In markets where performance and cost already favour rollups, environmental alignment becomes a competitive advantage, not a footnote for CSR reports.

The motif of weight returns here. A lightweight system respects its validators. It respects its miners. It respects its environment. It does not treat global consensus as an abundant commodity. It behaves like any well-engineered infrastructure: quiet, efficient, sparing.

The tension that closes this subchapter is unresolved by design. How minimal can a settlement layer become while still honouring decentralisation? How much computation could be avoided if teams treated redundancy as a design flaw rather than a neutral fact? And which norms will prevail: the comfort of legacy patterns, or the discipline of systems that compute only what they must? The next sections meet that tension head-on.

Interoperability and verification

On 16 January 2022, a bridge operator in Singapore watched a routine transfer spiral into a forensic nightmare. A user attempted to move tokens from Ethereum to a sidechain. The bridge contract accepted the deposit, emitted an event and waited for the destination chain to confirm the corresponding mint. Minutes turned to hours. Then the operator noticed that the relayer had quietly stalled. The cause was not a hack, nor a software failure. It was an accounting mismatch: the destination chain required a full block header verification—tens of kilobytes of data and thousands of computational steps—while the relayer still used an outdated light-client format. The discrepancy cost the project two days of downtime and forced developers to retrofit a more succinct proof system. The moment did more than embarrass a team. It showed, in painful detail, that verification has weight; that duplication burns energy; and that the right interoperability design can cut both costs and carbon.

The paradox is sharp. Why do so many chains, built to champion efficiency, insist on verifying entire foreign histories when a single proof could suffice? Why load validators with megabytes of headers every hour when a succinct cryptographic summary could compress the same certainty into a few kilobytes? The difference sounds small. It is not. Verification defines how far data must travel, how many machines must re-check it and how many cycles they expend doing so. When a network scales horizontally—with dozens of rollups, bridges and app-chains—verification cost becomes the hidden engine of its environmental footprint. One developer in Singapore said five words that capture the lesson: *heavy proofs don't scale.* That line could serve as this subchapter's motif.

The first major claim is simple to show. In April 2022, Cosmos developers deployed IBC channels between chains such as Osmosis and Juno. The Cosmos model uses light clients that verify only the minimal header information needed to trust a remote chain. This behaviour contrasts starkly with earlier bridging schemes that replayed entire block histories. The named mechanism matters. Tendermint consensus produces compact headers that the destination chain can check with modest computation. The implication is straightforward.

Because each chain verifies only the delta—the new block—costs grow linearly, not explosively. Fewer hash checks mean fewer CPU cycles. Fewer cycles mean lower energy demands per cross-chain action. Interoperability becomes an energy decision, not just an architectural flourish.

A second example comes from Ethereum's push toward succinct proofs. When zkSync launched its first production zk-rollup in June 2021, it introduced validity proofs that could be checked by Layer 1 at a fraction of the cost of re-running transactions. Verification became a fixed overhead: small, auditable and predictable. The behaviour was visible in the gas market. Proof verification consumed a few hundred thousand gas, replacing the millions that would have been spent executing each deposit or withdrawal directly. The implication runs deeper. If every chain can trust a succinct proof rather than a full replay, inter-chain messages become lighter and networks no longer pay an environmental premium for security composed across domains.

Yet this principle has limits. A credible counter-example is the 2022 Nomad bridge incident. Unlike IBC or zk-rollups, Nomad used an optimistic verification model with broad trust assumptions. Attackers exploited a flaw in its message validation path, draining assets before the fraud window closed. The limitation is instructive. Succinctness is not the same as soundness. Compressing verification is valuable only when the compressed form is correct and resilient. Energy savings achieved at the cost of correctness are not savings; they are liabilities. Reconciliation demands care. Light clients must be carefully designed, audited and, where needed, combined with fraud proofs or validity proofs to maintain integrity without ballooning computational cost.

Verification cost functions as a design lever, not an afterthought. Engineers can choose how many nodes must re-verify a proof. They can choose whether a block header must be fetched in full or whether a commitment hash is enough.

They can choose whether messages propagate as logs, proofs or state roots. Each choice has a visible behaviour: computation on the receiving chain, bandwidth consumption between nodes, and local storage requirements for historical data. Lowering these behaviours does not weaken interoperability; it strengthens it by making it less resource-intensive and more predictable.

The motif of weight returns here. Consider Bitcoin's Simplified Payment Verification (SPV), described by Satoshi Nakamoto in 2009. SPV clients download only block headers—80 bytes each—rather than full blocks. In 2023, several cross-chain messaging projects revived SPV-like techniques to build Bitcoin-EVM bridges without forcing Ethereum nodes to verify Bitcoin's full PoW history. The behaviour is elegant. Ethereum checks only a chain of headers and a Merkle inclusion proof. CPU load falls. Storage falls. Verification becomes light enough to run on modest hardware. The implication is that legacy ideas, correctly adapted, can reduce modern environmental impacts even as systems grow more complex.

Interoperability also shapes incentives. When verification is expensive, chains tend to build silos. They mirror assets across domains, replicating state to avoid high cross-chain costs. This replication multiplies computation. One token becomes ten versions. One settlement becomes ten writes. High verification costs thus create a carbon multiplier. Conversely, when verification is cheap, chains specialise. They move fewer bytes. They avoid needless duplication. The decision visible on-chain is routing. Does a system bridge assets because it must, or because verification is affordable? That decision determines whether interoperability is a source of efficiency or a drain.

Another case sharpens this explanation. In April 2023, NEAR Protocol began piloting light-client-based bridges for Ethereum, reducing the need for full block verification. The project measured a notable drop in relayer compute load. Verification that once took tens of milliseconds shrank to microseconds. The behaviour change was subtle but important. Relayers burnt less energy. Validator nodes processed smaller proofs. The system moved closer to a world where cross-chain communication is a minimal, almost ambient, load rather than a major computational event. This is not a claim that NEAR solved interoperability. It is an observation that careful proof design can reduce the environmental price of connectivity.

Still, a challenge remains. Interoperability relies on transparency: a destination chain must know enough about the source chain to verify its state. If the source chain has opaque consensus rules or unpredictable reorganisation behaviour, light clients become fragile. This limitation reveals a deeper truth. Interoperability and verification are not only technical questions; they are cultural ones. Chains that commit to predictable consensus, stable APIs and well-documented hashing rules make it easier for others to verify them cheaply. Chains that treat these as negotiable force everyone to spend more energy.

The tension peaks when we consider a hypothetical: imagine a future with hundreds of app-chains, each using a different proof system. Without convergence toward succinct, interoperable proofs, verifying state across them will be expensive. Validators will burn CPU hours just checking headers. Bridges will lag under the weight of full-block replays. The environmental footprint of "a million chains" becomes untenable. The question therefore becomes sharper: *Should networks coordinate on verification standards to reduce replicated work?* That is the unresolved test.

This subchapter leaves its closing thread intentionally open. Verification has costs. Interoperability spreads those costs widely. Succinct proofs, light clients and shared standards can cut the weight, but only if the ecosystem commits to them. The forward question is unavoidable: will developers treat verification cost as a strategic design lever, or will they accept duplication as inevitable? The rest of the chapter turns to this choice and its consequences.

Designing for sufficiency

In October 2020, at a shared workspace in Lausanne, the founders of a small blockchain payments firm stared at a dashboard that told an awkward truth. Their system, built to serve cafés and local retailers, produced more than 40,000 on-chain writes a day, each committing a few bytes of routine metadata. The workload generated no extra value for customers; it simply reflected a design habit the team had inherited from earlier prototypes. When the firm switched to a batched settlement model—settling hourly rather than instantly—the change cut daily writes by more than 95 per cent. Costs fell. Latency stayed acceptable. The unglamorous decision, made over a single whiteboard session, became a turning point. It forced the team to ask a blunt question that now threads through this subchapter: *how much is enough?*

The question echoes beyond Lausanne. In June 2021, engineers at StarkWare demonstrated a proof compression method that slashed verification data by megabytes per batch. Their breakthrough was not a race for throughput; it was an attempt to remove unnecessary bulk from every stage of the pipeline. By proving more with less, they showed a path to sufficiency grounded not in austerity but in clarity. The outcome—lighter blocks, lower gas, lower verification load—was measurable on-chain. The behaviour was visible: fewer bytes in each proof, fewer cycles to check them, fewer nodes pushed to their limits. Sufficiency became a design posture, a willingness to strip the system back to the smallest workable core.

The first major claim requires demonstration. Waste emerges not only from energy-hungry mining farms but from product choices that multiply work without proportionate benefit. The Lausanne example shows this directly. When 40,000 database-like updates become a few hundred aggregated commitments, the system moves from churn to discipline. Naming the mechanism matters. An hourly settlement window replaced per-transaction finality. The implication is clear. Reducing granularity reduced load, and lower load reduced emissions embodied in computation and hardware wear. Sufficiency is not restraint for its own sake; it is engineering that measures value relative to cost.

A second example names a different domain. In February 2022, Filecoin nodes in North America began adopting more selective replication policies after the Protocol Labs research team published findings on redundant storage. Many nodes previously mirrored the same popular datasets dozens of times, consuming terabytes of SSD capacity with little marginal gain in resilience. The change was behavioural. Operators adopted incentives that rewarded unique, socially useful data over brute replication. The implication was visible in node metrics. Storage growth slowed. SSD failure rates declined. Operators bought fewer disks. A cultural shift—valuing sufficiency over redundancy—produced environmental and economic benefits.

There is, of course, a credible counter-example. In late 2021, several DeFi projects pushed minimalism too far. One yield aggregator attempted to compress its entire strategy logic into a single contract with complex conditional flows. The contract became opaque. A bug in a rarely used branch led to mispriced withdrawals. The limitation reminds us that sufficiency must never collapse into fragility. Cutting too close to the bone can obscure assumptions and reduce fault tolerance. Reconciling this is essential. Sufficiency works when it removes redundant steps, not when it conceals necessary structure. Clarity and resilience must rise together.

To understand why sufficiency matters, we must observe concrete behaviours. Every extra commitment, every unnecessary proof, every redundant state transition triggers computation for hundreds or thousands of validators. Those validators burn CPU cycles, consume electricity and demand cooling. Each byte of avoidable data increases storage overhead across the network. The behavioural metric is simple: what is the marginal cost of an additional unit of state? When teams measure that cost rather than assume it is negligible, product design changes. They batch. They prune. They adopt compressed formats. The motif returns here: *how much is enough?*

Another claim demands naming. Consider Optimism's decision in May 2022 to separate data availability from execution using call-data compression. Their approach showed that reducing on-chain data volume does not weaken security; it sharpens it by making verification more streamlined. The behaviour was immediate. Gas fees for batched transactions dropped. Sequencers ran with lower memory pressure. L1 nodes processed less data. The implication extends beyond Optimism. Any protocol that separates essential from non-essential data can shrink its computational perimeter.

Sufficiency is as much cultural as technical. Teams that adopt "default minimalism" treat every new feature as guilty until proven necessary. They commit to measuring baseline load before adding complexity. They frequently ask whether a proposed improvement reduces total computational gravity or merely shifts it. One visible behaviour is analytical discipline. Engineers run load tests. They quantify write amplification. They instrument CPU hotspots. The implication is cultural stability: features ship only when they justify their footprint.

Naming a second cultural pattern clarifies the theme. In July 2023, a collaboration between the University of Cambridge and several European blockchain projects introduced the concept of *sufficiency sprints*: short design cycles where teams audit their systems for low-value computation. They removed unused API endpoints, deprecated redundant indexing jobs and rewrote slow routines. The behaviour shifted from reactive patching to proactive pruning. The environmental effect was modest but real. Fewer database calls. Lower memory churn. Reduced cloud egress. The lesson is that sufficiency thrives when teams treat absence—not accumulation—as a virtue.

Still, sufficiency confronts a hard limitation: market incentives often favour speed, novelty and throughput. A chain that markets itself as "fastest" may add layers of speculative complexity to chase benchmarks. A project that raises funds on hype may prioritise feature volume over structural elegance. The limitation is not hypothetical. In October 2022, a Layer 1 chain added multiple parallel execution paths to boost headline throughput. The system passed benchmarks but struggled to maintain consistency under real load. Nodes overheated; sync times ballooned. Sufficiency lost to spectacle.

Reconciliation demands a principle: measure what matters. If a product choice adds 1,000 extra writes a second, quantify the CPU and storage burden on full nodes. If a feature requires deep historical indexing, estimate the cost in terabytes over five years. If a consensus tweak increases message complexity, measure the extra bandwidth and its environmental footprint. Only then can a team choose deliberately rather than drift into excess. The motif sharpens: *how much is enough—and who pays for the excess?*

Sufficiency also pulls attention toward life cycles. Systems designed with modest footprints tend to have longer-lived components. They wear hardware less aggressively. They avoid architectural churn that forces frequent migrations. An engineer who designs for sufficiency does not chase marginal improvements that require rebuilding half the stack. They commit to components that endure. A system that avoids needless churn produces less e-waste, demands fewer server upgrades and allows data centres to plan capacity more responsibly.

The most mature teams channel sufficiency into governance. They document design rationales, justify resource budgets and revisit assumptions annually. They treat state growth as a public good—one that must be stewarded, not hoarded. The behaviour is visible when teams publish rational state boundaries or storage roadmaps. The implication is a culture that aligns technical decisions with long-term ecological responsibility, not short-term wins.

The unanswered tension remains. Sufficiency calls for disciplined restraint in a sector built on experimentation. The forward test is therefore sharp. When a team faces a choice between elegant simplicity and attention-grabbing excess, which path will they take? And can the sector build norms that reward those who choose enough?

The stewardship mindset

On 15 September 2022 in Berlin, a small group of engineers watched Ethereum's "Merge" countdown flick towards zero on a projector screen. The room was quiet, more hushed than celebratory. A few laptops ran live dashboards of client logs; another screen showed estimates of network electricity use dropping as proof-of-work rigs ceased to matter for consensus. The Merge was framed, correctly, as a technical achievement: years of research, coordination and rehearsal distilled into a few tense minutes. But something else shifted that evening. When later estimates from the Ethereum Foundation suggested a reduction in network energy use of more than 99 per cent after the move to proof-of-stake, the work acquired a different character. Those engineers had not only shipped a new consensus mechanism. They had taken responsibility for the external footprint of their design. The graphs told a story.

That story sits at the heart of stewardship. At some point, technical choices stop being ideologically neutral. They change who breathes cleaner air. They change which power plants run at midnight. They change what kind of generation a struggling grid operator is forced to dispatch first. A stewardship mindset is what emerges when practitioners accept that those consequences belong to them, not to some diffuse "market" or faceless "user base". The quiet question that stewards ask—*what follows from this code in the world?*—is the motif that threads through this subchapter.

Engineering has been here before. After the collapse of the Tacoma Narrows Bridge in 1940, civil engineers reshaped their profession around explicit safety obligations. They tightened codes. They created independent review processes. They embedded the idea that every design choice carries ethical weight. Nobody now celebrates a suspension bridge that is "innovative" if it wobbles in high winds. Good bridges are boring, stable, and long-lived. That is what stewardship achieved: a culture where safety is an assumed constraint, not a heroic afterthought. The blockchain world sits, uncomfortably, at an earlier stage. There is no shared code of practice for environmental stewardship. No peer expectation that energy and emissions must feature in every major design review. Yet the ingredients exist. The question is whether they will coalesce into norms.

The first claim to examine is that technical choices are already de facto ethical commitments, whether acknowledged or not. When a team chooses proof-of-work over proof-of-stake for a new chain in 2023, it is not making a purely security-driven decision. It is choosing to tie its security budget to a particular profile of energy use and hardware churn. When a protocol opts for maximum redundancy in cross-chain verification, it is deciding that doubled or tripled computation is worth the gains in perceived robustness. These decisions leave traces in the physical world: extra ASICs manufactured; additional data centres built; more gigawatt-hours pulled through transformers. The behaviour is measurable. The commitment is just rarely named.

Ethereum's Merge offers a named counterpoint. The shift to proof-of-stake was justified on multiple grounds—security, issuance policy, roadmap coherence—but its environmental impact was impossible to ignore. Analyses by independent researchers and by the Ethereum Foundation suggested energy use had fallen to a tiny fraction of the previous level. The behaviour of miners and validators changed visibly. GPU farms shut down or moved to other coins. Validators began running on commodity servers with modest power draws. A global network altered its relationship with electricity because its stewards decided the old model was no longer acceptable. That is stewardship in practice: recognising that a design inherited from one context has become indefensible in another, and doing the work to change it.

Stewardship becomes more concrete when we compare blockchain with sectors where safety culture is mature. In nuclear engineering, for instance, the concept of ALARA—"as low as reasonably achievable"—governs exposure to radiation. Engineers must show they have minimised risk within economic and technical constraints. The idea is not perfection. It is disciplined reduction. Environmental stewardship for distributed systems could adopt a parallel stance: energy and emissions should be as low as reasonably achievable, subject to security and function. That principle would appear not as a slogan but as a design habit. Teams would measure the power profiles of their nodes, compare alternatives, and commit to designs that move the numbers down without breaking the system.

The implication reaches beyond protocol design. A stewardship mindset changes how teams treat benchmarks and roadmaps. Instead of measuring success solely in transactions per second or "total value locked", they add metrics that capture hardware longevity, node diversity, and energy use per unit of useful work. They review these metrics regularly. They treat regressions as bugs, not footnotes. The visible behaviour is mundane: engineering meetings where someone asks, "What does this do to validator power draw?" or "How many additional full nodes can still run this on consumer hardware?" When such questions appear routinely, stewardship has begun.

There are, however, credible counter-examples. In 2021 and 2022, multiple chains rolled out extremely high-throughput designs that demanded powerful, data-centre-grade hardware. Sync times lengthened. Node operators without access to cheap hosting began to drop away. From a narrow performance lens, these networks looked impressive. From a stewardship lens, they signalled trouble. A chain that requires energy-hungry servers in specialised facilities has already made a choice about who can participate and how much energy its baseline demands. The limitation is not that high throughput is bad. It is that the design process treated resource demand as a secondary concern rather than a first-class constraint. Reconciliation would mean asking a harder question at each architecture decision: *can we achieve our goals on hardware that a typical steward could defend?*

Stewardship also shows up in small, almost domestic decisions inside teams. Which logging level is the default? How aggressively do nodes cache state? How often do background jobs recompute views? Does the team regularly prune unused indices? Each of these choices manifests as CPU heat somewhere. A steward does not track every watt, but they cultivate an instinct: if a process does not serve a clear purpose, it should not run.

One example comes from a Scandinavian mining company that, in 2020, began publishing not only its energy mix but also its curtailment logs. The firm operated in a hydro-rich area with frequent surplus generation. Instead of simply stating "we run on renewables", it showed when rigs ramped down to free capacity for the grid and when they took advantage of excess water flows. That transparency signalled something about mindset. The company was treating its operation as part of a shared system. It had moved from claiming purity to documenting interaction. The implicit ethical claim was that grid stability and community supply mattered at least as much as hash rate.

A second example comes from the design of rollups and Layer 2 systems. Some projects, when faced with the choice between more complex but more efficient proof systems and simpler but heavier ones, chose the former, accepting slower development and stricter auditing in return for lower long-term verification costs. The behaviour is telling. They were willing to delay launches to avoid locking in wasteful patterns. The implication is that stewardship changes the tempo of innovation. It prizes durable gains over rapid releases.

Still, stewardship has a hard time competing with hype. A culture that rewards announcements, token prices and short-term user growth will always be tempted to downplay energetics. Ethical commitments do not trend on social media. They manifest in quieter metrics: fewer rewrites, fewer forced hardware upgrades, a bias towards extensions rather than forks. In this environment, a credible stewardship norm must be collective. A single team that slows down for ethical reasons risks being outcompeted. A field that adopts shared expectations about what counts as responsible behaviour creates cover for those choices.

The analogy with safety culture helps here. Airlines compete aggressively, yet none boasts about trimming maintenance below regulatory standards. Nuclear operators do not advertise that they have "innovated away" key safety checks. The culture will not tolerate it. Environmental stewardship in crypto and digital finance could move in the same direction. Protocols could commit, publicly, to basic norms: publish energy profiles; design for ordinary hardware where possible;

document the reasoning when more demanding setups are chosen; participate in independent audits that consider environmental impact alongside security. The key behaviour is mutual reinforcement. When peers expect this, it becomes easier to justify the associated effort to investors and users.

The motif returns: *what follows from this code in the world?* A stewardship mindset requires that question to be asked continuously, not just during retrospective outrage after a crisis. It should be written into improvement proposals, raised in corridor conversations, framed in foundation blogs. Over time, it can become second nature. An engineer might think, "This new signature scheme is elegant, but does it double verification work?" A governance forum might debate not just throughput, but whether a proposed upgrade forces node operators into new data centres or allows them to remain on modest machines at the edge of the grid.

There is a deeper ethical strand here. Stewardship demands that practitioners see themselves not as neutral toolmakers but as participants in a shared planetary budget. That is uncomfortable. It cuts against a certain myth of technological innocence—the idea that builders provide options and that what follows is purely the user's responsibility. Distributed systems dissolve that separation. A consensus mechanism exists only because many actors run it jointly. No individual can meaningfully opt out of the environmental implications of a widely used chain. That is why stewardship must be collective.

Yet collective norms can become dogma. There is a risk that "stewardship" hardens into a justification for resisting necessary change. A community might reject an overhaul that truly improves security because it temporarily increases energy use. A governance process might treat any expansion as suspect, even when new functionality could enable others to reduce their footprint. Here lies a genuine limitation. Stewardship must remain analytical, not nostalgic. It should weigh trade-offs with evidence, not reflex. The right question is rarely, "Does this change consume more energy than before?" The better question is, "Does this change help the system deliver more useful security or functionality per unit of impact?" Reconciling care with progress is the central difficulty.

The unresolved tension, then, is not whether a stewardship mindset is desirable. It is what practitioners are willing to give up to live by it. Are teams willing to abandon architectures that are culturally familiar but environmentally extravagant? Will communities accept slower release cycles when rigorous proof systems or energy-aware designs demand more time? And when incentives pull towards quick wins, who will stand up in the room and ask, before the merge, before the launch, before the next hardware order is placed: *what follows from this code in the world, and are we prepared to own it?*

Chapter 10
A Practical Playbook for Builders and Policymakers

The first hint that the conversation had shifted came in February 2024, at a public hearing in Saratoga County, New York. A local hydropower operator—accustomed to defending its allocation of river flows—found itself fielding a different question entirely. Residents wanted to know whether a proposed crypto-mining facility could help the county avoid winter blackouts. The operator paused, surprised. For years, mining firms had been cast as energy takers, not grid partners. Yet the months prior had seen severe cold snaps and volatile demand, and the community had watched miners elsewhere throttle consumption within minutes to stabilise frequency. The question was genuine: *could this be an asset rather than a burden?* The shift in tone was subtle but unmistakable. It suggested that the future of digital infrastructure might hinge not on grand ideological battles but on practical arrangements that work for grid operators, builders, and citizens alike. Such moments illustrate the theme of this chapter: the move from abstraction to action, from sweeping claims to grounded judgment. The debate over crypto's environmental footprint has travelled a long arc—from alarm and dismissal to more disciplined scrutiny, and, increasingly, towards constructive design. Yet across that journey, one gap has persisted. Builders want clarity on what "good" looks like. Policymakers want confidence that measures will stick across boom-and-bust cycles. Communities want straightforward terms that protect their interests. What they share is a desire for something rare: a playbook that is ambitious enough to matter yet simple enough to use. The motif running through these pages is that practicality is not the enemy of principle. It is how principles endure.

Consider the paradox facing the sector today. Many of the environmental burdens associated with mining—spiky demand, uncertain siting, hardware churn—are not inherent. They are symptoms of choices, incentives, and weak coordination. The space is full of examples where different choices produced dramatically different outcomes. In Iceland, miners operating near geothermal plants have long been integrated into grid-balancing schemes, earning lower tariffs in return for rapid curtailment. In West Texas, by contrast, bursts of new demand collided with transmission bottlenecks, fuelling political backlash and emergency hearings. Neither story is definitive. But together they show that environmental impact is less a trait of mining itself than a product of how it is built, governed, and integrated. The path from controversy to contribution is neither speculative nor utopian. It is already unfolding—piecemeal, unevenly, but unmistakably—where the right agreements and incentives are in place.

This chapter attempts to give those choices structure. It begins by treating impact not as a matter of branding but of measurement. Builders often speak of sustainability as if it were an aura. In practice, it is a composite of four elements: *where* a facility draws power, *when* it operates relative to grid conditions, *what* hardware it uses and how long that hardware lasts, and *how* governance shapes incentives over time. Combine these and you can sketch a simple, legible score—one that is not a moral verdict but a diagnostic. The ambition is not to label actors as saints or culprits but to give them a way to see where marginal improvements will do the most good. A grid operator can use it to compare proposals. A policymaker can use it to prioritise incentives. A builder can use it to make early design decisions that avoid later regret.

From there, the chapter turns to procurement and partnership—the unglamorous but decisive agreements that dictate whether a project strengthens or strains its host system. Too often, negotiations between miners and utilities devolve into tariff haggling, missing the larger opportunity. The most durable deals are those that recognise mining's unique asset: controllable load. A miner that can ramp down within 90 seconds during peak hours is a different creature from one that must run flat-out. Structuring contracts around response times, emissions disclosure, curtailment windows, and community benefits transforms what might be a mere transaction into a shared framework. The point is not to produce model contracts but to highlight the clauses that matter most: commitments that can be monitored and enforced without requiring encyclopaedic expertise. Clarity is a public good.

The third movement of the chapter looks at roadmaps and milestones. Many environmental debates fail because they ask for perfection up front, leading either to paralysis or performative pledges. A more mature path is incremental. Builders can commit to staged targets: publishing node-level electricity demand within six months; adopting verifiable impact scoring within a year; phasing in hardware recycling partnerships by year three. Policymakers can do the same, tying benefits—like priority interconnection or lower congestion fees—to transparent progress rather than to technology mandates. What matters is not the glamour of the goals but the credibility of the tracking. Communities do not expect overnight transformation. They expect honesty.

The final movement explores the question that opened this introduction: when do miners stop being perceived as burdens and start being welcomed as flexible assets? The answer, as the Saratoga hearing suggested, is conditional. Flexibility alone is insufficient if the power source is dirty. Clean electricity alone is insufficient if the facility locks in congestion or shuts out local voices. Yet when all pieces align—sensible siting, time-aware demand, long-lived hardware, disciplined governance, and clear agreements—mining can fill a niche that few other loads can. It can absorb the excess energy that would otherwise be curtailed, release capacity during stress events, and anchor financing for new renewable buildout. But this favourable scenario is not automatic. It requires guardrails: rules and norms that prevent opportunism, ensure verifiable benefits, and preserve optionality for the grid.

At its heart, this chapter argues that environmental impact is not a fate but a function of choices made upstream. It invites builders and policymakers to trade overheated rhetoric for precise tools, to favour durable commitments over decorative claims, and to understand that credibility is cumulative. Each siting decision, each procurement clause, each disclosure, each roadmap milestone—taken individually—may seem small. But together they determine whether the sector evolves into a constructive partner in the energy transition or remains marginal and suspect. The opportunity is real, but so is the scrutiny. The work now is to meet both with steadiness.

What follows is not a manifesto. It is a map. And the value of a map lies not in its idealisation of the road but in its ability to guide travellers through the difficult sections: the trade-offs, the uncertainties, the places where judgment matters. As the industry stands at a moment when its environmental reputation is up for renegotiation, the way forward begins with a simple question—*what would it take for this project, this policy, this network to be genuinely welcomed by its neighbours and trusted by its regulators?* The pages ahead attempt to offer answers that are specific, practical, and built to last.

Impact scoring

In July 2021, the municipal utility in Plattsburgh, New York, released a short but consequential report comparing two proposed crypto-mining facilities. Both promised jobs, both claimed to run on low-carbon electricity, and both sought preferential tariffs under the city's longstanding hydropower allocations. Yet the report reached sharply different conclusions. One operator would consume most of its power during winter peak hours, when Plattsburgh's clean quota was already stretched, forcing the city to import expensive fossil-derived electricity from the broader New York grid. The other would run mainly in spring and early summer, when local hydropower flooded the system and spilled. The difference was not ideological. It was arithmetic. Plattsburgh chose the second proposal, citing measurable reductions in peak stress and imports. A simple comparison—*same technology, same town, different timing*—produced a radically different environmental profile and a clear outcome.

That episode crystallised an uncomfortable truth. Public debates treat mining's footprint as if it were monolithic. Yet the actual impact hinges on variables outsiders rarely see: the carbon intensity of the marginal kilowatt-hour, the seasonality of load, the longevity of the hardware, the incentives encoded in governance. The Plattsburgh report was austere in length—barely six pages—but rich in insight. It showed that impact is neither mysterious nor subjective. It is measurable when the right dimensions are chosen. The motif that guides this chapter—*clarity through comparability*—first appeared there. And it matters now because builders and policymakers desperately need a method that avoids both paralysis and greenwash. Impact must be calculable, not confected. The case also revealed something else. Conventional sustainability frameworks often smuggle in hidden value judgements through opaque weighting and sprawling indicators. Plattsburgh avoided this by grounding its analysis in straightforward, observable metrics: how much power, when, and at what cost to the grid. This chapter generalises that instinct. A credible impact score must be lean, legible, and anchored in behaviour. If the Plattsburgh example teaches anything, it is that small differences in timing or governance can outweigh large differences in rhetoric. *Small things change outcomes.*

A workable impact score begins with siting: the most visible, and yet often the most misunderstood, determinant of footprint. Show the decision first. Location establishes a facility's baseline carbon intensity because every grid has a marginal generator—the plant that ramps to meet incremental demand. Name the reality: in March 2023, the Electric Reliability Council of Texas (ERCOT) published hourly marginal emissions data, revealing that West Texas solar-rich regions frequently hit near-zero marginal intensity at midday, while evening peaks triggered gas turbines. Explain the point. A miner that operates predominantly during hours of near-zero marginal intensity has a dramatically different profile from one that runs through fossil-heavy peaks, even if both claim the same "grid mix". Implication: emissions depend on marginal consumption, not on annual averages. Scoring siting, therefore, requires measuring not theoretical greenness but the specific marginal response that the facility provokes. The second component is timing, already foreshadowed by Plattsburgh but deserving of sharper treatment. Show the behaviour. In November 2022, a mining cooperative in Alberta shifted its operating schedule after the Alberta Electric System Operator published real-time carbon intensity data. The cooperative throttled load during high-intensity hours and increased consumption during curtailment events, reducing its estimated emissions without altering its hardware or location. Name the mechanism: time-aligned operation. Explain it. Hourly carbon data allows facilities to optimise their run profiles, cutting emissions through scheduling rather than capital expenditure. Implication: timing and siting interact. A favourable site with poor scheduling can score worse than a middling site with disciplined timing. A robust impact score must therefore weight *temporal alignment* alongside geography. It must capture not where you are but *when* you draw power relative to system stress. Hardware enters as the third pillar, and here rhetoric often muddies the basics. Show the issue. In April 2020, Bitmain released the Antminer S19 Pro, a device whose efficiency (29.5 J/TH) extended its economic life compared with its predecessors. Many operators upgraded immediately, auctioning older units across secondary markets from Georgia to Kazakhstan. Name the underlying metric: efficiency per joule and lifespan. Explain the challenge. Rapid upgrade cycles produce e-waste and shift emissions to manufacturing hubs. The embodied carbon of an ASIC, while modest compared with operational emissions, becomes material when devices churn every 18–24 months. Implication: hardware longevity deserves explicit scoring. A miner operating high-efficiency units for five years, maintaining them, and declining unnecessary upgrades should receive credit. A miner accelerating hardware churn should not. Scoring must therefore consider not only the "headline" efficiency but the *upgrade cadence*, the resale pathway, and evidence of refurbishment.

Governance, the fourth dimension, is the most abstract but also the most decisive when understood through behaviour rather than rhetoric. Show the behaviour. In 2024, the Ethereum Foundation published validator performance metrics that included downtime penalties, signalling a culture of transparency around operational reliability. Name the principle: incentives and penalties. Explain the relevance. Protocol-level governance determines whether actors face costs for environmentally damaging behaviour—such as persistent high-load operation during stressed grid hours—or receive benefits for demand response. Implication: a facility embedded in a governance structure that rewards flexibility and disclosure should score higher than one in a governance environment that tolerates opacity or prioritises extractive incentives. Governance scoring must be tied to visible commitments: telemetry disclosure, curtailment participation, verifiable community agreements, and adherence to protocol-level norms.

These four elements—siting, timing, hardware, governance—form the spine of a lean scoring model. Yet a model is only as useful as its resistance to easy gaming. Two examples, one encouraging and one cautionary, show the tension. Show the encouraging case. In February 2023, Norway's energy regulator introduced enhanced disclosure requirements for data centres in Sørlandet, prompting several mining operators to publish granular hourly electricity consumption and curtailment data. Their disclosures aligned with the country's low-carbon grid, and independent audits confirmed the claimed reductions in marginal emissions. Name the mechanism: transparent data plus verifiable low-carbon power. Explain the value. Data made the scores credible.

Implication: transparency elevates honest actors.
Now the cautionary case. In 2022, a group of operators in the Republic of Georgia claimed near-zero emissions by purchasing unbundled renewable energy certificates (RECs) sourced from Norwegian hydropower producers. Yet their facilities sat in regions where marginal generation was dominated by imported gas-fired electricity. Name the discrepancy: book-and-claim versus physical reality. Explain the failure. RECs had no bearing on actual grid impacts. Implication: scoring must discount instruments that lack geographical and temporal alignment. It must reward real reductions, not financial abstractions.
A counter-example sharpens the argument. Some operators argue that scoring models should include social contributions such as local sponsorships or tax payments. The instinct is understandable, but the limitation is clear: such contributions, while valuable, do not directly change physical emissions or grid stress. A good scoring model should capture externalities that are mediated through energy or hardware pathways; it should not become a receptacle for public relations claims. Reconcile this by integrating community contributions only where they materially affect local impact—for example, co-funding transmission upgrades or contributing to shared curtailment infrastructure. The motif—clarity through comparability—demands restraint as much as inclusion.
A quiet motif runs throughout this subchapter: *the signal must outweigh the noise*. Every component of the score must map to a measurable behaviour. If timing matters, we measure hours of operation against carbon intensity. If hardware matters, we track upgrade cycles and refurbishment rates. If governance matters, we observe curtailment response times, data disclosure frequency, and protocol-aligned incentives. A score that cannot be reconstructed from transparent data is not a score; it is theatre.

The challenge, of course, is weighting. A miner located on a high-carbon grid but with impeccable hardware longevity and governance discipline may have a lower score than a miner on a low-carbon grid with poor scheduling. Should grid carbon intensity dominate? Or should flexibility be rewarded more heavily because it supports system stability? There is no single correct approach, but a pragmatic weighting emerges from operator behaviour. Siting and timing determine direct emissions and should therefore receive the largest weights. Hardware influences medium-term footprint and should follow. Governance shapes long-term incentives and should anchor the remainder. Weightings may vary by jurisdiction, but transparency about the weighting is non-negotiable. An unresolved tension remains. A simple score can guide decisions, but simplicity risks omitting nuance. A detailed score captures nuance but risks paralysis. The forward test is therefore straightforward: *does this score help a community, a regulator, or a builder make a better decision within an afternoon?* If not, it is too complex. The purpose of impact scoring is not to crown winners. It is to illuminate trade-offs clearly enough that actors can choose better paths. As mining intersects more deeply with energy systems, the questions sharpen. Should a miner that achieves flawless timing in a coal-heavy grid score higher than one that operates round-the-clock in a renewable-rich region? Should hardware longevity compensate for poor governance? These tensions will persist. But the existence of the tensions argues for impact scoring, not against it. Without a shared framework, decisions become hostage to lobbying, aesthetics, or sentiment. With one, even imperfectly calibrated, decisions gain structure. The path forward demands a scoring model grounded in measurable behaviour, resistant to gaming, and transparent enough that communities and policymakers can interrogate every claim. The final question, the one that lingers after the numbers settle, is simple: *is this facility making the system cleaner, more flexible, and more durable—or merely claiming to?*

Procurement and partnerships

In May 2022, the public utility district in Grant County, Washington State, voted on a contract that looked, at first glance, like any other large industrial supply agreement. A new crypto-mining operator was seeking tens of megawatts of power, promising jobs and local investment. Yet the document placed before commissioners differed in three quiet ways. It specified that the miner's tariff would spike during winter peaks. It bound the firm to real-time curtailment instructions during grid stress. And it reserved a portion of the revenue for a community fund dedicated to energy-efficiency upgrades in low-income homes. After a heated debate, the contract passed by a narrow margin. Months later, when an unusually cold spell hit and the utility needed rapid demand reduction, the same miner powered down within minutes, avoiding the use of expensive diesel peakers. The agreement had worked. Not perfectly, but visibly. Words on paper had shaped behaviour on the ground.

That episode captures the core argument of this subchapter: the environmental trajectory of mining is written as much in contracts as in code. Procurement choices and partnerships decide who carries risk during drought or heatwaves, who benefits from low-carbon build-out, and who pays when things go wrong. A miner that signs a fixed, inflexible tariff with no curtailment provisions becomes a blunt instrument on the grid. A miner that signs a contract recognising itself as a controllable load—paid less during stable hours, rewarded for turning off when needed—becomes a tool for system stability. The difference is not semantic. It is operational, and it is measurable in megawatts and tonnes of CO_2. Contracts decide.

The motif that threads through these pages is simple: *credibility lives in clauses*. Grand public promises about "green mining" or "community benefit" matter little if the agreements that bind parties ignore timing, emissions, and local impacts. To understand procurement and partnerships, we must therefore scrutinise the anatomy of deals that have passed real-world tests, and the shortcomings of those that have not.

Begin with procurement structure. When a mining operator approaches a utility or an independent power producer, the relationship often pivots around three numbers: price per megawatt-hour, contract duration, and maximum capacity. But the Grant County case showed that when those are the only numbers that matter, the public interest is exposed. The district's revised contract tied price not only to volume but to *time*. During specified peak windows, tariffs rose sharply. At other times, especially when hydropower spilled, tariffs fell. This was not cosmetic time-of-use pricing; it was a mechanism that aligned the miner's incentives with grid conditions. The implication is clear. Any procurement deal seeking credibility must move beyond flat pricing. It must encode time, not just quantity.

A second example, from Iceland in 2018, illustrates another dimension: physical linkage to a specific energy source. Landsvirkjun, the national power company, faced surging demand from data centres and miners. In several contracts, it specified not only delivered power but the origin of that power in particular geothermal or hydro plants, alongside explicit curtailment conditions when reservoir levels fell. Operators knew which stations they depended on and under which circumstances they might be turned down. The behaviour that followed was instructive. Some facilities invested in additional on-site thermal management and flexible workloads, acknowledging that their supply was not an unconditional right but a partnership with a finite resource. The implication for procurement design is that source attribution—done honestly, without pretending electrons carry flags—can signal shared responsibility. It makes it harder to hide behind abstract national averages.

There is, however, a counter-example that shows how easily procurement can drift into theatre. In 2021, several miners in

Eastern Europe touted "100 per cent green" operations based on contracts with intermediaries who bought unbundled renewable certificates from distant markets while the actual facilities drew from coal-heavy local grids. The power purchase agreements contained no references to local marginal emissions, no curtailment rights, and no verification provisions. Energy procurement had been reduced to a financial overlay. The limitation is obvious. Such arrangements may satisfy accounting frameworks on paper, but they do little to change physical generation. Reconciling this requires a stricter standard: a credible contract ties payment to measurable behaviour in a specific grid, not just to abstract financial instruments.

If procurement establishes the energy frame, partnerships determine whether a mining project coexists with its host community or collides with it. The behaviour that separates the two outcomes is often encoded in a few key provisions. One is *transparency*: whether the operator commits to regular disclosure of its real-time or near real-time electricity use, curtailment history, and, where possible, local emissions factors. Another is *benefit-sharing*: whether some portion of the economic surplus funds tangible projects—insulation upgrades, substation reinforcement, youth training programmes—that citizens can see and evaluate. A third is *governance access*: whether local representatives have seats on advisory boards or regular consultation forums with the operator.

A useful template begins to emerge. In agreements that stand up to public scrutiny, you repeatedly see clauses that define five things with precision. First, *source and profile*: the primary generation sources, any backup supply, and the expected hourly or seasonal load profile. Second, *flexibility obligations*: minimum curtailment response times, maximum notice periods, and clear triggers for load reduction, ideally tied to system frequency or price signals. Third, *emissions and data disclosure*: requirements to publish consumption data and emissions estimates using agreed methodologies, with rights for the utility or regulator to audit those figures. Fourth, *community contributions*: earmarked funds or in-kind work for local infrastructure, explicitly linked to project performance rather than vague aspirations. Fifth, *review and adjustment*: scheduled intervals at which tariff structures, curtailment rules, and contributions are revisited in light of measured impacts.

Each of these template elements translates abstraction into behaviour. If a contract stipulates that an operator must reduce load by 50 per cent within five minutes when locational marginal prices breach a defined threshold, that requirement will show up in control code and alarms. If an agreement requires quarterly publication of energy use and marginal emissions, that duty will show up in dashboards and data pipelines. Words become processes. Processes produce traces. Traces can be checked.

Successful partnerships also attend to hardware and land. In Quebec, Hydro-Québec's 2018 moratorium on new crypto loads eventually gave way to a framework in which selected projects agreed to specific caps on power density per site and commitments regarding hardware refresh cycles, including reuse and recycling arrangements with regional e-waste handlers. The contracts did not micromanage component inventories, but they did require evidence that older ASICs would be refurbished or exported to regions with compatible grids rather than simply scrapped. This linked procurement—the allocation of clean, relatively cheap hydropower—to downstream impacts in metals and waste. The implication is that credible agreements treat energy and hardware as parts of the same ecological story.

By contrast, some projects have attempted to placate communities with glossy "community benefit agreements" that lack teeth. A mining firm might promise to sponsor a local sports team or fund a tech incubator without addressing noise, water use, or grid congestion. These gestures may generate headlines but rarely survive moments of stress. When the first extended heatwave or cold snap hits and residents see their bills rise or hear generators at night, the quality of the underlying procurement deal is revealed. If tariffs and load obligations are well structured, the miner will curtail and explain the behaviour in public meetings. If not, anger will focus on the weakest link: the perceived failure of promises. The motif returns: credibility lives in clauses, not in marketing.

For policymakers and builders seeking to structure better deals, the most practical move is to adopt a shared set of headings under which key clauses are expected. An agreement that covers "Energy Source and Emissions Profile", "Flexibility and Curtailment", "Data Disclosure and Audit", "Local Infrastructure and Social Contributions", "Hardware Lifecycle and Decommissioning", and "Review and Exit Conditions" signals, simply by its structure, that the parties have considered environmental and social dimensions beyond price. Within each heading, the language can remain concise. For example, under flexibility, a clause might specify that the operator shall participate in specified demand response programmes, with penalties for non-performance measured in clearly defined financial terms. Under hardware lifecycle, a clause might require that decommissioned units be processed by certified recyclers or transferred under documented resale arrangements.

There are limits, of course. Contracts cannot anticipate every shock. A hydropower-backed facility may face drought. A gas-linked plant may be hit by geopolitical price spikes. A grid may experience new forms of congestion as electric vehicles and heat pumps spread. Well-designed agreements recognise this uncertainty. They incorporate shared-pain mechanisms—temporary tariff surcharges, stepped curtailment tiers, renegotiation triggers—that avoid pushing all risk onto a single party. They also recognise political risk. Communities may elect new leaders hostile to previous agreements. Operators may change ownership. This is why sunset clauses and periodic renegotiation windows matter. They keep the partnership alive rather than frozen.

A credible counter-argument deserves attention. Some developers worry that too much contractual detail will deter investment by making projects look unpredictable. They argue for simple, long-term fixed-price deals that provide certainty. The limitation of this view is that it often mistakes hidden volatility for simplicity. A flat tariff with no curtailment rights may look clean on a spreadsheet, but it simply hides the fact that someone—usually the public—will bear the cost of buying extra peak power or suffering degraded reliability. Reconciliation comes from acknowledging that complexity cannot be eliminated, only allocated. Better to expose it in contracts, where it can be debated, than to bury it in externalities.

Throughout this, the quiet motif holds: credibility lives in clauses. The more specific an agreement is about what happens during stress, the more likely the partnership is to endure. The more measurable its promises, the easier it becomes for regulators and communities to distinguish genuine alignment from opportunistic spin. At the same time, a tension remains unresolved. How far can contracts carry the weight of environmental responsibility before they become brittle or unwieldy? Where should the boundary lie between what is codified and what is left to norms and trust?

For a builder preparing to sign the next power purchase agreement, and for a policymaker drafting the next tender, the forward test might be this: if every clause of this deal were read aloud at a town hall during a heatwave or a blackout, would it stand up? Or would the gaps become painfully obvious?

Roadmaps and milestones

In September 2021, Microsoft released the first public update on its carbon-negative programme, detailing how far it had progressed since its initial 2020 pledge. Buried in that report was a modest but consequential admission: several procurement commitments intended to deliver verified removals had slipped by months because suppliers lacked the monitoring systems to validate their own claims. The document did not hide this delay; it quantified it. It also reset intermediate targets accordingly. For a company of that scale to acknowledge missed milestones so directly was unusual. Yet that admission had an effect. Analysts recalibrated their expectations. Suppliers accelerated their data collection. The next year's update showed fewer gaps. The lesson was unmistakable: a roadmap that survives contact with reality is one that treats milestones as public commitments rather than private aspirations.

That ethos—transparent, time-bound, and revisable—matters acutely for sectors with volatile energy footprints. Mining operators have often promised sweeping environmental improvements, yet without the scaffolding of phased goals or the discipline of public tracking those promises float free of scrutiny. A miner that declares it will run "fully renewable by 2030" but declines to publish annual load profiles or hardware life-cycle data invites scepticism. Conversely, a miner that publishes its emissions intensity each quarter, sets defined thresholds for its next hardware refresh cycle, and discloses its real curtailment performance invites engagement. It may still fall short, but it falls short on the record. And that record is the basis for course correction. Roadmaps gain their force not from bravado, but from measurability.

A roadmap begins with a decision about *what counts*. Some firms base their primary metric on absolute emissions. Others choose emissions intensity per petahash or per megawatt-hour. Neither is self-evidently superior; what matters is consistency and clarity. When Argo Blockchain published sustainability figures for its Quebec operations in 2021, it emphasised emissions intensity, reporting a notably low figure due to its reliance on hydropower. The implication was clear: its progress could be tracked by comparing that intensity over subsequent quarters, alongside changes in hardware efficiency. Contrast that with operators who shift between accounting methods from one report to the next, alternating between territorial emissions factors and market-based certificates without explanation. Roadmaps founded on unstable metrics rarely survive. They erode confidence and blur the baseline from which future milestones are meant to depart.

Once metrics are fixed, staging begins. A credible roadmap sets near-term actions that are hard to fudge. One operator might commit to publishing hourly consumption data by a certain month, turning opacity into transparency. Another might pledge a minimum percentage of curtailment events executed within a specified response time, converting grid rhetoric into measurable behaviour. A third might establish a cap on annual landfill disposal of decommissioned ASICs, supported by contracts with certified recyclers. Each of these milestones translates aspiration into an act that can be observed, audited, and debated. These are acts, not slogans. They impose structure on decision-making. And they create pressure across the organisation, because missing a public milestone forces explanation.

Milestones also reveal internal priorities. A firm that sets early targets for emissions reporting but postpones hardware life-cycle goals may be signalling a preference for the visible over the difficult. Meanwhile, a firm that stages its roadmap around hardware—publishing expected refresh cycles, refurbish-to-retire ratios, and export pathways for older units—signals a deeper commitment to systemic impact. China's industrial data for 2019 revealed the scale of global e-waste flows; when miners in Kazakhstan and Russia acquired waves of second-hand ASICs during that period, hardware decisions materially shaped emissions intensity as ageing chips pushed energy use per hash upward. A roadmap that ignores this cycle misses one of the system's major levers. By embedding hardware milestones into the plan, firms acknowledge that climate alignment is not just about electricity procurement. It is about the physical assets that embody the four-to-five-year cadence of silicon obsolescence.

A second pattern recurs in successful roadmaps: the layering of milestones such that each stage depends on the previous one's data. Google's 24/7 carbon-free energy initiative, announced in September 2020, offers a useful model. The company began by publishing hourly location-based grid carbon data for its data centres. Only once that transparency was established did it set targets for hourly matching procurement, followed by milestones for new project development in regions with high marginal emissions. In mining, the analogue would be to publish the hourly load profile of each site, then commit to procuring time-matched clean energy for a specified share of those hours, and only then to commissioning new clean capacity. Each step builds on the previous one and avoids the trap of making later claims unverifiable.

Sceptics might argue that mining is too volatile an industry for such neatly staged plans. Hash prices fluctuate. Difficulty adjusts. Hardware markets seize or boom. Yet volatility strengthens, rather than weakens, the case for roadmaps. A firm that can withstand market swings while maintaining emissions transparency reveals organisational discipline. A firm that cannot is signalling fragility. Moreover, roadmaps can incorporate scenario planning. For example, an operator might publish two pathways: one assuming steady revenues and another assuming a 40 per cent price shock. In both, the firm would commit to minimum disclosure standards and hardware recycling thresholds. This dual-path commitment reveals which milestones are non-negotiable and which can flex. It distinguishes between principles and prudence.

Transparency is the spine of any roadmap. And transparency is not simply the act of publishing data; it is the act of publishing data that can be meaningfully interpreted. Hourly profiles matter because marginal emissions vary dramatically within a day. Reporting quarterly averages elides that reality. In 2022, the Electric Reliability Council of Texas (ERCOT) published granular emissions data for each of its zones, enabling analysts to identify when grid conditions were cleanest and dirtiest hour by hour. Several miners in the state, including Riot Blockchain, subsequently highlighted their participation in demand response programmes during high-emissions hours. A credible roadmap would make such disclosures routine, including timestamps of curtailment events and their estimated avoided emissions. The motif here is subtle but persistent: milestones must illuminate behaviour at the scale where impact actually occurs.

Hardware management must be woven into milestones with equal care. When Bitmain released the Antminer S19 Pro in May 2020, the efficiency improvement relative to its S17 predecessor encouraged a widespread hardware refresh. But many organisations lacked clear pathways for managing the resulting wave of older units. Without milestones specifying how many units would be refurbished, resold, or recycled each year, hardware churn became an environmental blind spot. In response, some large operators began publishing annual refurbishment rates, often expressed as the share of total fleet capacity replaced by second-hand units rather than landfill. A robust roadmap would build on this idea, with milestones mandating that every decommissioned unit be accounted for and its pathway documented. Numbers matter here: counts of units refurbished, tonnes of equipment recycled, and percentages of fleet energy intensity improved. These are concrete, verifiable, and immune to greenwashing.

There is a limitation to roadmaps grounded entirely in internal commitments. Firms may over-optimistically map a path that assumes cooperation from utilities, regulators, or suppliers that may not materialise. For example, a miner might commit to hourly carbon matching by 2026, only to discover that the regional ISO provides no hourly emissions factors. Or a recycler might lose its licence, derailing hardware milestones. This is where the roadmap must include *external dependencies*—conditions that the firm cannot fully control but must communicate. Including these dependencies is not a weakness. It acknowledges reality. It also helps external stakeholders understand whether a missed milestone reflects organisational failure or systemic constraints.

A counter-example clarifies the risk of ignoring dependencies. Several renewable developers in the UK in the mid-2010s published aggressive build-out timelines that assumed rapid grid connection approvals. When those approvals stalled, the developers quietly shifted their targets without explanation. Investors and local communities lost trust. Mining firms that silently revise milestones when external conditions shift repeat this error. Reconciliation lies in pre-emptive transparency: milestones should include notes specifying which external datasets, programmes, or approvals they rely on.

Across these examples runs a recurring image: the *timeline* as both an anchor and a test. A roadmap is not a prediction; it is a commitment to a sequence of decisions. Missed milestones happen. The question is how the miss is disclosed and what corrective action follows. A miner that publishes a roadmap and then demonstrates quarterly how each milestone is progressing builds a form of credibility no marketing campaign can buy. A miner that hides its slippages forfeits its claim to responsible operation.

The unresolved tension is this: how granular should roadmaps become before they collapse under their own weight? If milestones become too detailed, firms may spend more time reporting than improving. If they remain too vague, they invite scepticism. The forward test, then, is simple. Could an informed outsider track progress using only publicly available data and the milestones themselves? If the answer is yes, the roadmap is doing its work. If no, the milestones may be markers in name only.

From controversy to contribution

In February 2021, during a cold snap that strained the Texas grid, ERCOT issued urgent calls for load reduction. One of the first industrial operators to respond was a mining facility outside Rockdale run by Bitdeer. Its operators curtailed within minutes, pulling tens of megawatts off the system at a moment when hospitals and water treatment plants were approaching emergency thresholds. The move was not heroic; it was contractual. But it was visible enough to cut through the usual rhetoric. For a few hours the familiar narrative inverted. A sector often blamed for stress on the grid demonstrated—quantitatively, not rhetorically—that flexible demand can matter. A miner became a grid asset.

That moment did not eradicate the controversy surrounding mining in the state. Nor should it have. Rockdale had witnessed the rise and fall of several industrial players before Bitdeer arrived, and many residents remained wary of promises. Yet the response in 2021 broke a pattern: it showed that mining's footprint is not fixed. It can contract at speed. It can synchronise with system needs. It can absorb surplus. Its effect on a grid is contingent on its design and its commitments. And that contingency is the hinge on which the industry's movement from burden to contributor will turn.

The central claim—that mining can evolve into a valuable form of dispatchable demand—must be shown, not asserted. Consider another moment: in May 2022, during high-runoff weeks in Washington State's Columbia River basin, hydro generators faced the prospect of spilling clean energy that could not be transported across congested transmission lines. A local miner contracted with the utility agreed to ramp up to absorb a portion of that surplus, reducing spill and providing the utility with a paying off-taker when wholesale prices collapsed. Here the effect was measurable. The utility reported that spill volumes dropped relative to the same hydrological conditions the year before. This was not an abstraction. It was a contract tied to hourly flows, prices, and physical operations.

Both episodes reveal a subtle motif that threads through this subchapter: *directionality*. Mining's effect swings with context. It can amplify strain or relieve it. It can mask marginal emissions or reduce them. Directionality is shaped by siting, timing, hardware decisions, and the governance choices described earlier in this book. These determinants are not incidental; they are the fulcrum on which the public case for mining balances.

To understand the design space clearly, we must name both its constructive and destructive poles. A constructive pole appears when miners act as controllable load. The Rockdale case and the Columbia basin case show miners adjusting their consumption in line with grid conditions. This behaviour requires transparent telemetry, predictable curtailment windows, and operational discipline. The implication is straightforward: grids benefit from load that can disappear faster than new generation can appear. The United States Department of Energy highlighted this in a 2022 report on flexible demand, noting that industrial loads able to curtail at sub-five-minute intervals confer measurable system value. When miners participate meaningfully in these programmes, they contribute a service distinct from their core commercial activity.

The destructive pole appears where miners behave as rigid load. In parts of Kazakhstan in 2021, when informal and under-regulated mining operations proliferated, grid operators recorded sudden frequency deviations as unmetered facilities powered up or down. These deviations increased wear on equipment and complicated the dispatch of thermal plants. Here mining was not a flexible asset; it was a destabilising force. The limitation is stark. Flexibility cannot be assumed. It must be engineered, contracted, and monitored. And where governance is weak, commitments to flex are unverifiable.

The reconciliation lies in the choices embedded into operations. Measurable curtailment, published demand-response logs, and contracts that define response times convert flexibility from marketing to mechanism. When integrated into a roadmap—as argued in the previous subchapter—these signals can shift public perception. Not by charm, but by evidence.

Mining's potential contributions extend beyond grid balancing. They emerge in waste heat utilisation, hardware circularity, and local industrial symbiosis. In 2023, a district heating trial in Boden, Sweden, used miner-generated heat to warm municipal buildings during winter months. Sensors recorded stable inlet temperatures even during peak hashing periods. The pilot lowered heating costs for the municipality and gave the miner a predictable heat sink. This is not a universal template; many climates and building configurations preclude such use. But it offers a tangible instance of mining's by-products being integrated into local systems rather than discarded. The motif of directionality returns: heat can be a waste or a resource, depending on design.

Another example appears in hardware refurbishment. In 2022, CleanSpark reported extending the life of several thousand ASIC units through board-level repairs and selective underclocking. This increased efficiency per unit when measured against energy use per terahash. It also reduced procurement of new, more resource-intensive equipment during a period of volatile supply chains. The behaviour was visible: counts of units refurbished, measured efficiency gains, and timelines for redeployment were published. The implication is instructive. Mining's footprint is inseparable from the hardware churn beneath it. When operators treat equipment as repairable rather than disposable, they influence the embodied emissions of their fleets.

Yet we must admit a counter-example that complicates the narrative. During the 2021–22 cycle, several miners pursued aggressive expansion in regions with high coal intensity and fragile transmission networks, especially in parts of Siberia and Inner Mongolia. Local outages followed. Residents reported voltage drops. In some cases, authorities seized unpermitted equipment. These episodes illuminate a persistent limitation: mining can move faster than governance. Even where operators intend to contribute positively, siting decisions made under short-term incentives can overwhelm local systems. The implication is that contribution demands alignment with constraints that miners do not control. Transmission capacity, generation mix, and regulatory enforcement shape the feasibility of beneficial participation.

From these examples, a principle emerges: contribution is contingent on verifiable behaviour at the margins. A miner that curtails during extreme events offers a measurable benefit. A miner that overstresses a grid during peak demand imposes a measurable cost. The directionality depends on context, time, and operational discipline. And this is where the quiet motif of *guardrails* becomes visible.

Guardrails are not metaphors. They are contractual clauses, data-sharing commitments, response-time thresholds, emissions disclosure standards, and siting constraints. Guardrails are the conditions under which mining shifts from burden to asset. Without them, the system reverts to its contentious state.

Consider the design of guardrails that genuinely constrain behaviour. The most effective combine three properties: clarity, auditability, and consequence. Clarity ensures that operators know the precise triggers for curtailment and the metrics by which success will be judged. Auditability ensures that third parties—grid operators, local authorities, or independent auditors—can review logs and verify behaviour. Consequence ensures that non-compliance carries costs, whether financial or operational. This triad mirrors the safety culture of mature engineering fields. And it pushes mining beyond voluntary codes towards accountable participation.

Governments experimenting with performance-based incentives demonstrate how guardrails can shift industry norms. In 2022, Quebec's energy regulator introduced mechanisms allowing utilities to contract directly with energy-intensive industries under conditions that protected grid reliability and local residents. Contracts required firms to accept curtailment during specified conditions and to publish annual data on consumption and emissions intensity. While not aimed solely at mining, these rules influenced miners' siting decisions. Several projects adjusted their operational profiles to meet the criteria. The effect was directional: operations became more predictable for utilities and less contentious for residents.

The transition from controversy to contribution unfolds through repeated, verifiable acts. Each act shifts the narrative incrementally. But the transition remains contingent. Mining will always be a substantial electrical load. Its physical footprint and hardware churn cannot be erased. The opportunity lies in whether those characteristics can be shaped to deliver system value rather than undermine it.

The open question is unavoidable. Under what conditions should a community, utility, or regulator regard a proposed mining operation as a contributor rather than a burden? The forward test might be this: if the miner disappeared tomorrow, would the grid, the community, and the local economy be materially worse off? If the answer is yes, the miner contributes. If the answer is no—or worse, if the answer is "better off"—the guardrails have failed.

About the Author

Tarek Omraneh writes at the crossroads of technology, energy, and ethics, helping readers see how design choices reverberate in the physical world. He has worked alongside engineers, policymakers, and community advocates to translate complex systems into practical decisions for people building and regulating them. A long-standing curiosity about how societies balance innovation and stewardship runs through his work, shaped by histories of water management and communal resource care across North Africa and the Mediterranean. His mission is simple: make the environmental consequences of digital infrastructure legible, testable, and open to better choices.

www.ingramcontent.com/pod-product-compliance
Lightning Source LLC
Chambersburg PA
CBHW031339230926
51848CB00002B/311
9789374599358